Praise for **THE BORDEN MURDERS**

An ILA Young Adults' Choice

A *Reader's Digest* Best Biographies You Should
Have Read by Now Selection

An ALA-YALSA Quick Pick

A CCBC Choices Book

A Volunteer State Book Award Nominee (Tennessee)

"This thriller by Sarah Miller was written for middle schoolers,
but its grisly details, as well as its focus on turbulent and tense
Borden family relationships, make it an intriguing and gripping
read for any adult fan of true crime." —*Reader's Digest*

★ "Fans of the podcast *Serial* will find much to enjoy here. . . .
Sure to be a hit with true crime fans everywhere."
—*School Library Journal*, Starred

"The high-appeal topic will attract many readers, and the
suspenseful account will have them trying to solve this still
unresolved murder mystery." —*Kirkus Reviews*

"[Will] engage readers in their own debate as to Lizzie Borden's
guilt or innocence." —*Publishers Weekly*

Also by Sarah Miller

Miss Spitfire: Reaching Helen Keller
The Lost Crown

THE BORDEN MURDERS

LIZZIE BORDEN & THE TRIAL OF THE CENTURY

SARAH MILLER

A YEARLING BOOK

A NOTE ON CONTINUITY

Careful readers will notice that some police officers' ranks vary from one point in this book to another. A number of policemen were promoted during the course of the Borden investigation and trial, such as William Medley, who was a patrolman in 1892 but had been awarded the rank of inspector by the time of the trial in 1893. The apparent inconsistencies in the text reflect these promotions.

Also, standards of spelling and punctuation were more idiosyncratic in the 1890s than they are today. For instance, "clue" was commonly spelled "clew" in the newspapers. Spellings in transcripts often differ from one court proceeding to the next, depending on who did the recording. (At the inquest, stenographer Annie White recorded, "O, Mrs. Churchill, do come over, somebody has killed Father," while at the trial, stenographer Frank Burt rendered the same sentence as "Oh, Mrs. Churchill, do come over; somebody has killed father.") Quotations from court documents and newspapers retain the spelling and punctuation of the original source material.

—•—

Text copyright © 2016 by Sarah Miller

All rights reserved. Published in the United States by Yearling,
an imprint of Random House Children's Books,
a division of Penguin Random House LLC, New York.
Originally published in hardcover in the United States by Schwartz & Wade Books,
an imprint of Random House Children's Books, New York, in 2016.

Yearling and the jumping horse design are registered trademarks of Penguin Random House LLC.

Visit us on the Web! rhcbooks.com

Educators and librarians, for a variety of teaching tools, visit us at RHTeachersLibrarians.com

Library of Congress Cataloging-in-Publication Data is available upon request.

ISBN 978-1-9848-9244-7 (pbk.)

Printed in the United States of America
10
First Yearling Edition 2019

TO W.

Partner in crime

CONTENTS

Honor and shame from no condition rise.
Act well <u>your</u> part: there <u>all</u> the <u>honor</u> lies.

—ALEXANDER POPE

Is the legend true?
I question not
But seek its proof.

—EDITH MATILDA THOMAS

WHO'S WHO

THE BORDEN FAMILY

Abby Borden: Andrew's second wife

Andrew Borden: Lizzie and Emma's father

Emma Borden: eldest daughter of Andrew and Sarah Morse Borden

Lizzie Borden: youngest daughter of Andrew and Sarah Morse Borden

Hiram Harrington: Lizzie and Emma's uncle (by marriage) on their father's side

John Morse: Lizzie and Emma's uncle on their mother's side

FRIENDS AND NEIGHBORS

Dr. Seabury Bowen: the Borden family physician; first doctor on the scene

Mary Ella Brigham: Lizzie's childhood friend

Reverend Edwin Buck: missionary at the Fall River Central Congregational Church

Adelaide Churchill: the Bordens' next-door neighbor; first witness on the scene

Marianna Holmes: a Borden family acquaintance; mother of Lizzie's schoolmate

Alice Russell: friend and former next-door neighbor of the Borden sisters

Bridget Sullivan: the Bordens' maid, called Maggie by the Borden sisters

POLICE AND CITY AUTHORITIES

George Allen: first policeman on the scene

Dr. John Coughlin: mayor of Fall River

Dennis Desmond: headed the search of the Borden cellar on August 8

Dr. William Dolan: Bristol County medical examiner

John Fleet: assistant marshal

Philip Harrington: questioned Lizzie on August 4

Rufus Hilliard: city marshal of Fall River

Joseph Hyde: guarded the back of the Borden property on the evening of
August 4

William Medley: questioned Lizzie Borden and searched the barn on August 4

Michael Mullaly: discovered the handleless hatchet on August 8

Hannah Reagan: matron at Fall River's Central Police Station

George Seaver: searched the clothes press on August 6

Deputy Sheriff Francis "Frank" Wixon: searched the Borden yard
on August 4

LAWYERS AND JUDGES

Colonel Melvin Ohio Adams: associate counsel for the defense

Josiah Blaisdell: justice of Bristol County District Court; presided over the
Borden inquest and hearing

Caleb Blodgett: associate justice of Massachusetts Superior Court; presided
over the Borden trial

Justin Dewey: associate justice of Massachusetts Superior Court; presided
over the Borden trial

Andrew J. Jennings: associate counsel for the defense

Hosea M. Knowlton: district attorney of the Southern District of
Massachusetts

Albert Mason: chief justice of Massachusetts Superior Court; presided over
Borden trial

William Henry Moody: associate counsel for the prosecution

George Dexter Robinson: former governor of Massachusetts; head of Lizzie
Borden's defense team

KEY WITNESSES

Thomas Barlow and Everett Brown: passersby on Second Street

Eli Bence: clerk at D. R. Smith's drugstore

Hannah Gifford: cloakmaker

Hymon Lubinsky: ice cream peddler

Edward Wood: professor and chemist at Harvard University

LIZZIE BORDEN TOOK AN AXE . . .

It happened every spring in Fall River, Massachusetts. Behind the curtained windows of the stately house she shared with her sister on French Street, Miss Lizbeth Borden heard the children skipping rope on the sidewalk, chanting a rhyme to the once-popular tune of "Ta-Ra-Ra Boom-De-Ay":

> *Lizzie Borden took an axe,*
> *Gave her mother forty whacks.*
> *When she saw what she had done,*
> *She gave her father forty-one.*

Year after year, she listened to them butcher her family's tragic past. A new century had dawned since the brutal hatchet murders of Miss Lizbeth's father and stepmother captured the nation's attention. She had altered her name from Lizzie to Lizbeth and left the family home on Second Street, where the terrible deed was done, and still the ditty followed her.

Most of Miss Lizbeth's well-bred neighbors up on Fall River's posh "Hill" refused to speak about the Borden slayings, let alone the fact that the Bordens' own daughter, Miss Lizbeth herself, had been accused of them. And yet their children never failed to learn the rhyme. The youngsters singing it now had not even been alive on August 4, 1892, but that didn't stop them from contributing new verses:

> *Andrew Borden now is dead.*
> *Lizzie hit him on the head.*
> *Up in heaven he will sing.*
> *On the gallows she will swing.*

Miss Lizbeth's sensational murder trial, the jury's momentous decision, the time she spent behind bars, none of that mattered. In the decades that followed, the citizens of Fall River—young and old—enacted their own sentence upon her.

The members of the Central Congregational Church, where Miss Lizbeth had been a member of the Christian Endeavor Society and taught immigrants at the Central Mission Sunday School, publicly shunned her. Friends, even those who had testified to her innocence, quietly broke away.

Over the years mischievous children trampled her lawn and lobbed rotting eggs at the clapboards of her home. Handfuls of sand and gravel rained upon her windowpanes. They tied her doorknobs and stuck pins in her doorbell to make it ring non-stop. At least they did not chant their jump-rope rhyme to her face when she answered the bell. Instead, they called her vile names before dashing from the porch.

Gawkers in Oak Grove Cemetery—adults, no less—rubbernecked at the sight of Miss Lizbeth Borden, come to tend the graves of her supposed victims. "Miss Borden, don't pay any attention to them," Terrance Lomax, the grounds foreman, often told her as he accompanied her to the plot where her parents lay alongside the baby sister she had never known. Certainly Miss Lizbeth was grateful for Terrance and the discreet handful of others who were kind and respectful to her in spite of her past. Everyone had heard the rumors about her beheading trouble-some kittens and baby birds, but only a few knew of the tender notes and thoughtful gifts she dispensed—people like the coal delivery man who always found a slice of chocolate cake waiting inside Miss Lizbeth's basement, or the sick little girl who received a pretty painted bowl full of gumdrops with a five-dollar bill hidden at the bottom from "Auntie Borden." There was little that Miss Lizbeth treasured above loyalty, and contrary to her public image, she delighted in doting upon those, like Terrance, who graced her later years with their companionship.

But did Miss Lizbeth realize that even Terrance, the sympathetic groundskeeper who made sure the paths to the Borden family plot were cleared in winter and was too polite to accept her persistent attempts to tip him, had gone to witness the spectacle of her trial as a young man?

In the same way the children chanting outside her windows marked the arrival of spring for Miss Lizbeth, the newspaper headlines heralded summer's peak. Every August, the *Fall River Daily Globe* observed the anniversary of Andrew and Abby Borden's deaths by printing another front-page tirade against the "incarnate fiend in human form [who] rained cruel, vengeful, bloody blow after blow upon Andrew J. Borden's venerable head." Always, the *Globe* was at pains to remind the citizenry that the man—or *woman*—who had committed the crime still wandered among them. There was no need to print a name. Every man, woman, and child in Fall River knew perfectly well who the *Globe*'s pointing finger accused.

> *Lizzie Borden took an axe,*
> *Gave her mother forty whacks.*
> *When she saw what she had done,*
> *She gave her father forty-one.*

Today, everything most people know of Lizzie Andrew Borden is contained in those four singsong lines of doggerel. And nearly everything in those four lines is wrong.

MURDER!

"SOMEBODY HAS KILLED FATHER"
Thursday, August 4, 1892

Lizzie could hardly look past the blood, there was so much of it. Blood soaked Mr. Borden's neatly folded Prince Albert coat. It dripped from the slick horsehair cushions to the flowered carpet below. It arced in a fine spatter across the wall and picture frame above. In the midst of it all, her father lay stretched out on the couch with his face so carved and bloodied that she did not know whether he was alive or dead. "I did not notice anything else, I was so frightened and horrified. I ran to the foot of the stairs and called Maggie."

Bridget Sullivan—nicknamed Maggie by Lizzie and her sister—had barely managed to drift to sleep when the shouting woke her. Bridget did not dally an instant. A housemaid had no business stealing a few winks at eleven in the morning, and besides, that scream was too loud, too strident for any ordinary reprimand.

"What is the matter?" Bridget shouted back.

"Come down quick!"

Down three flights of stairs Bridget came pounding to find Miss Lizzie Borden in a state such as she'd never seen before—backed up against the screen door as though she were about to flee the house entirely.

"Go for Dr. Bowen as soon as you can," Lizzie commanded. "I think Father is hurt."

Instinctively Bridget moved toward the sitting room to see what was the matter with her employer, Mr. Andrew Borden. "Oh, Maggie, don't go in," Lizzie cried. "I have got to have a doctor quick. Go over. I have got to have the doctor," she insisted.

Bridget dashed across Second Street and "rang violently" at Dr. Bowen's door, only to have Mrs. Bowen inform her that the doctor was out making house calls. Back Bridget hurried with the bad news. Lizzie had not budged from the doorway.

"Miss Lizzie, where was you?" Bridget ventured to ask. "Didn't I leave the screen door hooked?"

"I was out in the backyard and heard a groan, and came in and the screen door was wide open."

But Lizzie Borden did not want to answer questions. She wanted help. If she could not have the doctor, she wanted her friend, Miss Alice Russell. "Go and get her," she begged. "I can't be alone in the house."

Bridget yanked her hat and shawl from their hook and took off toward Borden Street.

Lizzie Borden waited, alone—as far as anyone knew. There were three locks on the front door. No one intent on harming her father could have gotten in that way. And anyone who might still be lurking inside could not possibly escape without her notice now.

"Lizzie, what is the matter?" said a voice from behind her. But it was only Mrs. Adelaide Churchill, the young widow next door. On her way home from her marketing she'd noticed Bridget crossing the street from Dr. Bowen's house, "running, and she looked as if she was scared." Mrs. Churchill went straight home and laid her groceries on a bench in the kitchen. Through her kitchen window she caught a glimpse of Miss Lizzie leaning against the doorway of the back screen, rubbing her face "as if she was in great distress." The young woman looked so much out of sorts, Mrs. Churchill had opened her window and called across the fence.

"O, Mrs. Churchill," Lizzie answered, "do come over, somebody has killed Father."

By the time Mrs. Churchill hurried across the yard, Lizzie had sunk down onto the second step, "pale and frightened."

"O Lizzie, where is your father?" she asked, laying a hand on Lizzie's arm.

"In the sitting room."

Mrs. Churchill did not go in. Instead, she asked, "Where was you when it happened?"

"I went to the barn to get a piece of iron."

"Where is your mother?"

"I don't know," Lizzie said, her words spilling out now, "she had a note to go and see someone that was sick this morning, but I don't know but they have killed her too. Father must have had an enemy, for we have all been sick, and we think the milk has been poisoned. Dr. Bowen is not at home, but I must have a doctor."

"Shall I go, Lizzie, and try to find someone to go and get a doctor?" Mrs. Churchill asked.

She answered yes, and Mrs. Churchill ran across the street to L. L. Hall's Stable for help.

Lizzie Borden did not want to be alone in that house. She had told Bridget so, and still Bridget had brought her neither the doctor nor Miss Russell. Where could that girl be?

"I DON'T KNOW BUT WHAT MR. BORDEN IS DEAD"

It was no more than quarter past eleven when Alice Russell saw the Bordens' maid hurrying up her front steps. Right then Alice knew there was trouble. Only last evening her friend Lizzie had come calling with worrisome news. She and her father and stepmother, Lizzie said, had all been taken sick Tuesday night—very sick indeed.

Alice laid aside her work at once and met Bridget at the door.

"What is it, Bridget? Are they worse?" Alice asked.

Bridget did not take time to explain. She hardly knew herself just what had happened. "Yes," the young Irishwoman said. "I don't know but what Mr. Borden is dead." She paused only long enough to hear Alice say she would come before taking off again. To Bridget's relief, Dr. Bowen was just stepping from his carriage as she ran back up Second Street.

"What is the matter, Lizzie?" Dr. Bowen asked as he entered the house.

Under any other circumstances, the sight of his familiar face with its graying mustache and side-whiskers might have calmed Lizzie. After all, he had lived across the street from the Bordens for twenty years; she had known him since she was a girl of twelve.

Lizzie answered that she was afraid her father had been stabbed or hurt.

That one word—*stabbed*—took him aback. He expected sickness, possibly bad, judging from the way his wife had called out *They want you quick over to Mr. Borden's!* before he stepped from his carriage. Even poisoning would not have completely surprised him. The previous day, Mrs. Borden had arrived at his office before eight o'clock in the morning, nearly hysterical with fear that her family's bread had been tainted. But stabbing?

"Has there been anybody here?" Dr. Bowen asked.

Not as she knew of, Lizzie answered.

"Where is he?" the doctor asked.

Lizzie led him through the dining room and motioned toward the sitting room door. Not a sound came from the other side.

Steeled for the worst, Dr. Bowen went in.

Nothing in all his twenty-five years as a medical man had prepared Dr. Bowen for the sight that assaulted him as he stepped into the Bordens' sitting room. Before him on the sofa, Lizzie's father lay keeled sideways, the left side of his face so smashed that Dr. Bowen did not, could not, recognize him. The elderly gentleman's features were a pulp of chipped bone and razored flesh, his left eye cleaved in two.

The wounds were so violent, so obviously criminal, that they completely derailed Bowen's instincts as a doctor. Instead, his first thought was that of a policeman. Something in that room—something besides the obvious horror on the sofa—felt wrong. "Like a flash," it struck him to check the room to see if anything else was disturbed. Nothing. Not one thing was out of place, not even a speck of blood on the side table. It was not a particularly reassuring observation.

Only then did the doctor do what he had been called upon to do, and lifted one of Mr. Borden's hands from his lap to feel for a pulse. Still warm, but that was all.

"WILL SOMEBODY FIND MRS. BORDEN?"

Alice Russell had taken just enough time to change her dress before hurrying over the three blocks that separated her home from the Bordens'. There, she found Bridget, Mrs. Churchill, and a "dazed" Lizzie. "Sit right down here Lizzie in the kitchen," Alice told her friend, and led her to a rocking chair.

While Mrs. Churchill fanned Lizzie, Alice rubbed Lizzie's hands and bathed her forehead with wet cloths. No one informed Alice what was wrong with Mr. Borden, but seeing her friend in such a state must have told her that it was something dreadful. The Lizzie she knew was simply not the sort of person who came easily unhinged.

At this moment, however, Lizzie Borden was not herself at all. She seemed so much in need of comfort that Alice could not content herself with holding Lizzie's hand. Within minutes of her arrival, Alice Russell climbed into the chair beside Lizzie as though she were a child, and Lizzie laid her head on Alice's shoulder.

Then Lizzie's voice, drifting up from beneath the waving newspapers and cool compresses, stopped them all with one simple question:

"Will somebody find Mrs. Borden?"

Amidst all the frantic coming and going, the women realized, not one of them had seen Abby Borden.

Lizzie was insistent that her stepmother had received a note that morning. Somebody was sick, Mrs. Borden had told her, and she intended to call on the invalid when she went out to pick up the meat for that afternoon's dinner.

"Oh, Lizzie," Bridget said, "if I knew where [Mrs. Borden's sister] was I would go and see if Mrs. Borden was there and tell her that Mr. Borden was very sick."

"No," Lizzie replied, "I think I heard her come in."

But if Mrs. Borden had already returned from her errand, why didn't she come running herself when Lizzie screamed for Bridget? Mrs. Borden's second-floor bedroom was directly below Bridget's—the maid had rushed right by it on her way down. Wouldn't the repeated slamming of the screen door or the drumming of excited footsteps have attracted Mrs. Borden's attention as the neighbors arrived on the scene?

As the pitch of excitement rose, Lizzie's conviction wavered. "I don't know where Mrs. Borden is," she said to Mrs. Churchill. "I think she is out, but I wish you would look."

Someone must search the house for Mrs. Borden, the women decided, and it would not be Lizzie. She was plainly in no condition to do any such thing.

At that moment, Dr. Bowen came out of the sitting room, shaking his head as though he hoped to dislodge the image of what he had just seen from his mind. "That is awful," he said.

"O, I can't go through that room," Bridget said. From where they stood, there was no way into the front of the house but through the sitting room, where Mr. Borden's murdered body lay with the blood still oozing onto the haircloth sofa.

LAYOUT OF THE BORDEN HOUSE

When Andrew Borden bought Number 92 Second Street in 1872, it was not a single-family home. At that time the building was fitted out as upper and lower flats with identical floor plans: a front parlor, central dining room, rear kitchen, and two small side bedrooms. This compact arrangement accounts for both the lack of hallways and the peculiar interconnecting layout of the upstairs bedrooms during the Bordens' time—Lizzie's room had once been the upstairs family's dining room, with doors opening to the entry, parlor, kitchen, and one of the bedrooms.

Andrew Borden made two substantial changes to the house. He tore out the upstairs kitchen and converted the space into a master bedroom, and he joined the two downstairs bedrooms to create a large dining room. What had been the downstairs family's dining room then became the Bordens' notorious sitting room.

The most significant alteration, however—at least in terms of the murder—was not structural. It was the mutually locked door between Lizzie's room and the master bedroom. That door, with its bolt on one side and hook on the other, essentially became a wall dividing the second floor into two completely separate compartments. As long as both sides of that door were locked, no one in the front half of the upstairs could access the master bedroom, back stairs, back door, cellar, or attic without going down the front stairs and passing through both the sitting room and the kitchen.

"Get me a sheet, and I will cover Mr. Borden over," Dr. Bowen offered.

But the linens were stored upstairs in the small dressing room off Mr. and Mrs. Borden's locked bedroom. And the key to that bedroom lay on the mantel in the sitting room—just steps from Mr. Borden.

Again Dr. Bowen spared the ladies by going back into the sitting room to retrieve the key, and a reluctant Bridget, accompanied by Mrs. Churchill, set off up the back stairs.

"GO AND GET THE POLICE AS FAST AS YOU CAN"

"Doctor, will you send a telegram to Emma, my sister, for me?" Lizzie asked after he had draped Mr. Borden's body.

"I will do anything for you," Bowen gallantly replied. As a doctor, there was nothing left for him to do. He acted now as a friend.

Her mind suddenly astir with practicalities, Lizzie asked him to word the telegram as gently as possible, not just for her sister's sake, but because "the old lady where Emma was visiting was feeble, she had better not have the shock."

As Dr. Bowen headed out the back door, two men met him at the screen—one was Charles Sawyer, a neighbor from just a few doors down Second Street. Bowen balked at letting them in until Sawyer identified his companion, a burly, pork-faced fellow dressed in an ordinary suit of clothes, as Officer George Allen of the Fall River Police Department.

"All right, come right in," Bowen said.

Before he went any farther, Officer Allen deputized Mr. Sawyer and stationed him at the screen door with instructions that he must not allow anyone to come in, only police officers. Then Allen followed Dr. Bowen into the sitting room, where the doctor pulled the sheet from Mr. Borden's face. "You go down, and tell the Marshal all about it," Bowen instructed the policeman. "Go and get the police as fast as you can."

Meanwhile, in the kitchen, Lizzie's moments of clearheadedness were fading in and out.

Again Lizzie said, "I wish someone would go and try to find Mrs. Borden."

They could avoid it no longer. Once more Bridget and Mrs. Churchill screwed up their courage to creep through the house. There was no one else for the job.

Together, the two women went through the dining room to the sitting room door. From there they scurried kitty-corner toward the foyer, trying not to see the end of the sofa a few inches to their left, where Mr. Borden's head lay. Bridget was just ahead of Mrs. Churchill, leading the way. Down the hall and then up the open staircase they crept, uncertain whether a murderer still lurked within the house.

As the floor of the landing and then the open door to the guest room came into view, Mrs. Churchill turned her head, peering beneath the railing. Her nose was not quite level with the second floor. Through the spindles she could see across the landing and straight under the guest-room bed. Lying on the floor on the other side of the bed was something she did not want to recognize, but even in the dim light she could not pretend it was anything but the form of a person.

Mrs. Churchill went not one step farther.

Bridget, suddenly bold, continued. Drawn by the glimpse of a woman's dress on the floor, she ran as far as the foot of the spare bed before the dreadful sight stopped her: Mrs. Borden, splayed facedown on the red Brussels carpet between the bed and the bureau in a thick black pool of drying blood.

Mrs. Churchill did not wait for Bridget to react. She rushed downstairs into the dining room, so frightened she doubled herself up, and cried out, "O, Mrs. Borden!"

"Is there another?" Alice Russell asked.

"Yes," Mrs. Churchill gasped, "they killed her too."

"FOR GOD'S SAKE, HOW DID THIS HAPPEN?"

First her father, now her stepmother. Lizzie reeled at this second blow, appearing so "very much overcome" that Alice Russell was compelled to shepherd her friend out of the hot kitchen and into the dining room. There Lizzie "threw herself" down on the green-striped lounge at the end of the room.

Alice bustled and fussed over Lizzie, anxious to keep her cool and calm. Thinking she was faint, she started to loosen Lizzie's dress. But Lizzie suddenly rallied, refusing to succumb completely to Alice's ministrations.

"I am not faint," Lizzie declared.

Nevertheless, Alice and Mrs. Churchill strove to maintain an atmosphere of calm for Lizzie's sake, even as a rapid succession of policemen bombarded the Borden property.

ROCKY POINT

Not every member of the Fall River police force was at the Borden house on August 4. Far from it. It just so happened that the homicide at 92 Second Street coincided with the annual policemen's excursion to a popular amusement park. At 8:00 that morning, a number of officers and their families had boarded the steamer *Mt. Hope,* bound for Rocky Point in Warwick, Rhode Island. There, on the shores of Narragansett Bay, they could partake of theater, vaudeville shows, music, dancing, a Ferris wheel, a toboggan run, and various outdoor sports. The ferry would not return for them until 4:15 that afternoon.

Just how many policemen were absent that day? Accounts vary. The *Boston Advertiser* estimated only half the force was away, while in the *Fall River Globe*'s report the figure swelled to 80 percent. The more conservative *Fall River Daily Herald* settled on a non-specific "majority." Author Edward Radin, who busted many a Borden myth in the 1960s, was most conservative of all, saying the picnic was limited to off-duty patrolmen. Whatever the actual number, the on-duty policemen were at a distinct disadvantage.

First came Inspector Patrick Doherty and Deputy Sheriff Francis Wixon. Then Officer Allen returned to the scene with Officers Michael Mullaly and John Devine.

They swarmed everywhere—searching the barn, the yard, the cellar and attics. Virtually all of them angled for a glimpse of

Mr. and Mrs. Borden, and all of them wanted information from Lizzie.

Did you see anyone around here?

Is there any Portuguese working on the farm over the river for your father?

PORTUGUESE

To be Portuguese in Fall River in 1892 meant to be constantly under suspicion. As far as the middle- and upper-class citizens were concerned, members of the swarthy-skinned Roman Catholic immigrant population were the first to blame for any unsavory goings-on, and August 4 was no different. One Portuguese man was brought into the police station on the day of the murders for withdrawing his life savings of about sixty dollars (approximately $1,450 today) from the bank. Another was reported for asking directions to New York.

What motive?

Was it robbery?

Have you any reason, no matter how slight, to suspect anybody?

Even Lizzie's own relatives could not spare her their questions. Shortly after Mullaly and Doherty finished probing her for information, Lizzie's uncle John Morse burst in, demanding, "For God's sake, how did this happen?" Nothing had seemed amiss when he dropped in for an overnight visit the afternoon before.

Just three hours earlier Andrew Borden himself had unhooked the back screen door for him, inviting Morse to finish his errands in time to share their noon meal. Now both his hosts were dead.

Dr. Bowen, returning from the telegraph office just as Mullaly and Wixon arrived, did his best to shield Lizzie from the mounting commotion. He covered Mr. Borden again and instructed Alice Russell to take Lizzie upstairs. "She better go up to her room," the doctor said, "and stay there."

Alice readily agreed. Despite the admirable composure Lizzie had displayed with Mullaly and Doherty, the congestion and disorder on the first floor were becoming too much to expect her to handle. Alice herself was so bewildered by it all, she did not know anymore how many people were in the house.

Without the policemen buzzing around her, Lizzie's thoughts returned to practical matters. "When it is necessary for an undertaker I want Winward," she told Alice upstairs, wanting to make sure Dr. Bowen knew of her wishes concerning funeral arrangements. And there was another, even more personal matter, something she must tell her doctor about. If the policemen found it, they would surely jump to the wrong conclusions—a small pail of bloodstained cloths, soaking in the cellar. Incriminating as it seemed, the bloody little bucket had no bearing on the search. It was instead a spectacularly inconvenient coincidence: at the time of her parents' murder, with the whole of the Fall River police force mobilizing a hunt for a blood-spattered murderer, Miss Lizzie Borden had the misfortune to be menstruating.

With Alice gone to fetch Dr. Bowen, Lizzie stepped into her sister's room. Like many of the rooms on the second floor, the sisters' bedrooms connected. Emma had traded bedrooms with her sister two years ago, and Lizzie's things were now arranged in the larger of the two. What Lizzie gained in space, however, she'd lost in privacy: anyone who wanted to enter or leave Emma's room had to walk through Lizzie's to do so. Lizzie's bedroom also adjoined the guest room and her parents' bedroom. There were latches on both sides of her parents' door, though, and the guest-room door was not only locked and bolted but blocked by her tall writing desk. No one could enter her room unless she allowed it. Still, on either side of those other doors Lizzie could hear voices, footsteps. Occasionally the handles rattled as another police officer tried to turn them. Emma's room, with its single entrance, was the most private space she had access to just then, and Lizzie Borden wasted no time in taking full advantage of it.

"WE KNEW THE STATE SHE WAS IN"

When Alice returned, she found Lizzie just stepping out of Emma's room, tying a red ribbon at her waist. In the few minutes she was alone, Lizzie had changed from an old blue skirt and blouse into a pink-and-white-striped wrapper—a dress that crossed in the front like a robe and fastened with a bow.

It ought not to have seemed odd. No lady who expected to greet callers would remain in her work dress. Granted, a murder investigation is not exactly a social occasion, but even Alice herself had quickly changed into a fresh dress before running to the Borden house when Bridget came for help. Bridget Sullivan would also steal a few moments to do the same before the afternoon was over. There was something about that pink wrapper of Lizzie's, though. Perhaps it was the bright red ribbon, or the sheen of the pale fabric's finish, but everyone who saw Lizzie in that dress that day seemed to take particular notice of it.

If Lizzie's change of clothes struck Alice as strange at that moment, she brushed off her misgivings. With so many people in the house, she reasoned, Lizzie "wanted to get into a respectable appearance." It wasn't just the police who wanted to see her. By one o'clock, two visitors offering support and condolences arrived at 92 Second Street: the Reverend Edwin Buck and Mrs. Marianna Holmes, mother of one of Lizzie's former schoolmates.

Throughout the afternoon, the two of them helped Alice tend to Lizzie as though she were an invalid. Alice was grateful for the extra hands. She had no intention of leaving Lizzie alone again, knowing the state she was in. "When one was out, another made a point to be there." Lizzie stayed on her little sofa by the windows with Reverend Buck sitting quietly beside her and let them fuss over her. Her head ached. Dr. Bowen brought her a preparation of bromo caffeine—a medicine about as potent as aspirin—to blunt the pain and calm her nerves.

They kept her bedroom door locked, too. Retreating upstairs had gained Lizzie only a little more privacy. Her door stood right at the head of the steps. Everyone who came to view Mrs. Borden's body—policemen, medical examiners, reporters—passed by it on their way to the spare room, and if Lizzie's door was not kept locked, they were "apt to open it" on their way past.

The locked door did not prevent the police from gaining access to Lizzie, however. Two more policemen, first Medley and then Officer Philip Harrington, came knocking and interviewed Lizzie in her bedroom. Next, Mullaly returned with yet more questions. After Mullaly came Assistant Marshal John Fleet in plainclothes.

He asked more of the questions Lizzie had answered at least half a dozen times already: *Where were you? How long? Who has been in the house? Could your uncle or the maid have had anything to do with it?* Lizzie gave him the answers she had given to all the others. Her story, assembled from the hundreds of questions she answered over that first week, went like this:

There were a few trifling chores to do that morning—handkerchiefs that needed ironing, some clean clothes to put away, a bit of mending. The handkerchiefs lay ready and sprinkled on the little ironing board in the dining room, but her flatirons were not hot enough. As she waited for them to heat on the stove, Lizzie leafed idly through an old Harper's Magazine *at the kitchen table.*

The house was quiet.

Her father napped in the sitting room—she had just watched him fold his Prince Albert coat into a pillow and stretch out on the sofa. Her stepmother was upstairs making up the guest room, or perhaps by now downstreet doing the one or two errands she'd mentioned to Lizzie earlier. Bridget had finished washing the windows and gone up to her attic bedroom to snatch a catnap of her own before fixing dinner.

DOWNSTREET

Why "downstreet" instead of "downtown"? Because the heart of Fall River lay in a dimple in the landscape. Rising to the north was the Hill, where the mill owners and other well-to-do families had their grand homes. South was the Bordens' neighborhood, an area called the Flats, which ranged across another smaller hill that also pointed downward into the business district. Here, mostly middle-class families lived alongside small groceries, restaurants, laundries, churches, stables, and candy stores.

Whether they came from the Hill or the Flats, most citizens of Fall River had to literally descend the street to reach the city's center.

Lizzie grew bored with the magazine, and still the stubborn flatirons were not hot. She could not say what made her think, just at that moment, of her fishing poles. She had not used them for five years or so. But a party of friends had arranged a fishing excursion on Monday, and it seemed to Lizzie that there were no sinkers on her lines last time she used them. Perhaps she could find some lead or iron up in the barn for new ones. It was something to do, anyway, while the slow flats heated.

Lizzie left the kitchen and went out into the yard, leaving the side screen door unlatched behind her.

The Bordens' pears were ripe already, riper than the Chagnons' whole orchard just over the back fence. Lizzie dallied to gather a few from the ground beneath a tree near the barn before climbing to the loft. They were still cool from the night's chill, their flesh sweet and light—not at all like that mutton soup the family had been dining on since Wednesday noon. After the way she'd felt the day before, she did not even want to think about meat. She nibbled at one and then another as she straightened the curtain on the window in the west peak—the one that looked down over the house. There she lingered, for no reason in particular, munching on the last of her pears in full view of the side yard and screen door before crossing the loft to rummage through a box of old things on the workbench.

And then—was that a noise? The window was closed; she had heard nothing out of the ordinary before. But now . . . a peculiar noise, it seemed to Lizzie. Something like scraping. Or a groan?

By the time Lizzie Borden reached the screen door, it was wide open.

"A THOUGHT THAT WAS MOST REVOLTING"

Assistant Marshal Fleet listened to Lizzie's story, noting it all down. Then he asked, "Has your father or mother—"

"She is not my mother," Lizzie interrupted, "she is my step-mother; my own mother is dead."

It was a plain and simple fact, but under the circumstances the remark did not sit well with Fleet. To top it off, Lizzie's demeanor struck the assistant marshal as decidedly chilly. More troubling yet, not at any time during the interview had she been in tears.

Fleet's impressions dovetailed all too neatly with the intuitions Officer Harrington felt during his own encounter with the freshly orphaned Miss Borden. Harrington observed that in contrast to Alice Russell, whose deathly pallor; short, sharp breathing; and fidgeting hands had betrayed her anxiety,

> Lizzie stood by the foot of the bed, and talked in the most calm and collected manner; her whole bearing was most remarkable under the circumstances. There was not the least indication of agitation, no sign of sorrow or grief, no lamentation of the heart, no comment on the horror of the crime, and no expression of a wish that the criminal be caught. All this, and something that, to me, is indescribable, gave birth to a thought that was most revolting.

Right then and there, with no more evidence than that, Lizzie Borden became the prime suspect.

THE BORDENS

"SHE IS VERY STRONG WILLED"

Exasperating as it is to admit, pitifully little is known about Lizzie Andrew Borden's life before the morning of August 4, 1892. Even the color of her eyes is an uncertainty. As notorious as Lizzie Borden's name is today, that may be hard to imagine, but consider this: more than 125 Borden families lived in Fall River, Massachusetts, in 1892, and until her parents' murder, Lizzie did not attract much undue notice.

SPINDLE CITY

By 1892, no city in the United States produced more cotton textiles than Fall River, Massachusetts. Some 597,850,000 yards of cloth rolled from its mills every year, earning it the nickname Spindle City.

A bustling city of 83,000 people, Fall River owed both its name and its prosperity to the falls of the Quequechan River, which tumbles through its heart. Stretching from North and South Watuppa Ponds in the east to Mount Hope Bay in the west, the Quequechan (pronounced *"quick*-uh-shan" locally) provided an abundance of free energy to the mills, factories, and foundries that sprang up along its banks in the boom years following the Civil War.

A tiny handful controlled the vast majority of the city's wealth. Among the seven families who ruled over Fall River was the Borden clan, whose claim to the Quequechan shores dated to the seventeenth century.

Fall River's royalty—like Lizzie's distant cousin M.C.D. Borden, the "Calico King"—also owed its affluence to the tens of thousands of laborers who kept the great steam engines and looms running. From their estates on the Hill, the rich literally looked down upon the Irish, French Canadian, and Portuguese workers who crammed the tenements along the murky waterfront. In a town heavily prejudiced against Catholics as well as foreigners, these immigrants, though essential to Fall River's economy, found themselves doubly snubbed by its society.

Afterward there would be all kinds of rumors and speculations as the newspapers filled with so-called revelations about the Borden case. Everyone in Fall River—everyone in the nation— would soon have an opinion about what kind of person Lizzie Borden was. Here, however, is the scant handful of undisputed facts, bland though they may be:

Although police and newspaper reports often referred to her as a girl, Lizzie Andrew Borden was in fact a grown woman in August of 1892. She had been born thirty-two years earlier, on July 19, 1860, to Andrew Jackson Borden and Sarah Morse Borden, and christened Lizzie, not Elizabeth. When she was not quite three her mother died of "uterine congestion, 4 mos."—possibly a miscarriage—coupled with "disease of spine." Unlike her sister, Emma, who was almost ten years older, Lizzie grew up without the slightest memory of Sarah Borden. The only mother Lizzie knew was the thirty-seven-year-old spinster her father took for his second wife in 1865, Abby Durfee Gray.

The relationship between the new Mrs. Borden and Lizzie, however, was not especially maternal, even when Lizzie was small. As Lizzie herself explained, "I had never been to her as a mother in many things." When she wanted mothering, Lizzie said, she always went first to her sister instead. It was not simply a matter of habit. As their mother lay dying, Emma Borden had solemnly promised to "watch over baby Lizzie." The twelve-year-old could scarcely have imagined the implications of this pledge, but by all accounts it was a duty Emma never shirked.

"Baby Lizzie" grew up to become a cultured, reasonably well-educated woman, active in her church and community's charitable works. She had a weakness for orange sherbet, a noticeable fondness for pansies, and a fine hand at needlework. In 1890, she spent nineteen weeks touring Europe with five other young ladies. She taught a Sunday school for Chinese immigrants and served as secretary of the local Fruit and Flower Mission and treasurer of the local Young Women's Christian Temperance Union. If not considered beautiful, she was certainly not repulsive, with glossy nut-brown hair and eyes that were described as ice blue, light brown, or gray, depending on the source. Whatever color they were, Lizzie's gaze was undeniably striking, almost unnerving, even in black-and-white photos.

But what about Lizzie's personality? Never mind her favorite posy or how she spent her Sunday mornings, what was she really *like*?

Those who ought to have known her best left few clues. Mr. and Mrs. Borden had rarely spoken of family matters, and Emma Borden was so intensely private that she granted only one interview—more than twenty years after the crime.

So here is where things become slippery, where solid facts give way to the observations and impressions of those outside the Borden household: the friends, acquaintances, shopkeepers, and dressmakers who spoke out only after Lizzie Borden stood accused of committing a double axe murder in broad daylight. Imagine for a moment how that glaring circumstance might influence the details they chose to share.

Even keeping that in mind, two contradictory traits stand out: Lizzie's reserve, and her temper. Both of these aspects of Lizzie's personality pop up in multiple newspaper interviews and statements to police investigators.

Like her father, who simply "shut his teeth and walked away" when his opinions were challenged, Lizzie Borden tended from childhood to be aloof, particularly with new acquaintances. Neither was she one to make a spectacle of herself.

"A great deal is said about her coolness now," a friend told the *Boston Globe*. "That's exactly like her. Why, at the church sociable last winter, when the waiter that has been spoken about fell on her wrists—it was a heavy dumbwaiter filled full of dishes, so heavy that it took a strong man to lift it off her arms where it had fallen and pinned them under it—instead of screaming or fainting or doing anything that any other woman but Lizzie Borden would have done, she merely said in a low voice, 'Will someone come here?'"

Behind that cool exterior lurked a volatile temper. Lizzie's grammar school principal said it most gently, remembering her as "subject to varying moods." A former city marshal of Fall River, on the other hand, confided to a state police detective, "This girl Lizzie Borden is known by a number of people here to be a woman of a bad disposition if they tell what they know." Another Fall River citizen remarked to the same detective, "Lizzie is known to be ugly."

Ugly. Peculiar. Odd.

These words crop up again and again in the state detective's notes on the Bordens. Lizzie's uncle Hiram Harrington told police, "She is very strong willed, and will fight for what she considers her rights." In another interview he went even further, remarking on his niece's "repellent disposition." More than one informant suggested that Lizzie came by her forceful temperament naturally. "Mrs. Morse the mother of Lizzie Borden was a very peculiar woman," went one report. "She had a Very bad temper. She was very strong in her likes and dislikes."

Lizzie's friends, however, viewed the same traits in a different light. As they saw it, Lizzie's distinctive combination of frankness and fearless honesty created what one supporter called "a monument of straightforwardness. I never shall believe, even were she convicted of the deed, that she committed it," her friend continued, "unless she were to confess herself, and then the marvel would be greater to me that she had concealed her act than that she did it. That is her character. If she had a reason sufficient for herself for murdering those people, it would be like her to say she did it and give her reason."

And what about Mr. and Mrs. Borden? What might make anyone—much less their own daughter—want them dead?

You would not know it to look at him, but at the time of his death Lizzie's father, Andrew Jackson Borden, was worth close to $500,000—a fortune that today would equate to nearly $10 million. The medical examiner found $81.65 on his body, a respectable amount of pocket change even now, but equivalent to $2,000 in 1892. The son of a fish peddler, he was a classic self-made man, rising from cabinetmaking and undertaking to become president of the Union Savings Bank and a director of the B.M.C. Durfee Safe Deposit and Trust Company. He also served on the board of directors of two prominent local mills. Over the course of his nearly seventy years Mr. Borden had accumulated two farms in nearby Swansea, an entire corner of Main Street, and various other rental properties scattered throughout the area.

And yet he was not the richest man in town—not by a long shot. His house was not on the fashionable Hill at the north end of Fall River, nor did it have running water upstairs. Like most others of his day, he saw no need for gas lighting when kerosene lamps were cheaper and safer. The Borden home did, however, boast the luxury of central heating, as well as a flush toilet in the cellar, though its presence never completely broke Mr. Borden of the habit of emptying his morning slop pail into the yard. It was just that kind of thrift and indifference to convenience that helped earn him a reputation as a hard and tightfisted old fellow.

SLOP PAILS AND CHAMBER POTS

Don't think for a moment that Andrew Borden was flinging raw sewage onto his lawn. Slop pails—unlike chamber pots—did not contain nightly deposits of urine (or worse). Because the Borden house had no running water upstairs, each bedroom was equipped with a pitcher of clean water, a basin, and a slop pail. After washing and brushing their teeth in the basin, the Bordens would empty the soapy water into the slop pail and carry it down to the water closet—or in Mr. Borden's case, the yard. What he dumped on his grass each morning was no dirtier than bathwater.

There's no denying that he counted every cent, but there was more to Andrew Borden than penny-pinching. He was also every inch a gentleman, an old-fashioned Yankee to the core. Temperate. Industrious. Courteous. Thin-lipped, with pale blond whiskers, his manner was such that even his "shocking bad hats" and threadbare ties could not interfere with his dignity. Above all, he was unfailingly fair and upright in his business dealings, and expected no less than the same rigid honesty from others.

Then comes Mrs. Borden. Not a soul in Fall River had an unkind word to say about her. In fact, few had anything at all to say about Abby Borden. She was not much to look at, thickset and graying, and so thoroughly ordinary that her murder was perhaps more disturbing than her husband's. She had no personal property of any particular value. Abby Borden, to put it crudely, was not worth killing. Yet those who cared for her cared deeply. According to the *Fall River Daily Herald,* Mrs. Southard Miller "said that she had lost in Mrs. Borden, the best and most intimate neighbor she had ever met."

With those she loved Mrs. Borden was not stingy with her affections. "Sit right down," she had said to John Morse when he came unannounced to their door not long after the dinner hour Wednesday afternoon, "we are just through and everything is hot on the stove. It won't cost us a mite of trouble."

More than anyone in the world—more, perhaps, than her own husband and his children—she loved her half sister, Sarah Bertha Whitehead. "Bertie," as she was called in the family, was easily young enough to be Mrs. Borden's daughter—thirty-six years younger, in fact—and Mrs. Borden doted on her, walking the five blocks to the Whitehead house almost daily, sometimes with gifts of mince pies sprinkled with rose water, or cast-off clothing from Lizzie and Emma's closet for Bertie's struggling family. Bertie had even named her own little girl Abbie in Mrs. Borden's honor.

Like anyone else, the Bordens had their faults, but nothing that could begin to make such an act of butchery comprehensible.

"I DON'T KNOW JUST HOW TO PUT IT"

When questioned by police, most of Lizzie's neighbors were care-ful to declare they had never seen anything out of the ordinary among the Bordens. Even so, many of them leaked an acknowl-edgment of the unsavory rumors circulating through town.

Neither Lizzie nor Emma had ever cared much for their step-mother. Thanks to Lizzie's brusque tongue, her feelings had been common knowledge since her school days. Emma, though far more discreet than her sister in public, found it more diffi-cult than Lizzie to be cordial toward Abby Borden in private. Her distaste for Mrs. Borden is easy enough to imagine. At twelve Emma promises her dying mother she will watch over her baby sister, and for two years she devotes herself to that promise. Then comes Abby—not only taking her mother's place alongside Mr. Borden, but jeopardizing Emma's motherly relationship with five-year-old Lizzie. There's no telling what kind of emotional tug-of-war Emma and Abby Borden might have waged for the prize of Lizzie's affection.

On the other hand, it is equally possible that Emma resented what struck her as indifference from her stepmother. Lizzie's childhood friend, Mary Ella Brigham, described Abby Borden as "not at all affectionate or calculated to draw the children to her. She was simply mild and good, and so long as things went smoothly she would have very little to say." If young Emma had dared to hope that the new Mrs. Borden would ease her responsi-bilities, perhaps even mother *her* a little, she may have been sorely disappointed.

However much or little Abby Borden tried to win over her stepdaughters, she never succeeded. Emma and Lizzie, it was said, did not always eat from the same table with Mr. and Mrs. Borden. Instead, the Borden daughters kept to themselves, sometimes entertaining their friends privately in the spare bedroom upstairs rather than the downstairs parlor. Aside from the care of their own rooms, they left the majority of the household responsibilities to Bridget and Mrs. Borden. Neither of the girls called Abby Borden Mother. Emma called their stepmother by her Christian name, while Lizzie usually addressed her as Mrs. Borden, or Mrs. B.

This had not always been the case—at least, not where Lizzie was concerned. Although she was known to speak harshly of her stepmother behind her back, Lizzie herself had to admit that Mrs. Borden "never spoke or acted unkindly to either of us," and so for most of her life Lizzie had been willing to grant Mrs. Borden the courtesy of calling her Mother. In 1887, the relationship began to falter.

That spring, Abby Borden's own stepmother, the widow Gray, decided to move out of the Fourth Street duplex she shared with her daughter Bertie. Bertie's family could not afford to pay Mrs. Gray $1,500 for her half of the house, and the entire place was put up for sale. Abby Borden could not abide the thought of her beloved half sister being forced from her home, so in an uncharacteristic flourish of generosity, Andrew Borden bought Widow Gray's share of the house and deeded it to Mrs. Borden.

It was an extraordinary kindness. With a scratch of his pen Mr. Borden had granted Bertie Whitehead the security of a home far above her indolent husband's meager means and Mrs. Borden the assurance that her dearest relative would always remain within easy reach. The cost, however, would ultimately be more than Andrew Borden had bargained for.

Perhaps if they had heard of this arrangement from their father, or even their stepmother, Emma and Lizzie might have taken the news more gracefully. Instead, Lizzie said, they first learned of the purchase from "outsiders."

Emma and Lizzie were incensed—jealous and wounded with an intensity that is difficult to understand. We can only guess why. Perhaps they had never seen their father do something so lavish, and resented watching others benefit from such a gesture. "[W]hat he did for her people he ought to do for his own children," Lizzie had informed her stepmother. Most of all they seemed disturbed by the notion that Mrs. Borden had "persuaded" their father to buy the house. Perhaps they began to fear their step-mother's power over him.

Capitulating to fairness, Mr. Borden gave his daughters the deed to their grandfather's former home on Ferry Street. Emma and Lizzie would collect rent on the property for the next five years, until Mr. Borden purchased the home from them for $5,000 just weeks before his death. But the rift did not heal. After the dis-agreement, Lizzie only seldom addressed Mrs. Borden as Mother. Emma's relationship with Mrs. Borden, which by Emma's own admission had always been weaker than her sister's, continued to curdle.

Mrs. Borden's family sensed the resentment. When Lizzie or Emma saw Bertie on the street, they refused to acknowledge her. Widow Gray also felt the cold shoulders of the Borden girls on the rare occasions she tried to visit Abby at the Borden house. When Mrs. Borden herself went calling, she never complained about the situation at home. It was simply not in her nature. "A very close mouthed woman," as the widow Gray described her, Abby Bor-den "would bear a great deal, and say nothing." Something must have betrayed the strain, though, for Widow Gray had once told Mrs. Borden she "would not change places with her for all her money."

Maybe that was when the other rumors began seeping through Fall River. Despite the hundreds of dollars he'd spent to send Emma to a young ladies' seminary and Lizzie on a grand tour of

Europe, despite the pretty studio portraits, the big closet over the stairs filled with fine dresses, the sealskin capes hanging in the attic, and the weekly allowances equivalent to nearly one hundred dollars today, local gossip had it that Andrew Borden was a miser; his stingy habits left his daughters seething with frustration.

There was likely a kernel of truth in it. "He was close in money matters," Lizzie remembered, but would give her nearly anything she asked for, "though sometimes I had to ask two or three times," she added. If there was anything she didn't want to request directly, Lizzie explained, "I would go to Mother, and she would always see that he humored me."

Ample though his daughters' small comforts and luxuries were, there is no way around the fact that Andrew Borden's fortune was capable of providing much, much more. "Mr. Borden," Alice Russell struggled to tactfully explain, "was a plain living man with rigid ideas, and very set. They were young girls. He had earned his money, and he did not care for the things that young women in their position naturally would; and he looked upon those things—I don't know just how to put it."

When a friend suggested it would please his daughters to move into more fashionable quarters, Mr. Borden had replied, "What is wrong with the house? It is good enough for me—good enough for any one to live in." And indeed it was—a pleasant, sturdily built place with airy rooms, an abundance of tall windows, and five bedrooms, all within easy walking distance of his business contacts in town. Much as they would have preferred an ornate house on the Hill, Lizzie and Emma both had to agree that living on Second Street was more convenient for their father, so they did not urge him to move. But that could not keep them from noticing how lavishly other less well-to-do businessmen indulged their daughters' expensive tastes.

Whatever the cause of Lizzie and Emma's discontent, it could not be kept sealed behind closed doors. People noticed, and they talked. The Bordens were too well bred to quarrel in front of the maid, but like Bertie Whitehead and Widow Gray, Bridget Sullivan could not ignore the tension. Despite her light duties, Bridget had given her notice three times, staying first out of loyalty to Mrs. Borden and later after being offered a raise, likely out of Abby Borden's own pocket.

And there were other strange things about the household—"odd habits," Bridget called them. Those three locks on the front door, for starters. And that key on the mantel shelf in the sitting room. Mr. Borden was not the only one who kept his bedroom door locked—Lizzie did, too—but only Mr. Borden left his key in plain sight.

Just over a year before he was murdered, Mr. Borden arrived at the police station to report that someone had burgled his house in broad daylight with his daughters and the maid both at home, sneaking up the back steps, through the master bedroom, and into Mrs. Borden's adjoining dressing room. There the thief had broken open Mr. Borden's desk and made off with $80 cash, $25 to $30 in gold, Mrs. Borden's gold watch and chain, and a number of horse-car tickets. A six- or eight-penny nail, likely used to pick the lock, was found jutting from the bedroom's keyhole. No other room in the house was disturbed, and no one else's property was stolen. Nobody had seen a thing—not the three women inside the house, nor any of the neighbors Inspector Dennis Desmond questioned.

However clever the thief had been about slipping in unseen, swiping the horse-car tickets was a mistake. Mr. Borden had once been a director of the Globe Street Railway Company, and these free tickets were a perk—specially marked and easily identifiable. Once the conductors were alerted, anyone attempting to use them would be immediately linked to the robbery. Eventually there would be rumors that the tickets had indeed been used and traced to none other than Lizzie Borden, prompting her father to hush up any further investigation. Inspector Desmond, however, made no such claim in his report of the break-in. "So far as I know this robbery has never been solved," he concluded.

Why, then, with a thief still at large, would Mr. Borden triple-lock his front door, only to leave the key to his bedroom on the mantel shelf for anyone in the house to use? Some wondered if it was a subtle jab aimed at the real culprit—his way of silently proclaiming that the theft was an inside job.

But by the following spring, the barn had also been broken into—twice. The only thing of value inside was a flock of pigeons, but that did not change the fact that the Bordens' security concerns seemed to be mounting, nor did it quell the uneasiness spreading throughout the family as spring gave way to summer.

"LIZZIE'S" PIGEONS

Myths persist to this day that the pigeons in the barn were Lizzie's beloved pets. One day Mr. Borden beheaded them to punish her, the story goes, so a vengeful Lizzie hacked him to pieces with the very same hatchet.

There is no evidence, however, to suggest that the pigeons were anything more than livestock occasionally served at the Borden dinner table, and though Mr. Borden did slaughter them soon after the break-in— probably to deter future burglars—Lizzie herself testified that he'd wrung their necks.

INVESTIGATION

"TELL HIM ALL, LIZZIE"

August 4, 1892

Assistant Marshal Fleet stood beside the little sofa in Lizzie's bedroom, pencil poised over his notebook. "Has your father or mother ever had trouble with anyone that you know of?" he repeated.

Lizzie, literal-minded sometimes to a fault, claimed that she did not know of anyone—perhaps meaning that she could not name anyone as a certain enemy. Alice Russell disagreed. "Tell him all, Lizzie," she urged. "Tell him about the man that you was telling me about."

The very night before, Lizzie had knocked on Alice Russell's door. For two hours Alice had sat listening in amazement as a fretful Lizzie described a series of unsettling events: the daylight break-ins, the ill-mannered man she'd heard her father order out of the house after an argument over renting some property, the figure she'd seen skulking around the back of the house when she came home one night, and finally, the sickness that had struck her parents so much more severely than herself.

"I think sometimes—I am afraid sometimes that somebody will do something to him; he is so discourteous to people," Alice remembered Lizzie saying of her father. Mr. Borden had even been rude to Dr. Bowen that same morning when Bowen stopped in to check on the family, Lizzie admitted. Both Lizzie and Mrs. Borden had been ashamed of the way he'd dismissed the doctor's friendly concern—"mortified," Lizzie had said. "I feel as if I wanted to sleep with my eyes half open—with one eye open half the time—for fear they will burn the house down over us."

At Alice's urging, Lizzie told the assistant marshal a fraction of what she'd told her friend the night before: Two weeks ago she heard the front bell ring, and her father had let a man into the house. "I did not hear anything for some time, except just the voices; then I heard the man say, 'I would like to have that place, I would like to have that store.' Father said, 'I am not willing to let your business go in there.' And the man said, 'I thought with your reputation for liking money, you would let your store for any-thing.' Father said, 'You are mistaken.' Then they talked a while, and then their voices were louder, and I heard Father order him out." She did not know who he was, had not seen him, and could not tell all that he said—only that he sounded angry.

That was all the information she offered.

"HER ACTIONS WERE RATHER PECULIAR FOR A LADY"

Outside of the Borden home, news of the murder was flashing through the streets.

In the first scramble for a doctor, the sight of Mrs. Churchill as she sped across the street had caught the eye of John Cunningham, a reporter for the *Fall River Globe,* out collecting the weekly pay-ments from subscribers. "Her actions," he noticed, "were rather peculiar for a lady." Smelling a scoop, he circled back down the block, where a group of men had gathered around Mrs. Churchill as she stood relaying the initial fragments of information. Learn-ing there was trouble at the Borden house, Cunningham headed straight for the nearest telephone—at Gorman's paint shop about half a block farther north—to notify the city marshal. Before he left Gorman's he also phoned his editor at the *Globe,* as well as the *Fall River Daily Evening News.*

At about the same time, Charles Gardner, a stable keeper driv-ing a customer down Second Street to change a hundred-dollar bill at the bank, became one of the first to hear a garbled sliver of the news: "[A] young lad told me that there had been a fight." His customer remembered, "Some one said there was a man stabbed another one."

By the time the pair had made their transaction and headed toward the train depot, Mr. Gardner spotted John Manning, a reporter for the *Herald,* "on the run going up Second Street." When the first volley of police officers arrived, Manning was already sitting on the Bordens' doorstep, hopeful that he would be able to pass inside along with them. He did. In the ten minutes he was in the house, Manning saw it all—Lizzie sitting in the kitchen surrounded by her neighbors, Dr. Bowen displaying Mr. Borden's wounds for Deputy Sheriff Wixon, and Inspector Doherty examining the position of Mrs. Borden's body on the floor upstairs. On his way out he spoke with Bridget Sullivan, who was sitting on the attic steps.

Outside, two other reporters were already searching the yard: John Cunningham of the *Globe* and Walter Stevens of the *Evening News.* Together Manning and Stevens inched along the fence line looking for footprints, peered into the old well, and tried the outer cellar door but found it fastened. Then they parted, Stevens heading for the house, while Manning had a look into the barn before returning to his office.

The first newspaper report would be on the street in two hours, sold out within minutes.

"THE [MOST] GHASTLY THING I HAVE EVER SEEN"

In a thoroughly improbable coincidence, Dr. William Dolan, the county medical examiner, happened to be passing down Second Street at 11:45 the morning of the murders. Noticing the commotion, he made his way inside and into the very center of the action—viewing the bodies, arranging for the crime scenes to be photographed, collecting hair samples, and sealing up milk specimens in jars bound for Harvard, where a chemist would verify whether any attempt at poisoning had been made. Upon his arrival, Dolan had taken only a cursory look at the victims; now it was time to examine them thoroughly.

Dr. Dolan's was by far the most professional examination of the bodies thus far, but even he was startled by the ferocity of the wounds. Mr. Borden's face, he said, was "the [most] ghastly thing I have ever seen." Although there were ten distinct cuts in all, at that time Dr. Dolan could not differentiate each of them. One blow sliced straight through the nose, lips, and chin. Another dented the forehead, split the left eyeball in two, and carved the cheekbone in half. Whole slivers of bone were missing entirely; others were driven into Mr. Borden's brain. In all, the murderer had opened a gap two and a half by four inches in the left side of Andrew Borden's skull.

Abby Borden's wounds, though slightly less gruesome to the eye, were even greater. Dolan counted eighteen blows to the back of the head—four to the left side, fourteen to the right. Only the blows on the right side had penetrated the skull. The cuts in this cluster were so near to one another they had effectively become crushing wounds, smashing shards of bone into Mrs. Borden's brain as though she'd been clubbed by a blunt instrument. The bleeding was so profuse she was soaked halfway to the waist, clear through to her underclothes. Even the canvas backing of the carpet on which she lay was saturated with blood.

"IT IS NO USE IN SEARCHING THIS ROOM"

Down cellar, police were unearthing a slew of weapons capable of inflicting exactly those injuries. They hardly had to look for them. Mr. Borden was particular about keeping his tools all in one place, and Bridget led them straight to a box on a shelf in the wood room alongside the chimney. She reached up and fished out two hatchets, which she handed down to Officer Mullaly. The larger of the two, a claw hatchet, had a rust stain on its head and a smudge of something red along the handle that looked as though it had been washed or wiped. Two axes, their handles coated with ashes, were also retrieved from the south wall of the cellar. Mullaly gathered them all up and laid them on the brick floor of the washroom, standing guard until Assistant Marshal Fleet arrived.

The big claw hatchet with its peculiar stains interested Fleet most. He took it aside and set it behind some boxes in the adjoining room under the stairs, where Mr. Borden kept shingles and vinegar barrels. Then Fleet searched the rest of the cellar, checked the outer cellar door, and looked into the barn long enough to satisfy himself that no one was there. The time had come, Fleet decided, to search Lizzie Borden's room.

Fleet summoned two officers to accompany him and went upstairs to Lizzie's bedroom door. It was locked. Fleet rapped. The bolt turned and Dr. Bowen appeared, opening the door just wide enough for the assistant marshal to see his face. His fearful expression, and the way he held the door, made Fleet think something was the matter inside. Fleet told the doctor that they had come to search the room.

"Just wait a moment," Dr. Bowen said without explanation, and closed the door.

Fleet waited, his suspicion mounting.

When the door opened, it was Bowen again. "Is it absolutely

necessary that you should search this room, Lizzie wants to know?"

"Yes," Fleet said, "I have got to do my duty as an officer, and I cannot leave the premises until I have searched the whole of this house."

Once more the door shut in Fleet's face before he was allowed inside.

Lizzie Borden lay on the sofa beside the windows, her eyes scarcely open. "It is no use in searching this room," she said. "Nobody can get in here, or put anything in. I always lock my door when I leave it. How long will it take you?" she asked as the officers began searching her bureau drawers, her bed, her shelves, the little curtained alcove she used as a toilet room, and anything else they could get at in both her room and Emma's.

"It won't take me long," Fleet said. "I have got to search it, though."

"I do hope you will get through soon," Lizzie replied, ruffling the assistant marshal yet again with her blunt manner. "It will make me sick."

"I wish to ask you some questions," Fleet said.

"Please be brief," Lizzie answered, "for I am very weary. I have answered a great many questions."

"You said this morning that you was up in the barn for half an hour," Fleet said. "Do you say that now?"

"I don't say a half an hour, I say twenty minutes to half an hour."

"Well, we will call it twenty minutes, then."

"I say from twenty minutes to half an hour, sir," she informed him with the same sharpness she'd used when he referred to Mrs. Borden as her mother. If Fleet had had any sympathy for Lizzie Borden prior to that moment, it all but vanished.

"I DON'T LIKE THAT GIRL"

Out in the barn, the city marshal himself, Rufus Hilliard, was overseeing the search. The police hoped to find one of two things: confirmation of Lizzie's alibi—her claim that she'd been up in the loft when her father was killed—or evidence of the murderer. It was about three o'clock in the afternoon and his men were "stifling hot" in their blue woolen uniforms as they rifled through the dusty workbenches and piles of hay. Officer Philip Harrington was among them.

It had been more than two hours since Harrington had spoken with Lizzie, and still suspicion nagged at him. "I don't like that girl," he told Hilliard.

"What is that?" the marshal asked.

"I don't like that girl," Harrington said again. "Under the circumstances she does not act in a manner to suit me; it is strange, to say the least."

He did not elaborate for the marshal just then, not about the surprising calm she'd displayed under questioning, or about how she'd dismissed Harrington when he tried to caution her about the firmness of her answers. It would be well, he'd advised, for her to be careful what she said, owing to the excitement. Perhaps on the morrow, she would be in a better frame of mind to give a clearer statement of the facts as she knew them. Lizzie had curtsied, saying, "No, I can tell you all I know now just as well as at any other time."

Harrington silently followed the marshal to the loft, where three more officers were already searching. "I want you men to go give this place [a] complete going over," Hilliard ordered. "Every nook and corner must be looked into, and this hay turned over."

"If any girl can show you or me, or anybody else what could

interest her up here for twenty minutes, I would like to have her do it," Officer Harrington remarked.

Marshal Hilliard shook his head. "Incredible," he agreed.

"AS IF SHE HAD RUN AROUND THE BED AS FAR AS SHE COULD"

Up in the guest room, photographer James Walsh was preparing his camera equipment for what would become the most famous images he would ever capture. Famous, but imperfect. Ideally, a crime scene photo ought to depict an untouched room, exactly as it appeared at the moment of discovery. Photographer Walsh was already too late for that.

When she was first found, Abby Borden lay with nearly a foot of her body wedged under the bed. A yardstick was beside her. Possibly she had been using it to get the bedspread perfectly smooth when the murderer came upon her. To Charles Sawyer, the position of her body made him think she had been trying to get "away from the door, as if she had run around the bed as far as she could."

One wound, a slice of skin two to three inches long, was flapped back over her left ear like a hinge, suggesting that she'd taken one blow—the first?—while facing her killer. Whether she was attacked before or after cornering herself no one would know for certain, but bruises on the bridge of her nose and above each eye marked where her face had struck the floor. Nose to the carpet, arms up around her face, she had evidently flailed and kicked until one of the eighteen blows to the head rendered her senseless.

None of this apparent struggle shows in the iconic crime scene photos snapped that afternoon, however. By the time Mr. Walsh arrived, the bed had been moved, and so had Abby Borden.

Walsh's photos depict her lying neatly centered in the space between the bed and the bureau, as though she keeled straight over like a tree trunk, pinning her arms beneath her. Her skirts are straightened demurely to her ankles, her face completely hidden by the shadow of her shoulder and a mass of blood-blackened hair. The yardstick is nowhere to be seen. The bed had not only been moved, but stripped, searched, and remade—and rather sloppily, too—before the photographer's arrival.

Andrew Borden's body—or more precisely, the sofa on which it lay—had been moved as well. Mr. Borden's splintered face distracts so thoroughly from the rest of the photo, it's not hard to overlook how drastically off-center the sofa is compared with the picture frame hanging above it, or the way its arm juts into the dining room doorway. If Abby Borden was indeed the kind of housekeeper who smoothed her bedspreads with a yardstick, it's difficult to imagine her abiding such an off-kilter arrangement of furniture. A closer look reveals the culprit: small casters on the sofa's feet. For whatever reason, the sofa was scooted sideways on its wheels, the movement hinted at by Mr. Borden's tipped knees and feet. Whether these shifts obscured any vital evidence is anybody's guess.

TURN-OF-THE-CENTURY FORENSICS

Glaring blunders, like repositioning the bodies and failing to secure the crime scene, insured that the Fall River Police Department's investigation was less than ideal even by nineteenth-century standards. Yet if the police had done everything right, they still would have neglected a great deal of what is considered fundamental evidence in the twenty-first century.

In 1892, forensic methods common today were only beginning to germinate in countries such as England, Scotland, and India. The very idea of identifying a criminal from hair, clothing fibers, or fingernail scrapings was unheard of. Even fingerprint evidence, which had been suggested as a unique identifier as early as 1880, was not in widespread use and would not be admissible in court in the United States until 1911.

So while the police almost certainly destroyed or overlooked the minute bits of evidence that might easily crack the case today, that same evidence would have been virtually useless to investigators in 1892.

Photographer Walsh took one view of Mr. Borden and two of Mrs. Borden—the first from behind, and another with the bed moved completely out of the frame to show the full length of her body. That done, Dr. Dolan continued his grisly work.

One at a time, Dolan stripped the bodies and placed them on lightweight folding examination tables called undertaker's boards: Mr. Borden in the sitting room and Mrs. Borden in the dining room. He sliced open their abdomens and removed their stomachs, carefully tying them off at each end to keep whatever remained of their breakfasts inside. Each organ was put into its own airtight jar, sealed with wax, and shipped by express to Harvard along with the milk specimens he'd gathered that morning. Partway through the process, Mr. Walsh took two more photos—close-ups of the Bordens' injuries as their bodies lay half opened on the undertaker's boards. The image of Mr. Borden is easily the most disturbing, showing wounds so profound it is difficult to discern his features, while Mrs. Borden's are obscured by the clotted mess of her hair. Their blood-soaked clothes were bundled up and sent down to the wash cellar, the naked victims themselves stitched back up before being covered and sequestered in the dining room for the night.

By the time Emma Borden arrived on the 3:40 train from New Bedford, the interior of 92 Second Street was returning to some semblance of order. Dr. Bowen had worded his telegram perhaps too softly, for Emma "had no thought of a greater calamity than that her father was sick." At what moment did she begin to realize her life had forever changed—at the sight of the crowds in Second Street, or the policeman standing guard at her front door? How did she react? What did she say? There is hardly any record of it—only that she was "overcome" by the recital of the details of the murder.

However awful the shock, she did not give way for long. True to form, Emma immediately began to shoulder responsibility of the household. She summoned her father's lawyer, Mr. Andrew Jennings, and asked Bridget two questions: whether the maid would stay on with them, and whether she had seen a boy come with a note for Mrs. Borden.

And what did she say to her sister, her beloved baby Lizzie? Were there tears between them, tenderness and grief? Again, no one seems to know. At the inquest less than a week later, Emma herself claimed not to remember what Lizzie had said to her about the murders. "[T]here was so much going on," Emma explained.

Indeed there was.

"RATHER A SINGULAR COINCIDENCE"

Word was out. All of Fall River was talking about the Borden slaying. To Eli Bence, a clerk in D. R. Smith's, a drugstore barely three blocks from the scene of the crime, it seemed that his customers had spoken of nothing else all afternoon. "Why, I understand they are suspecting Miss Borden, the daughter," one lady remarked.

"Is that so?" Bence asked.

"That," as Frank Kilroy put it when he arrived a few minutes later, "was rather a singular coincidence."

Both men had been in the store the previous morning, Wednesday, August 3, when a woman Bence knew only as a Miss Borden came in requesting ten cents' worth of prussic acid. She wanted it, she said, to put on the edges of a sealskin cape, presumably to discourage moths or vermin from nibbling the expensive fur. When Bence informed her that it was not sold except on a physician's orders, the woman protested that she had bought it several times.

"Well my good lady," Bence replied, "it is something we don't sell unless by a prescription from the doctor, as it is a very dangerous thing to handle." (In fact, it is one of the more deadly poisons, also known as hydrogen cyanide. Diluted to a strength of just two percent, more than four drops might be fatal.)

With that, she turned and went out.

"That is Andrew J. Borden's daughter," Frank Kilroy told Bence as she made her way to the door.

By itself the incident had been unusual enough to stick in his memory. Bence had never been asked for prussic acid over the counter. Now it was stranger still.

—•—

At the Borden place, the hubbub had died down somewhat. Three policemen ringed the property, standing guard. Between eight and nine o'clock, Officer Harrington arrived at the back door. With him was Eli Bence. But Bence did not follow Harrington all the way in. He hung back in the doorway to the hall, listening as Harrington spoke to Lizzie in the kitchen. Bence stood within Lizzie's view, but whether Lizzie noticed him or was made aware of his presence is unclear. For Harrington's purposes, it did not matter. Bence was there not to talk but to listen. Exactly what Harrington and Lizzie said is also not known—the particulars of the conversation were not important. Officer Harrington simply needed to get Lizzie talking within Bence's earshot. Bence himself never said a word to Lizzie. He did not need to speak to her to make up his mind. That voice, the druggist thought—low, and a little tremulous—matched the voice of the woman who had asked him to sell her a deadly poison only the day before. He was sure of it.

THE DRUGSTORE CRUSADERS

Could Eli Bence have been mistaken?

According to the local papers, the wife of state police inspector McCaffrey had been operating a sting in Fall River at the beginning of August, testing whether clerks would illegally furnish poison to a customer without a prescription. Just three days before the Borden murder, she and another woman inquired at a nearby drugstore for both arsenic and prussic acid. Their requests were refused. According to the *Fall River Herald*, one of the women was said to resemble

Lizzie Borden. Lizzie's friends pounced on the story, eager to prove Eli Bence was wrong.

That, countered the *Fall River Globe,* was absurd. As far as the *Globe* was concerned, Lizzie Borden resembled the drugstore crusaders as much as she resembled heavyweight champion John L. Sullivan.

"WHAT SHE DID I DON'T KNOW"

There was nothing left to do in the Borden house but go to bed. Alice Russell stepped outside to tell the nearest guard, Officer Joseph Hyde, that they were going to retire for the night and were locking the door. If the policemen needed anything, they could knock.

Wearily, Emma and Lizzie Borden climbed the front stairs to their own bedrooms. Bridget Sullivan had retreated across the street to the home of Dr. Bowen's in-laws, bunking with their servant girl, while Alice, in a stalwart act of friendship, took the murdered couple's bedroom for the night. Uncle Morse, some would later whisper, slept in the very room where Mrs. Borden had been killed. This proved to be no more than a macabre rumor; Morse actually slept in the third-floor bedroom he had been known to occupy on previous visits. Body or no body, the guest chamber was still very much a crime scene. Drops of Abby Borden's blood stained the marble top of the bureau and its wooden drawers, the molding, wallpaper, bed rail, and linens. The blood-blackened carpet on which she'd lain, at least, was gone—pulled up and put in the cellar with the victims' clothing.

Sometime that day, the door between Lizzie's room and her parents' had been unhooked, connecting her now to Alice as well as Emma. Before the three women began undressing for the night, Lizzie took up the slop pail and began to collect the afternoon's wash water from their basins.

"I will go down with that," Alice offered.

"I will go," Lizzie said, "if you will go and hold the lamp."

Down the stairs and through the dark house they went, Alice in front with a kerosene lamp and Lizzie just behind with the pail. They could no longer avoid the sitting room with its blood-spattered doors and wall—it was either that or go through the dining room, where Mr. and Mrs. Borden's corpses lay.

Alice stepped aside at the foot of the cellar steps. Lizzie passed by her, continuing across a little walkway to the water closet, where she dumped the soapy water down the toilet. Then Lizzie went to the washroom sink at the southeast corner of the cellar to rinse the pail.

The light wavered a little. Alice was nervous now. The wash-tub filled with Andrew and Abby Borden's bloodied clothes stood just a few feet away; nearer still, the trio of hatchets and axes lay on the brick floor where the police had left them.

Lizzie ran some clean water into the slop pail, and the two women went back the way they'd come.

From his post at the end of the house, Officer Hyde had observed it all through the big back windows—the light gliding toward him through the dark sitting room and kitchen before disappearing and reappearing in the cellar, the sound of water running in the washroom sink. At that moment, he thought little of it. The women had done nothing unusual, nor made any attempts to conceal their business. The light Alice carried burned brightly the whole time, bright enough that he could see them plainly.

Ten, perhaps fifteen minutes later, the light reappeared. This time it was Lizzie Borden—alone. Hyde watched through the cellar windows as Lizzie emerged into the wash cellar, set the lamp on a small stand just inside the door, and stooped down in front of the sink. What she did there, Hyde did not know. Whatever it was took less than a minute. She did not open the cabinet under the sink, did not run any more water, did not touch the washtub full of her parents' clothing. Hyde knew the small pail of blood-stained cloths he'd seen soaking by the sink earlier that day must be right next to her, below his line of vision. Any married man would understand what that pail was meant for—Hyde's own wife likely kept just such a pail in their own cellar. But if that was all Lizzie was attending to, why hadn't she done so while Alice was there to hold the light for her?

Upstairs, Alice knew nothing of Lizzie's return to the cellar. She had closed the connecting door to do her bathing, then read an account of the murder in the *Evening News*. Finally, she climbed into Mr. and Mrs. Borden's bed, where she lay awake all that long night, listening to the policemen whispering below her open windows.

"LYNCH HIM!"

After the tumult of Thursday, 92 Second Street was strangely quiet on Friday. A Fall River Police sergeant came to collect the axes and hatchets from the cellar, and a detective from the Massachusetts District Police also searched the barn and cellar. That was all.

Undertaker Winward arrived that evening. The bodies were still on the boards in the dining room. No preparations had been made for their funeral, which was to be held the following morning. Winward had his work cut out for him. Not only did he have to dress the Bordens and put them into their caskets, he had the daunting task of making them look somewhat presentable. As was customary, the caskets were to be left open at least long enough for the immediate family to view the departed one last time.

—•—

Lizzie, so the papers said, did not leave her room all day. Twice Dr. Bowen had been summoned to attend to her; at midnight he would come for a third time. Bromo caffeine was no longer relieving Lizzie's distress. Dr. Bowen prescribed morphine. The dosage was a relatively mild ⅛ grain—about 8 milligrams by modern standards.

No one seems to have mentioned how Emma was bearing up. Because she took the strain better? Because she had not been the one to discover her father's body—perhaps had not seen it yet at all—and therefore played a minor role in the unfolding drama? Or because she was not the one suspected of murder?

Nothing but an arrest would soothe the nerves of the city itself. Everyone in Fall River was on edge. The papers fairly seethed with stories about the killing, most of them rife with misinformation. All anyone knew for certain was that a murderer roamed among them, and likely a thoroughly demented one, judging by the descriptions of the corpses. *Horrible Butchery,* the headlines said. *Hacked To Pieces At Their Home. Mutilated Beyond Recognition.*

All day long a building crowd milled restlessly in Second Street, hungry for news. "At almost any moment startling developments may be given to the public," the front page of the *New Bedford Evening Standard* promised. There would probably be no arrests until after the funeral, the paper said, hinting that the family was suspected. Other headlines were far more blunt:

Suspecting The Daughter Lizzie
Members of the Family Are Shadowed
The Suspected Man; John V. Morse

The newspapers' fevered tone had thoroughly pervaded the streets by the time Uncle Morse stepped out of the house at seven o'clock that evening, apparently oblivious to the 600 to 1,500 people loitering in the street. A detective writer would hardly dare invent a more suspicious character than Lizzie's horse-trading uncle, John Vinnicum Morse, with his dark collar-length beard and eyes that seemed to want to bulge from their sockets. The afternoon before the killing he had turned up unexpectedly without so much as a toothbrush—in spite of the fact that he planned to visit for a number of days—and stayed the night in the very room where Mrs. Borden was found with the back of her skull cracked open. His original vocation? Butcher.

As he headed down Second Street for the post office, the throng followed, gaining size. Then someone said his name. At the sound, the crowd's curiosity turned venomous. "That's the murderer!" they cried. "Lynch him!" Lucky for Morse, two plainclothes policemen were also following him. With clubs drawn, they escorted Morse to the post office and back.

There was no escaping the public eye now, and not just in Fall River. As far as Boston and New York City, the Friday evening papers would carry this notice:

$5000 REWARD:

The above reward will be paid to anyone who may secure the arrest and conviction of the person or persons who occasioned the death of Andrew J. Borden and his wife.

Emma J. Borden

Lizzie A. Borden

With that, the Borden sisters had elevated every citizen to detective, judge, and jury.

"HER NERVES WERE COMPLETELY UNSTRUNG"

Lizzie came downstairs Saturday morning in a black silk dress with beaded trim, her dark bonnet adorned with small flowers. No other mourners had arrived. Mrs. Holmes led her into the sitting room and up to the identical caskets—cedar, with three silver handles on each side. There, beside her father's casket, Lizzie Borden cried. Not only cried, but leaned over and kissed Mr. Borden's face. What could Undertaker Winward possibly have done to make such a thing possible? It was a perfectly simple solution: he turned Mr. Borden's head so that only the uninjured side showed.

MOURNING DRESS

Newspapers took special note of Lizzie Borden's funeral attire, remarking that she "was not in mourning"—meaning that despite her obvious grief, her clothing did not follow the conventions of the day.

In 1892, dressing for the funeral of an immediate family member was far more complicated than pulling a black dress from the closet. Very specific types of fabric, trimming, and jewelry were used as public emblems of grief, making the bereaved immediately recognizable. An orphan was expected to wear "deep mourning"—black wool trimmed with crepe—for a full year. Only then would silk with crepe trimmings become acceptable.

So although Lizzie did wear black, it seems her dress was neither wool nor trimmed with the traditional crepe—a somber, lusterless fabric that, as the author of Lizzie Borden's own 1884 etiquette manual,

Manners and Social Usages, explains, "is alone considered respectful to the dead." Lizzie and Emma also did not wear veils, mainstays of bereaved women. Either of these two omissions would have been enough to raise eyebrows.

The service was small and private—only a few friends and relatives, among them Dr. and Mrs. Bowen; Mrs. Churchill; Abby Borden's stepmother, the widow Gray, sister Priscilla, and dear half sister Bertie; Andrew Borden's sister, Luana, and cantankerous brother-in-law, Hiram Harrington; and of course, Uncle John Morse. Reverend Buck and Reverend Dr. Adams read scriptures and prayers. There were no songs, no eulogies.

Outside, onlookers crammed the entire block. Nearly a dozen officers, overseen by Marshal Hilliard and Assistant Marshal Fleet, worked to hold back a crowd estimated at anywhere from two to four thousand people as the front door of Number 92 opened and the pair of caskets appeared, borne by twelve of the town's most prominent businessmen. The caskets were draped in black broadcloth now. A plain wreath of green ivy was the only decoration for Andrew Borden; upon Abby Borden's lay a circlet of white roses, sweet pea, and fern, tied up with a white satin ribbon.

VICTORIAN FLOWER LANGUAGE

Whether for courtship, weddings, or funerals, flowers were not simply something pretty to look at. By the end of the nineteenth century, the Victorians had developed an extensive language of floral symbolism. Some of these associations are familiar to this day,

such as red roses for romantic love or lilies for purity,
but the Victorians went much further, combining multiple varieties and colors into bouquets capable of con-
veying complex messages.

What, then, did the flowers atop the Bordens' caskets represent?

Mr. Borden's plain and simple ivy wreath stood for
fidelity. The blossoms chosen for Mrs. Borden are more
enigmatic. Sweet pea represented simple pleasures, or
sometimes departure. In the context of a funeral, ferns
likely stood for sincerity, but they could also convey
fascination. White roses often expressed the sentiment
I am worthy of you; they might also signify sadness, innocence, purity, or, most intriguing, silence.

And then, perhaps, the most coveted sight of all: Miss Lizzie
Borden herself, leaning on the arm of Undertaker Winward. "Her
nerves," the *New York Times* reported, "were completely unstrung,
as was shown by the trembling of her body and the manner in
which she bore down on her supporter." Behind her came Emma.
Noticeably calmer than her sister, she walked quickly to her carriage, hardly acknowledging the jostling spectators.

All along the procession's route, one black hat after another
silently rose and was lowered—associates of Andrew Borden,
paying their final respects as slowly the long string of carriages
containing the mourners, pallbearers, and clergy swung west
and then north, making their way past the big Andrew J. Borden
building at the corner of Anawan and South Main.

Hundreds more onlookers awaited the cortege beyond the
granite archway of Oak Grove Cemetery. Lizzie and Emma did
not leave their carriages as the caskets were carried from the

hearse to the Borden family lot, nor were they expected to. Standing before a wide-open grave was considered too much to ask of grieving Victorian ladies. Fir boughs covered the tops of the freshly cut graves, and dark fabric screened their sides from view. Only John Morse and the clergymen emerged for the reading of prayers. Within two minutes, all was said and done.

The somber carriages pulled away, but no one stepped forward to lower the caskets into the graves. Unbeknownst to Lizzie and Emma Borden, a message from Medical Examiner Dolan had arrived for Undertaker Winward at 92 Second Street before the funeral service. His orders? Do not inter the Bordens' bodies. Instead, they were taken to the receiving vault.

This large stone tomb, built into the side of a hill near the cemetery's entrance, was most often used to hold coffins through the winter months until the ground thawed sufficiently for burial. Andrew and Abby Borden's remains entered the receiving vault on August 6. They would not leave for nearly two weeks.

"AS THOROUGH AN EXAMINATION AS POSSIBLE"

The moment the funeral cortege left Second Street, Marshal Hilliard and a few of his men entered the Borden house. They had a search to make, a search that Alice Russell had instigated and that Emma and Lizzie Borden almost certainly knew nothing about.

Something in Mr. and Mrs. Borden's bedroom had frightened Alice nearly to pieces that morning. As she turned, fastening her waist, an object on the floor just under the head of the bed caught her eye. Alice was horrified at the sight. Immediately, she fetched both Mrs. Holmes and Officer Hyde. "I slept here last night," she told Hyde as he examined the thing. "If that was there last night, I don't see how I missed seeing it."

It was a wooden club, twenty inches long—not the least bit sharp, but plenty big enough to bash a person's head in. "I was terribly alarmed, because I felt as if in some way it implicated me," Alice said, begging Hyde to tell no one but the city marshal about it.

Now, with no one remaining in the house but Alice and Mrs. Holmes, Marshal Hilliard targeted Lizzie's bedroom, then Emma's, and the guest chamber. Every bit of linen was stripped from the beds and the beds themselves lifted to see whether anything might be hidden inside or underneath. Nothing. The men were gone before the mourners returned.

At three o'clock, Hilliard was back. This time he brought Assistant Marshal Fleet, Captain Desmond, and Detective George Seaver of the state police. Medical Examiner Dolan and the Borden family lawyer, Andrew Jennings, met them there. Small and prone to scowling, Lawyer Jennings had "a body that might rightly be designated as a bundle of nerves." Only two years older than Emma, he had been acquainted with the entire Borden family from boyhood; now in his early forties, he was "considered one of the ablest corporation lawyers in the state."

The authorities intended to search the place literally from top to bottom, beginning with the attic. The Borden sisters had just buried their parents—at least as far as they knew—but they made no objection to this unexpected intrusion. Emma told the men that she wanted "as thorough an examination as possible" of every part of the house. Any door or box they could not open, any lock that baffled them, they needed only ask and the keys would be given.

In the attics, the search party "handled most everything that was moveable." They found nothing of interest in Bridget's room, nothing in the old wooden water tank in the clothes press. Also nothing in the narrow bedroom Morse had been sleeping in. Nothing in the two storage rooms at the front of the house, though two obstinate trunks briefly aroused suspicion. None of the keys they had been given fit the first of them. The other, once unlocked, simply would not open. All the men puzzled over it until they were confounded to the verge of breaking the thing open. Finally, they sent downstairs for help. Both Emma and Lizzie went up to show them the trick of it—a sly little spring release of a sort none of them had encountered before. The key to the first trunk, one of the sisters pointed out, was tied to the side of the trunk itself.

Not one thing in any way connected to the murder was up there, except, perhaps the sealskin capes hanging in one of the two front rooms—just the sort of garment the woman who had asked Eli Bence for prussic acid had described. Assistant Marshal Fleet even went out on the roof, clear up to the ridgepole, and found nothing.

Down they went to the second floor, where Fleet and Detective Seaver personally examined the dresses in the clothes press on the landing directly opposite Lizzie's room. Eighteen or nineteen dresses hung in this large closet, all but one belonging to Lizzie and Emma.

One at a time Detective Seaver took each dress down from its hook and passed it to the assistant marshal to examine before the big front window. The Bordens' murderer must have been spattered with blood, and if that murderer was Lizzie Borden, one of her dresses must be stained.

Fleet and Seaver noticed no stains of any kind. One or two heavy silk dresses they left untouched. If a lady were to go on an axe-wielding killing spree, it stood to reason that she would not put on her best silk to do so.

Stains or no stains, there was one dress Marshal Hilliard decided he must have as evidence—the one Lizzie Borden had been wearing the day of the murders. Lawyer Jennings relayed the marshal's request to Lizzie, and within a few moments she retrieved three garments from the clothes press: a dark blue blouse and skirt of patterned or "figured" fabric, as it was called at the time, and a white underskirt.

Room by room, the search party slowly spiraled its way down to the cellar, where the intensity of the inspection fizzled. The men had been at it for three hours. They could not have been more thorough, Medical Examiner Dolan told Emma, "unless the paper was torn from the walls and the carpets taken from the floor."

So when they finally came to the cellar, Marshal Hilliard did not order his men to dismantle the wood and coal piles or sift through the bushel baskets of ashes. He let it go at looking into each room and examining the foundation and chimney to be sure no bricks or stones had been removed. But he would send a mason to dismantle the base of the chimney first thing Monday morning, he told Lawyer Jennings as they climbed the cellar steps to the kitchen, in case anything had been thrown down it.

"IS THERE ANYBODY IN THIS HOUSE SUSPECTED?"

At quarter to eight that same evening, a knock came at the back door of 92 Second Street. It had already been an exhausting day. The funeral, the searches. And now what?

Once again, it was Marshal Hilliard. Beside him stood the mayor of Fall River, Dr. John Coughlin, a sweet-faced man with a full beard and turned-up mustache.

"I have a request to make of the family," Mayor Coughlin said once the Bordens had assembled in the front parlor, "and that is that you remain in the house for a few days, as I believe it would be better for all concerned."

"Why, is there anybody in this house suspected?" Lizzie asked.

The mayor hedged. "Well, perhaps Mr. Morse can answer that question better than I, as his experience last night, perhaps, would justify him in the inference that somebody in this house was suspected."

Such a roundabout reply did not satisfy Lizzie Borden. "I want to know the truth," she said.

Mayor Coughlin hesitated.

"I want to know the truth," Lizzie said again.

"Well, Miss Borden," Coughlin said, "I regret to answer, but I must answer yes, you are suspected."

"We have tried to keep it from her as long as we could," Emma said.

"Well," Lizzie answered without hesitation, "I am ready to go any time."

Whether Lizzie's surprising reply betrayed her guilt or demonstrated complete confidence in her innocence is debatable. Either way, it created a terribly awkward situation. She was, after all, a woman of impeccable reputation, and there they sat in her formal parlor, practically accusing her of double homicide. Hilliard and Coughlin did not even have a warrant, and Lizzie Borden had all but volunteered for arrest.

If the curiosity seekers outside the house bothered them in any way, the mayor told the family, they should inform him or the marshal. "I shall see that you receive all the protection that the police department can afford from the annoyance and the disturbance of the people congregating about the streets," he promised.

As he rose to leave, the ever-accommodating Emma responded

with equal good faith. "We want to do everything we can in this matter," she said.

It all sounded so courteous, but in fact the entire Borden household was now under house arrest.

"I WOULDN'T LET ANYBODY SEE ME DO THAT, LIZZIE"

When Alice Russell came downstairs Sunday morning, Lizzie stood at the foot of the stove near the dining room door, a skirt hanging over her arm.

Emma turned from the sink, where she was washing up the breakfast dishes. "What are you going to do?"

"I am going to burn this old thing up," Lizzie declared, "it is covered with paint." She held up the edge of the skirt, displaying a hem soiled with drab green house paint.

Emma could not recall her exact answer later—something like *You might as well,* or *Why don't you.* At any rate, she agreed, and turned back to the dirty dishes without another word about it.

Alice left the room.

When she returned, Lizzie had moved to the opposite side of the stove, into the corner beside the window. The door to the wood closet hung open, a bit of blue material visible on an upper shelf—an odd sight among the fuel and flatirons and other kitchen utensils Alice was used to seeing there. A small piece of fabric was in Lizzie's hand. Alice could not tell if Lizzie was ripping up the skirt or tearing something down from the shelf.

Whatever she was doing, Alice did not like the looks of it. "I wouldn't let anybody see me do that, Lizzie," she said, and left the kitchen again.

Lizzie took a single step back toward the closet. There was

almost nothing she could do to conceal herself. The three big kitchen windows stood wide open, with their blinds open. Any of the policemen in the yard could look inside without so much as standing on tiptoe. If Lizzie Borden had something to hide, she could hardly have picked a worse time or place to do it.

"WHY DIDN'T YOU TELL ME?"

Monday morning, August 8, the Borden property rattled and shook with the sounds of yet another search. Down cellar, a mason chiseled bricks from the base of the chimney. Four police officers under the command of Captain Desmond pulled barrels, boxes, and shingles from under the steps. They dismantled the woodpiles, shoveled through boxes of ash and cinder, and emptied out the coal bins.

They also searched the barn, its privy, and the vault beneath it. They tore a foot of boards from the top of the lumber pile against the back fence and peered down through its center to the ground. They searched the old well behind the barn and examined the yard for any sign of the sod having been turned. Again, nothing.

But in the cellar, in the same room—the very same box—where Bridget had retrieved a pair of hatchets for the police on Thursday, Officer William Medley made a most interesting find. In his excitement Medley "sung out" to Captain Desmond, who stopped what he was doing to come and see.

It was a small hatchet, its handle broken off near the head. That break was curiously fresh—what the authorities termed a "bright" break due to its light color—while the head was coated front and back in an ashlike substance that did not seem to match the texture of the dust on the rest of the tools in the box. Medley rubbed at one of the dark spots on the blade, but whether it was stained with rust or blood he could not tell. Then, handling it carefully to avoid rubbing off any more dust than had already been disturbed, they wrapped it up in a sheet of paper from the water closet. Medley put the bundle into his pocket and took it straight to Marshal Hilliard's office.

Upstairs in the parlor, a private detective from the famous Pinkerton Detective Agency was interviewing Alice Russell. Detective Hanscom had been hired on the advice of Lawyer Jennings, in hopes that the Pinkerton man could help unravel the crime. Both Lizzie and Emma had taken their turn with him and waited in the dining room.

When Alice emerged from the parlor, that hope dissolved in a single sentence. Alice's conscience was in turmoil. She had lied, "told Mr. Hanscom a falsehood."

"What," Emma wanted to know, "was there to tell a falsehood about?"

The detective had asked whether all the dresses that were there the day of the tragedy were still in the house. Out of loyalty to her friend, Alice had answered yes.

Emma was so frightened she hardly heard the rest of the conversation. To bring a private detective into their home only to have him lied to? It was a disaster.

"I am afraid, Lizzie, the worst thing you could have done was to burn that dress," Alice said.

"Oh, what made you let me do it?" Lizzie said. "Why didn't you tell me?"

Alice must confess her lie to Detective Hanscom, the women decided. Not only confess, but tell the detective she was doing so at Emma and Lizzie's insistence. Alice did.

It made no difference. At noon, a warrant was sworn for the arrest of Lizzie Andrew Borden.

"LET US OURSELVES CURB OUR TONGUES"

From the outside, it appeared the police were at a standstill. Forty-eight hours had passed since the funeral, and the hinted-at arrest had not been made. Marshal Hilliard had not breathed a word of the warrant. "At this moment I can say there is nothing to connect any members of the family with the murder," he said, stalling.

It seemed everyone but the police wanted to talk about the murders. "[M]en walked slowly with papers before their faces, absorbing the news," the *New Bedford Evening Standard* reported, "drivers of delivery wagons allowed their horses to pick their own way and went over 'the latest, all about the murder,' and on every corner and in almost every doorway were groups of three, four and half a dozen, explaining and arguing, and driving home their own private convictions with their forefingers."

Unlike the police, the newspapers did not have the choice to remain silent on the matter. The public was in such a frenzy for news that even the sight of Emma Borden bringing in the morning milk made the papers.

FALL RIVER'S NEWSPAPERS

Fall River had three newspapers in 1892: the *Daily Evening News,* the *Daily Herald,* and the *Daily Globe.*

People like the Bordens read the *Evening News*—a respectable, conservative paper favored by mill owners and other well-to-do businessmen.

In between came the *Herald,* another reliable, Republican-leaning newspaper that appealed to the middle class.

The *Globe* was the workingman's paper, Democratic, sensationalistic, and somewhat more reliable than a modern-day tabloid.

Competition between the three kept fresh news available constantly. Some papers published in the morning, others late in the day. The most sensational news—news like the Borden murders—produced special, or extra, editions that hit the streets at all hours, as quickly as the type could be set and the paper inked. Some were no more than a single one-sided sheet.

Finding accurate, unbiased news, especially on the Borden case, posed more of a challenge. John C. Milne, editor of the *Evening News,* was a friend of Andrew Borden and believed firmly in Lizzie's innocence. The *Globe,* almost from the moment of the murders, sided with the police and used a mixture of inside tips (probably from Officer Harrington) and outright hogwash to send its circulation rocketing. Though the *Evening News* had more integrity, both papers were guilty of emphasizing the evidence that favored their verdict on the case. "Two interpretations are not placed side by side so that readers can make their own choice," the *Herald* complained. The *Herald* may have been the least biased paper in town, but it was not above using the Borden case to boost its own numbers. Not at all. "34 Columns of reading matter," its weekly edition advertised in big bold print, "comprising the latest developments in the Borden affair."

From his pulpit on Sunday morning Reverend Jubb of the Central Congregational Church begged, "Let us ourselves curb our tongues and preserve a blameless life from undeserved suspicions." The Bordens' pastor had every reason to be concerned. In spite of her friends' attempts to defend Lizzie's character, juicier stories were making the rounds. An indelible image of Lizzie Borden was emerging, one her nearest and dearest could barely recognize—a cold, conniving Lizzie Borden obsessed with wealth and privilege.

Lizzie, so a pair of local hatmakers heard, had been practicing in a gymnasium, boasting of building her strength. Mrs. Churchill, said a clerk at Troy Mill, had seen something in the Borden house the day of the murders that she would never repeat, even if they tore her tongue out. And everyone in town seemed to know that Lizzie had tried to coax Bridget out of the house just before Mr. Borden's murder by offering her money to buy one of the dress patterns on sale at Sargent's dry goods shop.

These second- and third-hand tales might have been dismissed as absurdities if not for unsettling remarks coming from those who were indeed acquainted with Lizzie Borden. Mrs. Borden's brother-in-law told police he believed Lizzie and her uncle John Morse had "concocted the deed, and hired someone to do it." Worse yet, the *New York Herald* quoted Uncle Morse himself admitting "that there had been ill-feeling between Mrs. Borden and her step-daughters."

One of the most scathing interviews came from another of Lizzie's uncles, Hiram Harrington, who claimed to have spoken with her at length on Friday evening. Whether the visit actually took place is hard to say. Harrington's story is a maddening mixture of the kind of intimate details only a family member might be expected to know and flagrant exaggerations—if not outright lies. He appears to be the first to verify the daylight robbery, for example, but he embellished the story with the claim that diamonds had been among the items stolen. Harrington also tried to convince the *Herald* that Lizzie had refused to see anyone but him since the murder—a claim at least half a dozen friends and neighbors could disprove.

In a manner clearly evoking suspicion, Harrington described the uncharacteristic tenderness with which Lizzie helped Mr. Borden take off his coat and lie down for his nap Thursday morning: "She told me she helped him to get a comfortable reclining position on the lounge, and asked him if he did not wish the blinds closed to keep out the sun, so he could have a nice nap," he said. "All these things showed a solicitude and a thoughtfulness that I never had heard was a part of her nature or custom before," Harrington added, almost, but not quite, suggesting that she'd deliberately positioned her father for his murder.

When asked what motive for the crime, Harrington replied, "Money, unquestionably money. If Mr. Borden died he would have left something over $500,000, and all I will say is that, in my opinion, that furnishes the only motive, and a sufficient one, for the double murder." He had managed to say, without actually using the words, that Lizzie Borden slaughtered her own parents for her inheritance.

If a member of her own family suspected her, the public wondered, why couldn't the police arrest Lizzie Borden? The officers had followed every outside lead—even those given by gossips, drunkards, and children—and come up with nothing. They'd hauled in the usual suspects—peddlers, Portuguese, Russian Jews—and been forced by lack of evidence to set them all free. They'd searched for a man seen with a monstrous cleaver and questioned Mr. Borden's troublesome tenants. Nothing.

Every dead end forced the police to turn right back toward Miss Lizzie Borden of Number 92 Second Street. Everyone knew

Lizzie had refused to let the officers search her room—the *New York Herald* had said so. What more did the authorities need?

In his private office at the central police station, Marshal Hilliard sat considering the evidence. The press was watching, criticizing his every move. "The Fall River police are making a dreadfully bungling mess," a Rhode Island editor said, mocking the officers as "country bumpkins." Even the residents of Fall River had begun grumbling that if Lizzie Borden were a poor man's daughter, she'd have been locked up days ago.

The warrant alone was not enough. It would do no good to arrest anyone if he did not also have enough proof to hold them, and what Marshal Hilliard had told the press was true. He did not have one atom of direct evidence linking Lizzie Borden to the crime.

Lizzie Borden, about twenty years old.

Collection of Fall River Historical Society.

Taken in the early 1890s, this portrait was the basis for most newspapers'
sketches of Lizzie Borden and remains the most recognizable image of her.
The pansy pin seems to have been a favorite; Lizzie also wore it on the first
day of her trial, where it was remarked upon by more than one reporter.

Collection of Fall River Historical Society.

Emma Borden and her mother,
Sarah Morse Borden.

Collection of Fall River Historical Society.

Emma Borden around the time she promised to
"watch over Baby Lizzie."

Collection of Fall River Historical Society.

Emma Borden. Likely taken in the 1880s,
this is the last known photograph of her.

Collection of Fall River Historical Society.

Andrew Borden, about a year before his death.

Collection of Fall River Historical Society.

Lizzie's stepmother, Abby Durfee Gray, three years before her marriage to Mr. Borden.

Collection of Fall River Historical Society.

Uncle John Vinnicum Morse.

Collection of Fall River Historical Society.

Bridget Sullivan.

From The Fall River Tragedy; *collection of the author.*

92 Second Street, as it appeared in the winter of 1892–93. The Borden barn stands at the rear corner of the property, and the edge of Mrs. Churchill's front porch is just visible at left.

Collection of Fall River Historical Society.

Steps leading to the screen door on the north side of the Borden house, where Mrs. Churchill noticed Lizzie "in great distress." Dr. Bowen's house is visible across the street.

Collection of Fall River Historical Society.

The Bordens' backyard. At right, the pear tree and the door Lizzie used to enter the barn.

Collection of Fall River Historical Society.

The south side of the Borden house, showing the sitting room windows with their shutters open. Before washing them, Bridget stopped to chat over the fence at left with the neighbor's maid.

Collection of Fall River Historical Society.

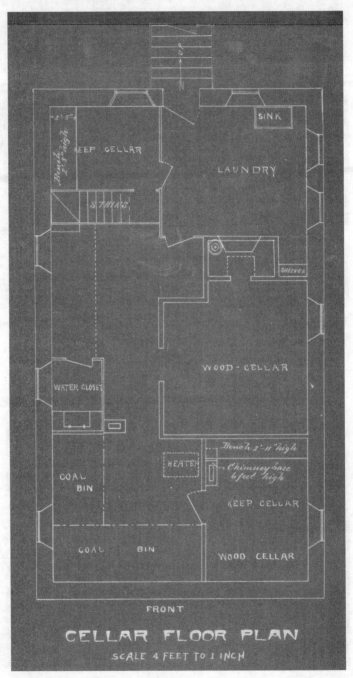

The cellar of 92 Second Street. The hoodoo hatchet was found in an alcove off the large room marked "Wood-Cellar." The sink where Officer Hyde observed Lizzie on the night of the murders is at the upper right.

Collection of Fall River Historical Society.

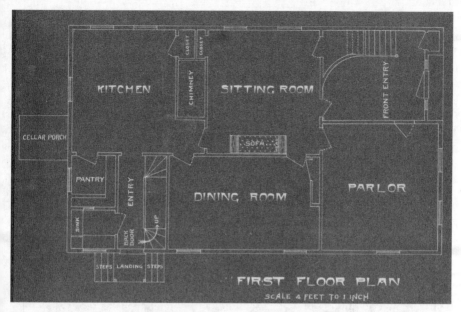

The ground floor. The sofa marks the spot where Andrew Borden's body was found, his head resting on the arm nearest the front entry.

Collection of Fall River Historical Society.

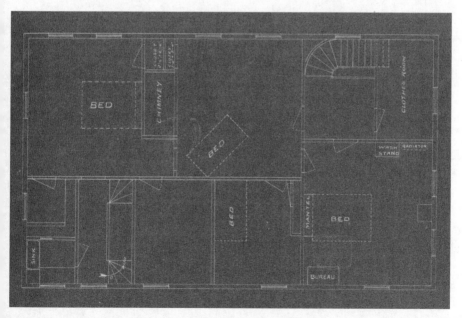

The second floor. Mrs. Borden was found between the bed and the bureau in the front bedroom. Lizzie's bedroom is at the head of the stairs, with the bed angled into the corner.

Collection of Fall River Historical Society.

A bird's-eye view of Second Street, *Boston Globe*, June 6, 1893.

KEY

I: Borden house
II: Borden barn
III: well
IV: fence
V: side entrance
VI: Churchill house
VII: Bowen house
VIII: Chagnon house
IX: Kelly house
X: yard where police kept watch over the Borden property
XI: Crowe barn
XII: Chagnon orchard

INQUEST

"IT WAS HARD TO BE WATCHED SO CLOSELY"
Tuesday, August 9, 1892

By now it was not unusual for Bridget Sullivan to find a police-man at the Bordens' door. She was not, however, accustomed to them asking for her. She must come down to the police station, Inspector Doherty informed her, either by foot or by carriage.

Bridget began to cry. Just the day before, she had tried to pack up her things and get out for good, but the police would not let her go. Her tearful pleading, her begging that she couldn't sleep nights, that she was afraid to remain in the house any longer, made no difference. She had broken down so utterly that Marshal Hilliard himself had come to reason with her. What was a poor Irish girl of twenty-five to do but obey the marshal's orders and pass another night in that house? And now Inspector Doherty had come to arrest her.

But Bridget was wrong. It was only an inquest, Inspector Doherty explained. The police wanted nothing more than to ask her questions. In that case, Bridget told Doherty, she was willing to have the police or anyone else examine her every action since she arose Thursday morning.

Bridget had no way of knowing it, but convening an inquest was an odd choice on the part of the authorities. Inquests are most commonly held in the event of a suspicious death to deter-mine whether there is evidence of foul play. In the Borden case, that was the single fact that had been completely clear from the instant the bodies were discovered. What, then, were the police hoping to uncover?

By law the police were permitted—even encouraged—to conduct inquest proceedings in absolute secrecy to prevent pre-trial publicity from tainting potential jurors' opinions. But Fall River, as the *New Bedford Evening Standard* remarked, was a "leaky place," and it could be no secret that something important was going on within the closely guarded doors of the central station. The papers had already noted the arrival of the district attorney, Mr. Hosea M. Knowlton. A few lucky reporters had also spotted Medical Examiner Dolan pulling up to the back door of the police station to unload a box from his carriage. When the lap robe covering the box slipped, the newspapermen were treated to a glimpse of a dress and hatchet and something else they could not quite make out.

It did not take much sleuthing to deduce what the authorities might be discussing, and once again, an eager crowd gathered in Second Street Tuesday afternoon in anticipation of a spectacle.

They were not disappointed. Following Bridget's examination, Marshal Hilliard and Inspector Doherty arrived at the Borden house at 1:40 with a subpoena—a summons for Lizzie to appear as a witness at the inquest upon the deaths of Andrew and Abby Borden. Immediately. Instead of Lizzie, Mary Ella Brigham, Lizzie's childhood friend, emerged from Number 92 and crossed the street to Dr. Bowen's house. The crowd rippled with excitement—had one of the Bordens fainted from the shock of the summons? But Mrs. Brigham returned without the doctor, and within a few minutes, the marshal and Inspector Doherty escorted Mrs. Brigham and Miss Lizzie into the waiting carriage.

Since the funeral, the strain on Lizzie had begun to crack through her famously rigid exterior. "In the past few days Lizzie has terribly aged," the *Fall River Herald* reported. "The full round cheeks that friends of her former days remember have entirely disappeared, although the bright eyes and haughty expression are still retained. There was not a falter in the step as she came down the stairs." Again the public noted that although she dressed in black, she still was not wearing deep mourning.

As the carriage set off north up Second Street, the news that

Miss Lizzie Borden was headed toward the police station outran the horses. Hundreds of spectators swarmed the entrance, grinding business in the center of town to a near standstill. Pale-faced and biting her lower lip, Lizzie made her way through the crowd and into the station.

The doors locked behind her.

"I DON'T KNOW HOW TO ANSWER IT"

Lizzie Borden stepped up to the witness stand. The second-floor courtroom was all but empty. The doors had been shut, an officer stationed on the landing to keep onlookers out of earshot. Beside her, Judge Josiah Blaisdell sat presiding. District Attorney Knowlton stood before her—a bearded man with a "disinterested expression" and a colossal build. His credentials were as formidable as his stature. A former Massachusetts state congressman and senator, Knowlton would one day become the state attorney general. The table alongside his, customarily occupied by the defense, was empty. Lawyer Jennings's petition to be present during Lizzie's questioning had been refused. No one but Marshal Hilliard, Medical Examiner Dolan, State Detective Seaver, and the district attorney's stenographer, Miss Annie White, had been permitted to enter the courtroom. None of them advised Lizzie that she was not obligated to testify regarding anything that might incriminate herself. Presumably, Lawyer Jennings had already gone over the particulars of the procedure during the brief private conference the authorities granted them before Lizzie took the stand. No one mentioned the warrant for her arrest held by Marshal Hilliard, which allowed him to take her into custody at any moment. Even Lawyer Jennings did not know about that.

Bridget Sullivan had already testified for two and a half hours and, despite her repeated requests to go home, was now sequestered in the matron's room. What Bridget said, what she might have divulged, Lizzie had no way of knowing. Whatever it was had been interesting enough to delay Judge Blaisdell's habitually prompt noon dinnertime by a full thirty minutes.

"Give me your full name," Knowlton began.

One startling fact must be acknowledged: the first volume of the original inquest transcript has been lost. The official record of the one and only time Lizzie Andrew Borden was ever directly questioned in court—gone. What remains is a copy printed in the *New Bedford Evening Standard* on June 12, 1893. District Attorney Knowlton himself provided the transcript, which is believed to have been reprinted verbatim. It is impossible to know if the *Evening Standard* made any significant changes to Lizzie's words; other newspapers certainly did. At any rate, it is the most complete and accurate version known to exist.

THE *EVENING STANDARD* VS. THE *DAILY JOURNAL*

Another frequently quoted source for Lizzie Borden's inquest testimony is the *Providence Daily Journal*. Since the 1920s, prominent Borden scholars have asserted that the *Daily Journal*'s version "does not differ widely" from the *New Bedford Evening Standard*'s, claiming that "the two vary only in slight detail."

In reality, anyone can see at a glance just how different they are. The *Daily Journal* printed less than 5 percent of Lizzie's testimony, reducing the number of words from 15,535 to 651. Nearly one hundred of District Attorney Knowlton's questions are missing, and Lizzie's answers have been condensed into long paragraphs full of disjointed sentences that ricochet from one subject to another. As a result, Knowlton's wording is often attributed to Lizzie, such as when she states, seemingly out of the blue, "I made no effort to find my mother at all." The *Evening Standard*'s version reveals that it was actually Knowlton who asked, at the end of a series of questions regarding Mrs. Borden's whereabouts, "You made no effort to find your mother at all?" Lizzie answered simply, "No, sir."

Despite its alterations to the inquest text, the *Daily Journal* made only a handful of factual errors. Nevertheless, the *Daily Journal*'s version of Lizzie's testimony created a distorted view of Lizzie Borden's voice and state of mind that has spanned three centuries.

Whether she was guilty or innocent, Lizzie Borden's inquest testimony was nothing short of catastrophic. Her answers appear so evasive, contradictory, and obstinate, it's hard to imagine anyone attempting to prove his or her innocence more ineffectively.

And yet Knowlton had his work cut out for him. Lizzie was astonishingly ignorant of her own family's affairs. She was not certain of her stepmother's age or how much real estate her father owned. She could give no useful information about Andrew Borden's financial worth or say whether he had a will.

"Not that I know of," she said more than once, and "I cannot locate the time exactly." "I think, I am not sure, but I think . . ."

It was chore enough to extract plain facts from her. Trying to get an idea of more abstract notions, such as the feelings between her and her stepmother, proved a daunting task. Lizzie testified that she had never had trouble with her stepmother in her life. There was "simply a difference of opinion," she said, regarding Andrew Borden's purchase of Bertie Whitehead's house.

"You have been on pleasant terms with your stepmother since then?" Knowlton asked.

"Yes sir," Lizzie said.

"Cordial?" Knowlton pressed.

"It depends upon one's idea of cordiality, perhaps."

"According to your idea of cordiality?"

"We were friendly, very friendly."

"Cordial, according to your idea of cordiality?"

"Quite so."

"What do you mean by 'quite so'?"

"Quite cordial. I do not mean the dearest of friends in the world, but very kindly feelings, and pleasant. I do not know how to answer you any better than that."

Knowlton was not satisfied. Round and round they went, Lizzie conceding a bare minimum of information to each question, forcing Knowlton to prompt and pry for more.

"You did not regard her as your mother?"

"Not exactly, no; although she came there when I was very young."

"Were your relations towards her that of daughter and mother?"

"In some ways it was, and in some it was not."

"In what ways was it?"

"I decline to answer."

"Why?"

"Because I don't know how to answer it."

"In what ways was it not?"

"I did not call her mother."

"What name did she go by?"

"Mrs. Borden."

"When did you begin to call her Mrs. Borden?"

"I should think five or six years ago."

"Before that time you had called her mother?"

"Yes sir."

"What led to the change?"

"The affair with her stepsister." (Mrs. Borden had no stepsister. Lizzie of course meant Bertie Whitehead, Abby Borden's half sister.)

"So that the affair was serious enough to have you change from calling her mother, do you mean?"

"I did not choose to call her mother."

"Have you ever called her mother since?"

"Yes, occasionally."

"To her face, I mean?"

"Yes."

"Often?"

"No, sir."

"Seldom?"

"Seldom."

Knowlton prodded a while longer, then abruptly changed his line of questioning to Lizzie's whereabouts the morning of the murders. Just as suddenly, Lizzie began answering more freely, even volunteering information.

Lizzie had been the last to rise that Thursday morning. Everyone had eaten, and Uncle Morse had gone to call on another relative in Fall River. Mr. Borden sat in his large chair, reading the *Providence Daily Journal,* while Mrs. Borden dusted in the dining room. Bridget was just bringing in the brush and bucket to wash windows. Lizzie had been ill most of the day before and did not care much about breakfast. She might have eaten half a banana, perhaps a molasses cookie—she did not remember. Her father went into town while the women continued their various chores. Lizzie set up a little ironing board on the dining room table, laid out eight or ten of her best handkerchiefs, and put the flatirons on the stove to heat.

Knowlton worded his next questions very carefully, for he knew that Medical Examiner Dolan believed Mrs. Borden had been dead for an hour to an hour and a half when he first saw her body at 11:45. That meant whoever murdered Abby Borden had done so while her husband was out on his morning errands— exactly the time Lizzie was about to describe.

How long had she spent ironing her handkerchiefs? Knowlton wanted to know.

"I did not finish them," Lizzie said, "my flats were not hot enough."

"How long a job would it have been if the flats had been right?" Twenty minutes, Lizzie guessed.

"How long did you work on the job?" Knowlton asked again.

"I don't know, sir."

What Knowlton had really asked was *Where were you when your stepmother was killed?*

Lizzie Borden had given no alibi.

"I AM SO CONFUSED I DON'T KNOW ONE THING FROM ANOTHER"

"Where were you when [your father] returned?" Knowlton continued.

With that one question, Lizzie Borden's testimony fell apart.

"I was down in the kitchen," she said. "Reading an old magazine that had been left in the cupboard, an old *Harper's Magazine*."

Even if the original inquest transcript were available, it would not convey the atmosphere in that room at that moment. Everyone but Lizzie must have understood the significance of what she had just said. Whether the authorities reacted, whether Lizzie sensed any astonishment or suspicion, is impossible to know.

Her answer had flatly contradicted the version of Mr. Borden's arrival Bridget Sullivan had given only a few hours before.

What exactly had Bridget said? No one knows for sure. Once again, the answer is in that missing volume of inquest testimony, and in Bridget's case, there are no newspapers to resurrect it from. The nearest approximation is her preliminary hearing testimony, given two weeks later. District Attorney Knowlton himself considered it "almost identical" to what she said at the inquest, so what is known of Andrew Borden's return home is taken from Bridget's earliest surviving testimony, given August 26 and 27.

According to that testimony, when Mr. Borden turned his key in the front door's spring lock, it did not open. Bridget, washing windows in the sitting room, heard him trying to unlock the door and went to open it for him. The interior key and bolt, which normally were unlocked each morning, were still fastened. Puzzled and fumbling, Bridget cursed the door. From upstairs came the familiar sound of a laugh—Lizzie's.

That information alone had been remarkable. If Dr. Dolan was right about the time of Mrs. Borden's death, then Bridget Sullivan's testimony meant Lizzie Borden was not the only one on the second floor at that moment. Abby Borden was up there, too, probably still bleeding onto the Brussels carpet. If Lizzie had not done the killing, then the murderer might have been lurking upstairs as well.

And now Lizzie Borden stood at the witness stand, swearing under oath that she had been in the opposite end of the house entirely. One of the women must be wrong—or lying. District Attorney Knowlton had to find out which.

"Are you sure you were in the kitchen when your father returned?" he asked, leaving her an opening to change her mind.

"I am not sure whether I was there or in the dining room," Lizzie said.

Knowlton began to nudge his questions toward Bridget's testimony. "Did you go back to your room before your father returned?"

Yes, Lizzie remembered carrying up some clean clothes, staying only long enough to make a quick repair to one of the garments.

"Was that the time when your father came home?"

"He came home after I came down stairs."

"You were not up stairs when he came home?" Knowlton asked outright.

"I was not up stairs when he came home; no, sir."

Bridget Sullivan had not given Knowlton one reason to doubt her. Bridget's responses had been so clear and consistent, so forthright, that she'd been dismissed as a suspect almost immediately. Lizzie, with her terse, vague answers, had not inspired the same confidence. Anyone standing in Knowlton's shoes would have been skeptical of Lizzie's claim. He diverted her with a few questions about the locks, then returned to the upstairs-downstairs issue from a different angle:

"Where were you when the bell rang?"

"I think in my room up stairs," Lizzie said, contradicting herself as plainly as she'd contradicted Bridget's testimony only moments before.

"Then you were up stairs when your father came home?" Knowlton asked.

"I don't know sure, but I think I was."

"What were you doing?"

"As I say, I took up these clean clothes, and stopped and basted a little piece of tape on a garment."

"Did you come down before your father was let in?"

"I was on the stairs coming down when she let him in."

"Then you were up stairs when your father came to the house on his return?"

"I think I was."

Lizzie Borden's credibility evaporated. First one story, then another, as though Knowlton's questions were not connected to each other. She did not seem to be thinking at all.

Since Friday night, Lizzie had been taking morphine, a highly addictive sedative and painkiller made from opium, capable of causing troublesome side effects such as confusion and hallucinations, for "mental distress and nervous excitement." Saturday, the day of the funeral and the search, the day Lizzie learned she was a suspect, Dr. Bowen had doubled the dose. By today's standards the prescription was unremarkable; Lizzie had been taking approximately 16 milligrams of morphine a day since Saturday, August 6.

Of course, there is no way to prove whether the inconsistencies in Lizzie Borden's inquest testimony were caused by morphine. It is a fact, however, that today, testimony given by a witness under the influence of any narcotic would be questionable, if not inadmissible.

Knowlton in all probability knew nothing of this, so it is hard to tell whether his tone was sarcastic or patient when he asked, "You remember, Miss Borden, I will call your attention to it so as to see if I have any misunderstanding, not for the purpose of confusing you; you remember that you told me several times that you were down stairs, and not up stairs, when your father came home? You have forgotten, perhaps?"

Lizzie finally seemed to realize the bind she was in. "I don't know what I have said," she admitted. "I have answered so many questions and I am so confused I don't know one thing from another."

Knowlton reminded her what she had said, then asked again: downstairs?

"I think I was down stairs in the kitchen."

"And then you were not up stairs?"

"I think I was not," Lizzie decided. She had carried the clothes up right after using the water closet, then had come down and stayed down. It must have been a different day that she'd been on the steps when the doorbell rang.

"I now call your attention to the fact that you had specifically told me you had gone upstairs," Knowlton said, "and had been there about five minutes when the bell rang, and were on your way down, and were on the stairs when Maggie let your father in that day—"

"Yes, I said that, and then I said I did not know whether I was on the stairs or in the kitchen."

"Now how will you have it?"

"I think, as nearly as I know, I think I was in the kitchen."

Knowlton had given Lizzie one more chance, and she had failed. That was the worst of it, but it was not the end. Lizzie could also not account for how she and Mrs. Borden could have spent the two hours from nine to eleven o'clock in the house together without crossing each other's paths, or for why she had not noticed that Mrs. Borden never came downstairs after going up to put fresh pillow slips on the guest bed—an errand that should have occupied no more than two minutes. Aside from Lizzie's brief trip to the water closet and then upstairs to put her clean clothes away, it was almost impossible for Abby Borden to have left the spare room or the house itself without Lizzie seeing or hearing her. Yet Lizzie supposed Mrs. Borden had gone up the back stairs to make up her own bed, or out marketing as she usually did—perhaps visiting her sick friend along the way—even though she would have walked right past Lizzie to do so. Nothing added up.

"YOU DID NOT ANSWER MY QUESTION, AND YOU WILL, IF I HAVE TO PUT IT ALL DAY"

On August 10, Lizzie returned to the stand for the second day in a row. Knowlton tried to begin afresh, asking her to relate Thursday morning's events once again.

Lizzie obliged. She had come downstairs, saw her father reading the paper, spoken briefly with her stepmother in the dining room about the day's marketing, and gone down cellar to the water closet for about five minutes. When she came back, Mrs. Borden was nowhere in sight, and Lizzie assumed she had gone out. That, at least, seemed feasible.

Then Lizzie began to confound him once more. Knowlton could get almost nothing useful from her regarding the critical minutes between 9:15 and 11:00, when Mrs. Borden was murdered. Her father, Lizzie thought, had left the house around 10:00, but Knowlton knew from police witness statements that Mr. Borden had been seen on his usual rounds downstreet as early as 9:30 that morning.

Again and again, Lizzie's answers were infuriatingly terse and matter-of-fact. She answered questions literally to the letter and no further, even when giving more information would have been in her best interest. She would not even commit to having seen Bridget washing the windows, driving Knowlton to the very brink of exasperation.

"Do you think she might have gone to work and washed all the windows in the dining room and sitting room and you not know it?" he asked.

"I don't know, I am sure, whether I should or not. I might have seen her, and not know it."

Knowlton gave up and began to prod at her whereabouts during the second murder. Without too much trouble, they established that her father had come home and settled down on the couch. Lizzie asked Mr. Borden if he wanted the window left open, then left him to his nap. The flatiron was still not hot enough for her handkerchiefs, so out she went to the barn to look for some lead to make sinkers.

Knowlton clearly could not fathom how Lizzie, who had not been inside the barn in three months and had not used her fishing lines in five years, just happened to choose the very hour of her father's murder to suddenly leave the house and go hunting for lead sinkers. Lizzie freely admitted that nothing in particular had prompted her: "I said to myself 'I will go and try and find that sinker; perhaps by the time I get back the flats will be hot.' That is the only reason." And why, an incredulous Knowlton wanted to know, did she begin preparing for Monday's fishing trip by looking for old sinkers when she admitted she had not even bought new lines yet?

"I thought I would find out whether there were any sinkers before I bought the lines," Lizzie explained with the frugal logic she'd learned at her father's knee, "and if there was, I should not have to buy any sinkers."

Knowlton dropped the subject and moved on to how Lizzie occupied herself in the loft of the barn while her father was being butchered in the house. Twenty minutes seemed an awfully long time to pick over the workbench for a handful of scrap metal.

It took longer, Lizzie explained, because she had eaten her

pears first. Knowlton balked at that, and once more they sparred, arguing almost like brother and sister, as though deliberately trying to irritate each other.

"You were feeling better than you were in the morning?" Knowlton asked, calling her upset stomach into question.

"I felt better in the morning than I did the night before."

"That is not what I asked you. You were then, when you were in that hot loft, looking out of the window and eating three pears, feeling better, were you not, than you were in the morning when you could not eat any breakfast?"

"I never eat any breakfast."

"You did not answer my question, and you will, if I have to put it all day. Were you then, when you were eating those three pears in that hot loft, looking out of that closed window, feeling better than you were in the morning when you ate no breakfast?"

"I was feeling well enough to eat the pears."

Lizzie's evasive manner had returned—splitting hairs and offering not one particle more information than Knowlton explicitly requested. Sometimes she gave him none at all. Asked why she had chosen to eat her pears in the one place where she could not see the house, Lizzie answered, "I cannot tell you any reason," though she did inform Knowlton that she could see the house from the barn window. It was after she finished the pears and turned to the workbench at the other end of the barn that someone might have gone in unnoticed. Then could she explain why she had spent a full ten minutes at the workbench with her back to that window? "No," Lizzie replied, "only that I can't do anything in a minute."

Regardless of whether her answers pointed toward guilt or innocence, District Attorney Knowlton had to ask and re-ask his questions to wrench the most trifling details from his witness. Even when his restraint gave way to badgering, Lizzie relinquished the barest minimum of information. Only when it came time to recount the discovery of her father's body did her composure falter.

"I opened the door and rushed back," she said.

"Saw his face?"

"No, I did not see his face, because he was all covered with blood." She'd seen nothing else—not the blood pooling on the floor, the gashes that laid her father's face open, his sliced and dangling eyeball.

"Nothing of that kind?"

"No sir," Lizzie Borden said, and covered her face with her hand. The court waited. It was nearly two minutes before she could go on.

"BEING ENTIRELY DECOMPOSED"

As the third and final day of inquest testimony was commencing on August 11, Medical Examiner Dolan and Dr. Frank Draper, medical examiner of Suffolk County, met at Oak Grove Cemetery. The time had come to perform full and official autopsies on Andrew and Abby Borden.

Once more the Bordens' bodies were stripped, laid out for examination, and reopened from chin to groin. They had not been embalmed, and so there had been nothing but the thick stone walls of the receiving vault to stave off the inevitable decay. After five days, their bodies were no longer stiff with rigor mortis, due to their "far advanced" state of decomposition. Mrs. Borden's brain, Dolan noted, "evacuated in a fluid condition, being entirely decomposed." Mr. Borden's brain had also liquefied but apparently remained inside his skull for the duration of the autopsy. The skin around the wounds had deteriorated enough that the doctors could no longer determine how sharply the edges had been cut. The residue of the couple's week-old breakfasts still remained in their bowels.

Painstakingly, Dolan and Draper measured, numbered, and assessed each wound. In Mr. Borden's case, the doctors determined, the half-dozen disfiguring blows to the face had not been fatal—it was the four to the temple that crushed his skull into his brain and killed him.

On Mrs. Borden they discovered a wound no one had seen before—a slice two and a half inches long and two and a half inches deep into the flesh of her back, just below the neck.

They shaved the back half of Mrs. Borden's head, exposing the severity of the trauma she'd suffered more clearly than ever before: at the crown of her skull, the skin and bone was slashed into a broad gap shaped like the number seven. And this was not the worst of it. Fourteen parallel blows to the right side of her skull had obliterated the bone behind Abby Borden's right ear, leaving a hole measuring four and a half by five and a quarter inches.

The doctors also noted a few internal idiosyncrasies of little consequence: Mr. Borden had a hernia in his groin, Mrs. Borden a small fibroid tumor on her womb. Both Bordens had worn false teeth in the upper jaw. Mr. Borden's right lung was glued to his front ribs, while Mrs. Borden's were "bound down behind but normal." Nothing out of the ordinary for an aged couple a full week postmortem.

But what Dr. Dolan did last of all was quite thoroughly out of the ordinary: he decapitated Andrew and Abby Borden and took their severed heads away with him.

"I DON'T KNOW AS I COULD PUT ENOUGH OF IT TOGETHER NOW"

On Granite Street, the throngs outside the police station were growing restless. "[A]t 3 o'clock the bulletin boards announced that no action had been taken and no verdict had been rendered, and the crowds muttered and grumbled," the *Evening Standard* reported. Twenty minutes later, yet another carriage pulled onto Granite Street. It was becoming a too-familiar sight: Emma and Lizzie Borden, accompanied by Mrs. Brigham. After two days of questions, District Attorney Knowlton still had a few more things to ask Lizzie.

"Miss Borden," Knowlton said inside the courtroom as he neared conclusion, "of course you appreciate the anxiety that everybody has to find the author of this tragedy, and the questions that I put to you have been in that direction; I now ask you if you can furnish any other fact, or give any other, even suspicion, that will assist the officers in any way in this matter?"

All Lizzie offered was the story she'd told Alice Russell about a man she'd seen creeping around the side door of the house when she returned from a visit one night.

"Is there anything else that you can suggest that even amounts to anything whatever?" Knowlton asked.

There was nothing. And with that, Knowlton was finished with her.

This time, Inspector Doherty and Marshal Hilliard did not escort Lizzie past the fretful crowds and into a carriage bound for Second Street. Instead, she was conducted across the hall to the matron's room, where she threw herself down on the lounge, visibly frazzled by the three-day ordeal.

Knowlton and Hilliard considered the evidence before them. Three days' questioning had provided little more than they already knew.

Those who had arrived first on the scene—Mrs. Churchill, Dr. Bowen, Alice Russell—were still shaken by the experience a week after the murder. By their own admission, their recollections were jumbled and confused, and all three ran into details they could not, or would not, swear to on the stand: *I am only guessing,* said Dr. Bowen; *I don't know, because I was so shocked,* said Mrs. Churchill. Both Alice Russell and Mrs. Churchill acknowledged that they were not very observant, but the gaps in Alice's memory are startling. Alice, who had tried to loosen Lizzie's dress to keep her from fainting, could not remember a thing about that dress—whether it was light or dark, one piece or two, all the same material or a combination.

Emma Borden had not been feeling well the day she took the stand, and after less than 150 questions (in contrast to the nearly 850 he asked Lizzie), Knowlton allowed her to step down. "I have omitted a good many questions I should have asked you on that account," he acknowledged for the record.

Uncle Morse answered everything asked of him as freely and confidently as Bridget Sullivan, incriminating no one. His alibi was watertight: the owner of Number 4 Weybosset Street confirmed that he'd been visiting relatives there from about 9:40 until 11:20 that morning.

UNCLE MORSE'S ALIBI

The rumor that John Morse's alibi was too tight to believe continues to circulate in Fall River and beyond—not only was he visiting relatives a mile across town who vouched for him, Borden enthusiasts say, but he remembered the number of the streetcar wagon he rode back to Second Street, the number on the conductor's hat, *and* the names of the six priests he spoke to while on board.

Although Morse's visit to Number 4 Weybosset Street was confirmed by police, the details about the streetcar and the priests really are too good to be entirely true. According to a *Fall River Evening News* story, a conductor on an eastbound wagon did recall passing a westbound wagon full of priests around 11:22 Thursday morning, but Morse never recited the litany of their names in any of his statements to police, or in his court testimony. The numbers on the wagon and the conductor's hat are also nowhere to be found in the official record.

Bertie Whitehead claimed not to know anything about the friction her house had caused within the Borden family. The girls, she thought, had simply never liked her.

Lizzie's uncle Hiram Harrington, whose newspaper interview had been downright vicious, became reluctant to speak so unkindly of his niece while under oath. Although he had "cut [Mr. Borden's] acquaintance" and the two men no longer spoke, Harrington explained, he remained on good terms with Abby, Emma, and Lizzie. When asked what he'd heard from Lizzie about the trouble over Bertie Whitehead's house, Harrington had nothing specific to say. "I don't know as I could put anything together now to tell you, any more than to tell you there was some difficulty some way." Yes, she sometimes spoke "sneeringly" about Mrs. Borden, but he could not recall Lizzie bringing the matter up since the previous winter. None of them spoke much of it, Harrington said, but the difficulties were sometimes "mentioned in a joking way." He even went so far as to point out that things had not always been disagreeable in the Borden household. "For several years, I guess, of his early marriage with her, everything was very, very pleasant, uncommonly so for a step mother."

The testimony of Augusta Tripp, a longtime friend of Lizzie's, also turned out to be a disappointment. Officer Medley's notes from August 7 recorded Mrs. Tripp's statement as follows: "Lizzie told me she thought her stepmother was deceitful, being one thing to her face and another to her back. Lizzie told me her stepmother claimed not to have any influence with her father. But she must have influence with my father, or he never would have given my stepmother's half sister such a very large sum of money. She said, I do not know that my sister or I would get anything in the event of my father's death."

But on the stand Mrs. Tripp disagreed with the officer's version. She did indeed believe those were Lizzie's feelings about Abby Borden, but Mrs. Tripp had never heard Lizzie actually say so outright—especially not the part about the Borden girls being left penniless upon their father's demise. Mrs. Tripp had heard that juicy tidbit from her invalid sister, a Miss Poole of New Bedford.

Only Mrs. Hannah Gifford, a cloakmaker, was willing to go on record and quote Lizzie's distaste for her stepmother directly. Mrs. Borden, Lizzie had once told her, was "a mean old thing."

"She said that?" Knowlton asked.

"She said that, yes."

"Anything more?"

"Well, she says, 'We stay up stairs most of the time; we stay in our room most of the time.' I says, 'You do, don't you go to your meals?' Yes, we go to our meals, but we don't always eat with the family, with them; sometimes we wait until they are through,' she says."

And of course there was the druggist Eli Bence, with his story of the young Borden woman who wanted to buy prussic acid the day before the murders. He had not known it at the time, but he was as sure now as he'd been when Officer Harrington brought him into the Borden house—that lady with the "peculiar expression around the eyes" had been none other than Andrew Borden's daughter.

In the end, no one's testimony was of as much consequence as Lizzie's and Bridget's. Bridget had laid out a clear framework of the hours leading up to the murder, and little that Lizzie Borden said fit well within it. Lizzie's words did not betray guilt, but they did almost nothing to suggest innocence. Her account of the morning of August 4 was, at the very least, worthy of suspicion.

It was not much for Knowlton and Hilliard to go on, but it was all they had.

ARREST

"I HAVE HERE A WARRANT FOR YOUR ARREST"

Fall River could no longer endure the teasing of the newspapers with their endless clues and hints and theories. For two nights a "grim and self-composed" Lizzie Borden, the only apparent suspect, had been escorted back to Second Street to sleep in her own bed. Packed around the central station, the people rumbled with impatience. A rumor leaked out to the reporters that the inquest was done and Lizzie Borden's arrest imminent, but none of them budged. The public, they seemed to sense, would not tolerate another false alarm.

Four o'clock, five o'clock, six. The inquest had been over nearly two hours when Marshal Hilliard and District Attorney Knowlton finally emerged. Without comment the two men ducked into a carriage.

The crowd could do nothing but wonder and wait. Perhaps Knowlton had given up after all, headed back on the Boston train?

The city hall clock struck seven before Hilliard and Knowlton returned. Not far behind came Attorney Jennings.

The moment had come.

Marshal Hilliard entered the matron's room. The supper that had been brought for Lizzie, Emma, and Mrs. Brigham sat untouched before them; Lizzie had not moved from the lounge where she'd collapsed after her questioning. Nor did she rise when State Detective Seaver entered, though there was no mistaking why the men had come. Marshal Hilliard held a paper in his hand. All of them could guess what it was, though only Hilliard knew it was actually the second warrant for Lizzie Borden's arrest, freshly sworn that afternoon. As gently as he could manage, he told Lizzie, "I have here a warrant for your arrest—issued by the judge of the District Court."

The long-dreaded words struck Emma Borden like a slap. Immediately, the tears began to stream down her face.

Lizzie said nothing. Her face turned pale and a sheen of tears glossed her eyes.

"I shall read it to you if you desire"—and here Hilliard addressed Lawyer Jennings—"but you have the right to waive the reading of it?"

"Waive the reading," Jennings instructed.

Lizzie turned to the marshal. Across her face, one newspaperman reported, flashed "one of those queer glances which nobody has attempted to describe, except by saying that they are a part and parcel of Lizzie Borden."

"You need not read it," she said.

Lizzie Borden was now under arrest. There was no dramatic slapping on of handcuffs, no dragging the struggling prisoner away.

Lawyer Jennings spoke a few hopeful words to brace her up, but it was clear to everyone that Lizzie's composure was giving way. She might hold her tongue and her tears in check, but she could no longer force the rest of her body to bear the strain. Lizzie was trembling—trembling so pitifully that Marshal Hilliard decided she would not be locked into the cell that had been prepared for her, but put up in the matron's apartment instead.

Emma Borden did not kiss her sister, did not even say goodbye. All Emma could do was cry as Mrs. Brigham and Lawyer Jennings led her downstairs and into the waiting carriage. She did not seem to see the curious throng pushing toward her, nor the police muscling them back.

Lizzie was searched, measured, and booked. Formalities complete, Matron Russell took her dazed and silent prisoner by the arm and led Lizzie to her quarters.

With no one but the matron left to see her, Lizzie shattered.

She sobbed herself sick, her pent-up emotions unleashing a fit of vomiting so violent that Matron Russell finally sent for Dr. Bowen.

The doctor succeeded only in relieving her physical suffering. Mentally and emotionally exhausted, Lizzie went to bed, while outside her window the newsboys' shouts carried the story of her arrest through the streets below.

"*NOT* GUILTY"

It was as if the crowd had never left, never slept. By eight o'clock the following morning, they were back in full force, despite "a drenching rain." The station doors, which had been barred and guarded for three long days, would today be thrown open, and no one wanted to miss their chance to get inside. At nine o'clock, Lizzie Borden would be arraigned before the Second District Court.

LEGAL PROCEEDINGS

INQUEST
Has a crime been committed? Inquests are convened in the event of a suspicious death, usually to investigate whether foul play is involved and, if so, to identify a suspect for arrest.

ARRAIGNMENT
Does the suspect admit or deny it? At an arraignment, a formal accusation against the suspect is read in court, and the suspect must enter a plea. Pleading *not*

guilty moves the case one step closer to trial, while a plea of *guilty* leads directly to sentencing. (Some suspects choose to plead guilty to a lesser offense to avoid the ordeal of a trial and make themselves eligible for a less severe sentence.)

PRELIMINARY HEARING
(ALSO CALLED A PROBABLE CAUSE HEARING)

Is the accusation legitimate? Serious crimes, such as murder, must be tried before the superior court. But first, the prosecution must demonstrate to a district court judge that there is enough evidence to support the accusation. If the judge decides the accused is *probably guilty,* the accused is either released on bail or bound over to police custody to await a turn before the grand jury of the superior court.

GRAND JURY

Is the case worthy of a trial? A large panel of thirteen to twenty-three jurors listens to the prosecution's evidence and then votes whether to formally charge, or *indict,* the accused with a crime. A majority of at least twelve jurors is required to indict and send the case to trial before the superior court. (A second arraignment before the superior court often follows this step.)

TRIAL

Guilty or not guilty? The prosecution and defense argue both sides of the case before a twelve-person jury. The prosecution must prove the accused guilty *beyond a reasonable doubt,* while the defense is under no obligation to prove anything. Nor is the defendant required to testify. The jury votes on whether the accused is guilty or not guilty—and in a murder case, the vote for a guilty verdict must be unanimous—and a sentence is delivered by the judge. For those found guilty of murder in Massachusetts in the 1890s, only one sentence was possible: death.

The mood in town had reversed entirely. No longer glancing over their shoulders for fear of the murderer they knew was somewhere among them, the people jostled for a chance to see the woman charged with the most brutal crime in memory, to be in the same room with her and hear her answer guilty or not guilty. They streamed into the upstairs courtroom, filling it so tightly that once again, officers were put on guard to turn people away—this time to keep the room from bursting at its seams.

At 9:05, the door to the matron's apartment opened and Miss Lizzie Borden appeared on the arm of Reverend Buck, her face flushed and her eyes inflamed—though her night's sleep, she'd told the matron, was the best she'd had since the tragedy. She had not eaten, had barely spoken all morning. Emma Borden, Reverend Buck, and Uncle Morse all sat nearby, yet Lizzie looked straight ahead as though there were nothing more interesting in the room than the corner of a desk.

To some, her unwavering gaze came across as cool and calm. Others thought she bore herself "more like one who did not fully understand her position than with the composure of courage." Those who sat nearest noticed Lizzie's lips moving nervously throughout the proceeding.

The clerk of the court called the case of *The Commonwealth of Massachusetts v. Lizzie A. Borden* on complaint of murder.

Here the arraignment took an unexpected turn. Lawyer

Jennings, busy with pen and paper at his desk, asked for a moment more. He finished writing, read the document to Lizzie, and she signed it.

"Your Honor, before the prisoner pleads, she wishes to present the following." Jennings read the document aloud—a motion declaring that Lizzie objected to Judge Blaisdell presiding over the arraignment, and furthermore that Blaisdell was "disqualified" to do so. The inquest had not been officially closed, Jennings argued, and if the evidence on the murder was not all in, Blaisdell should not be permitted to hear Marshal Hilliard's accusation against Lizzie. How could Blaisdell remain impartial toward any remaining evidence if he did?

This argument might have seemed odd to the spectators, for Lizzie Borden was already under arrest. Clearly the authorities saw no need for more evidence. But Lawyer Jennings was actually looking beyond the arraignment. His true concern about whether Judge Blaisdell could listen impartially to new evidence had to do with the next inevitable step: the preliminary hearing.

At first glance, Jennings's concern appears misplaced. No matter what happened next, Massachusetts law guaranteed that Judge Blaisdell would never preside over a murder trial against Lizzie Borden. (District courts in Massachusetts have jurisdiction only over cases that carry a maximum sentence of five years in prison. Homicides, then punishable by death, were heard by the superior court of Massachusetts.) Blaisdell did, however, have the power to decide whether Lizzie's case would proceed to the superior court at all. This would happen at the preliminary hearing—a one-sided dress rehearsal for a trial, where the prosecution presents its evidence against the accused in hopes of convincing a judge that the case is worthy of a place before the superior court. And the catch: the law requires a judge to hear only as much evidence as it takes to persuade him that the defendant is *probably* guilty.

Judge Josiah Blaisdell had already spent three days listening to the evidence that had led to Lizzie's arrest. Lawyer Jennings, who had not been permitted into the courtroom during the inquest, did not even know what that evidence was. Was it any wonder that Blaisdell was the last person Lawyer Jennings wanted to preside over Lizzie's preliminary hearing? The way Jennings saw it, Judge Blaisdell should be removed from the case entirely, and the sooner the better.

Knowlton stood up. Was this a ploy to delay the prisoner's plea? he wanted to know.

Blaisdell said it was not, and ordered the arraignment to continue.

The clerk of the court, Augustus Leonard, motioned for Lizzie to stand. "This is a complaint charging you with homicide," he called out in that queer singsong cadence heard only in courtrooms. "What say you? Are you guilty or not guilty?"

"Not guilty," Lizzie said in her low voice.

Clerk Leonard, whose age was apparent by his long white beard, had not heard her. "What is your plea, Lizzie A. Borden?" he sang out again.

Lizzie spoke up loud and clear. "*Not* guilty," she said, her emphasis lost on no one.

"LIZZIE BORDEN, STAND UP"

Plea or no plea, Lawyer Jennings was not about to give up on his motion. "It is beyond human nature to suppose that Your Honor could have heard all the evidence at the inquest and not be prejudiced against this woman," he told Judge Blaisdell. Blaisdell had already deemed Lizzie guilty enough to arrest. How could he possibly turn around and rule her innocent enough to release after listening to even more evidence against her at a hearing?

"The Commonwealth demurs to the plea," Knowlton said in a cool, metallic voice, "and asks that it be overruled. There is nothing extraordinary in these proceedings." He could think of nearly two dozen cases involving inquests and arraignments that had been carried out exactly the same way, and no one had protested.

Jennings was on his feet now. The difference in this case, he insisted, was "apparent and glaring." The Borden inquest had not been convened to root out the most likely culprit, Jennings argued. The police had decided on Lizzie Borden and instead of arresting her had used the inquest to extract information from her. It had been nothing but a secret trial dressed up as an inquest. Had he known that Marshal Hilliard held a warrant for Lizzie's arrest during the entire length of the inquest, Jennings would have had plenty to say on that score as well.

Technically, Knowlton's position was correct. Jennings could not deny that Judge Blaisdell had the authority to convene inquests, issue warrants, and preside over preliminary hearings. Unfortunately for Lizzie Borden, no law specifically prevented the same judge from performing all three roles in the same case. Whether a judge might be biased in such a situation was a matter of opinion, not law, and the decision belonged solely to Judge Blaisdell.

"The motion is overruled," Blaisdell announced.

"Exception!" Jennings demanded. Then, to everyone's surprise, "Your Honor, we are ready for trial."

District Attorney Knowlton was caught entirely off guard. "The evidence in this case could not be completed at once," he protested. "It could hardly all be gathered by next week."

"We are very anxious to proceed at once," Jennings said. "We ask for a trial at the earliest possible moment."

Chagrinned, Knowlton had to admit that he was not ready.

Judge Blaisdell granted a continuance to the following Monday, allowing Knowlton just ten days to assemble the evidence in preparation for a preliminary hearing.

"Lizzie Borden, stand up," said Clerk Leonard. "By the order of this court this case is continued until August 22 and you are ordered to stand committed without bail."

"THAT'S THE MURDERESS!"

Police held back the crowd as Lizzie Borden, escorted by Reverend Buck, Marshal Hilliard, and State Detective Seaver stepped into a curtained carriage bound for the depot. Two more carriages containing eight reporters took off after her, eager to cover her departure for the county jail at Taunton. Hilliard zigzagged across one block and down another rather than proceeding straight up North Main, but the tactic only allowed the newspapermen to arrive ahead of them.

And then the train was late. Lizzie waited in the carriage while the people outside gossiped and shouldered nearer. At the ticket master's announcement of the train's arrival, they surged forward, pressing so close to the carriage door that the police had to intervene yet again.

Suddenly, the engine bell clanged and Marshal Hilliard pulled open the curtains. It was time to go. For a moment Lizzie's strength deserted her. She swayed and might have tottered, but Reverend Buck and Marshal Hilliard's arms were there to support her. Leaning on the two of them, she made her way into the last car and took a seat beside a window. Reverend Buck sat next to her, Marshal Hilliard and Detective Seaver behind. Across the aisle were a pair of newspapermen. Again her blinds were drawn to shield her from the curious. No one spoke. Lizzie stared straight ahead.

Word traveled ahead of the locomotive, and curiosity seekers collected at every stop along the sixteen-mile trip to see the train pass. At Somerset a gaggle of mill girls waited on the platform. When the reporters raised their window to take in the scene, one of the girls spotted Lizzie across the aisle. "Oh, there she is! That's the murderess!" she squealed, and they all crowded closer to get a better look. Lizzie Borden did not flinch.

The train pulled into Taunton at 4:20. Hundreds of people choked the platform, swarming so thickly around every car it looked as if the whole town were there. Detective Seaver stepped from the train and went bustling off toward the north end of the station. Fooled, the eager throng followed. Reverend Buck and Marshal Hilliard then slipped Lizzie Borden around to the south and into yet another carriage.

They halted before a large picturesque building outside the city center. At first glance it might have passed for a library or private school, with neat flower beds and Boston ivy twining lazily across its two-toned stone walls. But though the windows were tall and ample, they were barred. This was the county jail—Lizzie Borden's home for the next ten days.

Lizzie had apparently steeled herself for this moment. "[H]er step as she alighted from the carriage at the entrance to the Taunton jail was firmer then at any time during the journey," the *New Bedford Evening Standard* noted with a mixture of admiration and surprise.

Marshal Hilliard, still shadowed by the newspapermen, conducted Lizzie to the corridor of women's cells. Here he left her to wait with Reverend Buck for the matron. Matron Wright, the sheriff's wife, turned out to be a kindly woman of late middle years, with gold-rimmed spectacles and silvering hair. The more she spoke with Lizzie, the more familiar the young woman seemed. Then the pieces began to fit together—Sheriff Wright had once been city marshal of Fall River. Not only that, the Wrights had been neighbors to one of the city's dozens of Borden families.

"Are you not the Lizzie Borden who used to play with my daughter Isabel?" Matron Wright asked.

It was so. The avid reporters watched the news sting the matron like a pinprick. Within hours her tear-rimmed eyes would be in all the papers.

Lizzie's childhood connection with the Wrights little mattered when it came to the admittance routine. She was subjected to a bath—"an inflexible prison rule"—and then committed to cell number three.

This was a whitewashed space nine and a half feet long, seven and a half feet wide—just enough for a bed, chair, and washbowl. A large window looked out across the garden. Lizzie had brought a box of books and church weeklies, and a valise of clothing. (Since she had not yet been convicted of a crime, Lizzie was not required to wear prison dress.) All of Mr. Borden's weekly newspaper subscriptions would be forwarded her; she did not care to see the dailies with their breathless minute-by-minute accounts of the tragedy. Her meals would be sent in from the City Hotel rather than the jail's kitchen—a luxury permitted to any prisoner who could afford it.

If the rumors floating about town were correct, if Lizzie Borden had truly committed murder to get her hands on her father's fortune, this was surely not how she had planned to spend it.

"SHE HOPED HE WOULD COME HOME A CORPSE"

The case had come to another momentary standstill, but the fascination, the greedy fever for news, grew steadily.

"No matter where a person goes—in the city, in the country, on the river or at the seashore—the murder continues to be the principal theme of conversation," the *Fall River Herald* reported.

Many were not content to simply talk when they could go see for themselves. Friends, sweethearts, and whole families went out of their way to pass Taunton Jail, trying to guess which window Lizzie Borden might be looking out of. A handful of women from as far away as Boston came knocking at Sheriff Wright's office that morning, asking to attend the jail's Sunday services—hoping for a chance to sing hymns alongside Lizzie Borden.

The whole thing disgusted Sheriff Wright. "I do not believe that the public has a right to know anything of this girl's life within these walls," he informed the *Herald,* when she gets up and when she lies down, and what she eats and drinks and when she does either. She herself wishes not to be disturbed, and I am not going to allow her to be disturbed. Nor shall I relate these petty incidents of her life here."

But someone with less integrity obviously blabbed, for the *Herald* reported that in spite of sleeping brokenly, Lizzie Borden arose refreshed at six o'clock with the rest of the prisoners and made her own bed. She did not partake of the fish hash served at seven o'clock, making do with only a cup of coffee and a nibble of bread until her dinner arrived from the hotel at noon.

Even Matron Wright was not above spilling a few scraps to the paper. By Monday most of Bristol County knew she had lent Lizzie one of her own big feather pillows, a rocking chair, and a stool. A white bedspread and pillow slip brought from home, as well as gifts of flowers and fruit, also softened the cell.

Did Matron Wright believe Lizzie guilty? the *Herald* wanted to know.

"No, I can't. I said so to her when she first came, and the only emotion she has shown came then. She looked up at me quickly, and said in a surprised way: 'Oh! you don't? Oh, Mrs. Wright!' and she threw her arms about me, as if it was more than she could stand of relief to find any one who had not turned against her."

Reporters also flocked to Second Street. "I believe firmly in my sister's innocence," Emma told them in her brief statement. "She will have my full support and cooperation, because I am certain she deserves it. The blow has been terrible for me to bear, but I cannot help it. My resources will be at her command."

Lizzie's arrest even subdued her "embittered" uncle, Hiram Harrington. Before, he had relished the chance to tantalize the papers with inside information. Now, with his niece behind bars, all his extravagant claims suddenly vanished. "I am sorry," he told the reporters as he turned them away. "I wish it could not have happened."

Public opinion had veered just as sharply. Lawyer Jennings's motion to remove Judge Blaisdell from the case had not budged the judge, but its effect on Fall River—and beyond—was remarkable.

For a week the people had demanded an arrest, talking as though nothing stood between Lizzie Borden and the gallows. "[F]rom Lizzie's face I read that she is deep as the bottomless pit and subtle as hell void of soul or feeling," read one anonymous letter to District Attorney Knowlton on the first day of the inquest.

Less than a week later, the street corners were hot with debates about the legality and justice of the whole affair. The question now was not whether Lizzie Borden had done it, but whether she would receive a fair trial. "The rights of a noble woman have been trampled upon by you and your blood-hounds who, having run your suspicions to their end, are gloating over their object," an incensed woman wrote to Knowlton after Lizzie's arraignment.

Jennings's criticism of the inquest had left the citizenry particularly riled. Demands for the facts crowded the newspapers. That inquest, they declared, ought to have been public from the start. People had a right to know what happened behind those doors, just as they had a right to know what had happened to Andrew and Abby Borden.

Facts were indeed in short supply. As the story of the murder spread across New England, details began to blur and tangle. The most sinister tale purported Andrew Borden had told a friend that Lizzie was so troublesome, she "ruined the peace of the household." She refused to eat at the same table with him; when he so much as accidentally walked in during her breakfast, she'd get up from the table and leave the room. And most damning of all: "[W]hen he left the house Lizzie told him she hoped he would come home a corpse," adding, "probably you will before long."

The chain of information was weak, the story secondhand at best—told by a stove salesman to a whaling captain on the porch of a Craigville hotel. Possibly it had come from a mill or bank administrator before that. But if a paper as respectable as the *New York Times* printed it, how could it be false?

The legend of Lizzie Borden was beginning to take root.

RUMORS AND FALSEHOODS

Incensed by the rumors, Lizzie's friend Mrs. Brigham told the *Fall River Herald,* "The story that she would not sit at the same table with her father is a falsehood of the blackest sort.

"It has been said that Mr. Borden was angry with

and did not speak to Lizzie upon her return from Europe. That, too, is a falsehood, distorted out of facts that were as contrary to the statement as could be." Lizzie came home so late, Mrs. Brigham explained, that her parents had already gone to bed when she arrived. She'd spoken only a few words to Emma before going to bed herself. "The next morning Mr. Borden found her steamer chair in the hall and bounded up stairs three at a time to see and greet her, and Lizzie told me her hand ached all day he pressed it so hard. Going down town he met a man who said to him: 'Well, I would guess that some one had come home judging from your bright face this morning.'"

In the absence of facts, newspapers were scrounging for anything to fill the gaps. The *Fall River Globe,* usually the last place anyone would look for a reasoned perspective, remarked in an editorial, "It is hardly necessary to say that the published stories of the proceedings are very incomplete and fragmentary, perhaps some of them mythical."

Before the week was out, Marshal Hilliard had accumulated a desk drawer filled with letters attempting to crack the case. Clairvoyants offered their services to the police for prices ranging from $8 to $2,000. One medium claimed to have received instructions from Andrew Borden himself. Another self-proclaimed detective told the marshal to examine the eyes of the murder victims, explaining that the last sight they saw remained imprinted on their retinas, plain as day. Clues, theories, and even confessions piled up. Most of them amounted to nothing—like the pond the police had been advised to dredge for the murder weapon, only to find a banana peel tied up in a paper sack—but to placate the public,

Hilliard sent his men chasing down one blind lead after another. He would give the newspapers no chance to say he had left a clue unexamined, no matter how absurd. He had seen enough complaints from the press already.

"You and every other citizen must remember that the newspapers have not given anything near the facts disclosed at the inquest," a red-faced Hilliard complained right back to the reporter who handed him a stack of fifty editorials denouncing the police department's conduct. "I think if you were to publish tomorrow the solid facts in the case and all of them," he told another, "you would find that before night a great many people would suddenly change their minds."

But no one who knew the facts was talking. Not District Attorney Knowlton, not Lawyer Jennings, and certainly not Lizzie Borden. "Under no circumstances will she open her mouth," said the *Fall River Herald*.

PRELIMINARY HEARING

"THAT IS THE FIRST THING THAT I UNDERTOOK TO DO THAT I NEVER COULD"

Monday, August 22, 1892

The thermometer had pushed past 80 degrees and continued rising. Inside Fall River's second floor courtroom it could only have been hotter. Spectators had been filling the seats since eleven o'clock—many of them ladies carrying their knitting and lunch baskets. Almost three dozen reporters sat wedged behind tables they had procured from local furniture stores. In all, three hundred people waited—not only to see Miss Lizzie Borden, but to finally hear the evidence against her firsthand and learn whether it would be enough to send her to trial.

The city hall bell struck two, and Judge Blaisdell arrived. Then all eyes turned to the door of the matron's room. Lizzie Borden did not appear. Almost twenty hushed minutes passed before Lawyer Jennings entered, a scowl on his face. With him was Colonel Melvin Ohio Adams, an eminent Boston lawyer with a razor-sharp memory, a genius for cross-examination, and "[a] record of unvarying success," who had been enlisted to Lizzie's defense team. The pair passed through to the judge's chamber, where they conferred so long with District Attorney Knowlton that even Judge Blaisdell could not keep his eyes from his watch. Another thirty minutes inched by before the three attorneys emerged and Knowlton addressed Judge Blaisdell.

"If it please Your Honor, there are some things used as evidence in this case which are wanting at the present time." The dress Lizzie had turned over to the police, among other things, was still being tested at Harvard. "Consequently we have agreed with the defendant's counsel to adjourn this hearing until Thursday, if it meets Your Honor's approval."

Blaisdell approved, and so for two more days Fall River drummed its fingers.

At her own request, Lizzie Borden waited out the continuance in Matron Hannah Reagan's room at the Fall River police station rather than return to the county jail at Taunton. Emma brought Lizzie's bedding from home and cooked her meals. Most of the time Lizzie lay on her cot and read. A few select visitors were permitted in, and one of the matrons was always on duty to see to Lizzie's comfort as well as guard her privacy. The reporters never stopped coming, no matter how often the matrons turned them away.

INSIDE 92 SECOND STREET

While Lizzie sat undisturbed in jail—"a sanctuary," as the *New York Telegram* wryly put it, "from the sleuth hounds of the press"—one reporter, a Mrs. Percy of the *New York Herald,* managed to talk her way into the Borden house for a look around. Goodness only knows who let her in—Bridget had long since gone, and Mrs. Percy's article clearly states she did not see any member of the family.

However she did it, Mrs. Percy got inside and was permitted to view the two rooms where the murders took place, as well as the parlor, dining room, and, most astounding of all, given Emma Borden's feelings about privacy, the Borden sisters' own bedrooms.

"I was surprised to find the house extremely pretty and refined in its appointments," Mrs. Percy wrote. "Easy chairs, shaded lamps, books, well-chosen bits of bric-a-brac, cushions and draperies, an open piano, a

> hundred comforts and pleasing trifles tastefully dis-
> posed bespoke pleasantly the character of the occu-
> pants." The only room she did not care for was the
> guest room, its expensive black walnut furniture being
> of a "heavy gloomy" style no longer in fashion.
>
> Lizzie's room held the most fascination—"as dainty
> and charming a place as any girl need ask for," with its
> hand-embroidered blue bedspread and wealth of books
> and pictures. "How could Lizzie Borden have come in
> the dainty place and removed the traces of such fear-
> ful work without marring all the delicate purity of
> everything with which she had contact?" Mrs. Percy
> wondered. "Why, the washstand even is in a recess
> veiled by a pale silken curtain. A soiled finger pushing
> it aside would leave a mark, and there is none."

Surrounded by her books and her friends and her sister's good cooking, Lizzie Borden passed the hours as pleasantly as could be expected under the circumstances. Even as the court date closed in, she could relax enough to enjoy a little merriment. The last afternoon before the hearing, she and Emma, Mrs. Brigham, and Mrs. Holmes sat laughing together over a bet Lizzie had made with Matron Reagan. The matron had wagered a dollar that Lizzie couldn't break an egg.

"Well, I can break an egg," Lizzie said.

"Not the way I would tell you to break it," Matron Reagan teased.

Lizzie negotiated the bet down to a quarter, and Mrs. Brigham fetched an egg. Lizzie followed the matron's instructions (hold the egg between two clasped hands and try to crush it) and to her astonishment, the egg would not break.

"There, that is the first thing that I undertook to do that I never could," Lizzie marveled, much to her friends' amusement.

In the middle of it all, Edwin Porter, a correspondent for the *Globe,* came up into the corridor, asking for Matron Reagan. The matron was not pleased to be interrupted for the umpteenth time that week. "That reporter has come after me again, and I told him that I had nothing to tell him," Mrs. Brigham remembered hearing her grumble when she returned to the room.

"LIZZIE WAS BACK TO HER OLD MOOD"

By nine o'clock on the morning of Thursday, August 25, the crowd gathered on Granite Street knew there was almost no hope of getting inside the courtroom. The seats had begun filling before eight, the officers on guard at the doors awarding most of them to well-dressed young women. Even gentlemen had to make do with standing room once inside. But the people choking the sidewalks outside the police station were not willing to give up. They watched keenly as a curtained carriage pulled up to the public entrance. Someone was about to get inside.

It was as if a silent signal passed among them. All at once the mob surged for the door, overwhelming the police and blocking the sidewalks and doorway entirely. At a gesture from Marshal Hilliard, the officers charged forward, pushing the crowd back at a run.

Miss Emma Borden stepped quickly out into the space they had cleared and went straight upstairs to the matron's room. There she found her sister calmly rocking in a chair by the window. Emma kissed her, and Lizzie replied with a squeeze of her hand. Immediately, they began talking as though they sat in their own front parlor instead of the police station. Not a word of the murder passed between them. Only Emma's tearful face betrayed the ordeal to come. It was nearly time.

The first and greatest revelation of the entire hearing came on the second morning. For a day and a half, Medical Examiner Dolan's questioning by District Attorney Knowlton and cross-examination by Colonel Adams had monopolized the stand. Adams, with his endless arsenal of rapid-fire questions, generated so much clinical talk of wounds and blood, spatters and gashes, that by the time Dolan began to describe the autopsies the court was nearly numb to it. And then Colonel Adams asked, "Did you remove anything from those bodies, or either of them?"

Dolan's eyes and voice both dropped. "Yes, sir," he said. "I removed the skulls, the heads."

Shock and revulsion careened through the courtroom. Every head pivoted toward the Borden sisters. Startled, Lizzie also looked to her sister. Emma could not cover her face or lower her head fast enough to hide her tears. Lizzie managed to mask herself behind her black fan. It was perfectly clear no one had told them, much less asked their permission.

"For what purpose?" Adams asked.

"Because I was instructed to do so." The state attorney general had given the order, Dolan explained.

"What did you do with them?" Adams asked.

"I cleaned them."

Cleaned was a comically delicate way of putting it. The man had boiled Mr. and Mrs. Borden's heads like soup bones until the flesh—their very faces—dropped off, exposing the battered and broken white skulls beneath.

Adams, who could swerve from cordial to sarcastic in the blink of an eye, matched his tone to the gravity of the news. "Do you mean to say these bodies are now buried without the heads?" he asked.

"Yes sir," Dolan answered.

The public was incensed. Barbarous, they called it. The argument that every means necessary must be taken to bring the murderer to justice, no matter how revolting, hardly made a dent in the outcry. "The bodies have been made sausage meat of," said one paper, proclaiming that the decapitation was more cold-blooded even than the crime itself.

There were dull moments, too. Both Bridget's and Uncle Morse's testimonies, though loaded with detail, left the public unsatisfied. They had hoped for splashy stories of the family's relations, of bitter arguments pitting parents against children. Instead, they got minute-by-minute accounts of the hours leading up to the murder—the meals, chores, and mundane morning habits common to most any family.

Dull as it was, this turned out to be some of the most damning testimony. Bridget in particular accounted for the Bordens' movements so thoroughly that it became difficult to imagine how anyone could have snuck into the household unnoticed, much less remained unnoticed during the interval between the two murders. The combination of intricate planning and sheer luck necessary to pull it off seemed awfully far-fetched.

The logic was simple: if no one from the outside could get in, that left no one but Lizzie Borden to do it.

As the testimony mounted, the public's attitude toward Lizzie's demeanor changed. Lizzie herself had not changed one bit—she never would—but the way the newspapers portrayed her did. Early on, many reporters had described her calm self-possession as *wonderful*, *dignified*, and *remarkable*. Now, with the shadow of guilt creeping ever closer, words like *strange*, *indifferent*, *unfeeling*, and *abnormal* appeared more often than not.

"Even at the recital of the gory details of the butchery of her parents she showed no emotion," the *New York Times* claimed. Another correspondent saw it differently. As Dr. Dolan described his first ghastly sight of Mr. Borden's face, the *New Bedford Evening Standard* observed, "Miss Lizzie closed her eyes with a look of real sadness, and placed a small palm-leaf fan which she had in hand over her face. The reporters all around her were nudging each other to look at Lizzie, but before they all had the opportunity to see the prisoner's grief the fan was lowered and Lizzie was back to her old mood."

Before her arrest the *Evening Standard* had consistently referred to her as *Miss Lizzie,* or at least *Lizzie Borden.* It was common courtesy. Once she was behind bars, that courtesy began tapering off. Then came the hearing, and suddenly she became almost exclusively *Lizzie*—as though she were a child or a servant. Consciously or unconsciously, the *Standard* (and other papers, too) were signaling to their readers that Lizzie Borden was unworthy of respect.

TRIAL BY NEWSPAPER

Without the newspapers' reports you would never know when the spectators gasped, when they laughed, or when they fell into utter silence. You would never get the slightest glimpse of the ladies' shawls and handbags draped over the gas jets; the tables jammed elbow to elbow with sweating, scribbling newspapermen; the constantly waving paper fans printed with advertisements featuring scantily clothed nymphs swinging a pressed ham in some festoons of ribbon. None of that is in the official transcript. Even if you read all 480 pages of the preliminary hearing, you will never see Lawyer Jennings's perpetual scowl; Knowlton sitting on his table, dangling his feet during lengthy cross-examinations; Dr. Bowen's wife fainting from the heat; or Lizzie Borden chewing the end of a pencil "to a fringe" during testimony, then leaning forward with her elbows on her knees and her chin in her hands to chat gaily with Mrs. Brigham and Mrs. Holmes during recesses. Only the papers can tell you how it looked and felt inside that courtroom.

Their coverage of the testimony was another story—sometimes quite literally. The words that came out of the witnesses' mouths and the words the papers printed did not necessarily match. Often the difference was negligible, and for that the reporters deserve a little slack. They did not have the advantage of digital voice recorders, or even typewriters. The only tools the press correspondents had were pencils, paper, and their own memories. And they could not print every last question and answer. There simply was not space. Most of it had to be shortened or summarized somehow. For example, the *New Bedford Evening Standard* condensed the twenty-six-question testimony of Joseph Shortsleeves, one of the last people to see Mr. Borden alive, to this: "Mr. Borden was in my place of business on the day of the murder. It was between 10:30 and 11 o'clock when I saw him." In the case of Mr. Shortsleeves, that really is all you need to know about what he said.

Other witnesses' testimony deserved more nuance but rarely got it. Take the opening lines of Alice Russell's testimony, as printed in the *Evening Standard:*

"I live on Main Street near Second. I have known

Lizzie Borden for some considerable time. I first heard of this affair about 11:15 o'clock on the day of the murder."

And here is how Knowlton actually got Alice to establish the time:

Q. Do you know what time of day that was?
A. I am not positive.
Q. As near as you can fix it, when was it?
A. I thought that day it was quarter past eleven; I do not know why I thought so, now.
Q. Have you come to any different opinion now?
A. No, sir. I have forgotten how I placed the time.

Yes, the final answer is basically the same in both versions: Alice Russell first heard of the murder around 11:15. But in this instance, Alice comes across as noticeably less sure of herself in the real testimony. In fact, Alice Russell was one of the most uncertain witnesses called to testify, yet you'd hardly know it from the *Evening Standard*'s rendition. Alice actually answered *I do not remember* to so many questions that Knowlton finally asked her, "Do you remember anything that took place at all?"

"I remember nothing very connectedly," Alice acknowledged.

What difference does it make how she stated that one plain fact? Think back to Lizzie's interview with Assistant Marshal Fleet. Many would argue that the way Lizzie Borden said *She is not my mother* changed the course of the entire investigation, and that was a plain fact, too.

"YOU GAVE ME AWAY, EMMA"

Believe it or not, the preliminary hearing itself wasn't the hottest news in the Borden case that week. On August 25, the very same day the hearing opened, a story more incriminating than any of the courtroom evidence claimed headlines all across New England:

THE TWO SISTERS.
Quarrelled in Fall River Police Station.

Matron Hannah Reagan had overheard every juicy word of the argument, so the story went, and somehow the conversation had found its way out of the central station and into the ear of the *Fall River Globe*'s Edwin Porter, who fed the scoop to a Boston paper before breaking the news locally. Almost instantaneously it boomeranged back to the *Globe*, then the *Herald* and the *New Bedford Evening Standard,* and by the next day readers across the country were eagerly lapping up Lizzie and Emma's stormy exchange:

"You gave me away, Emma, didn't you?"

"No, Lizzie, I only told Mr. Jennings what I thought he ought to know for your defense."

"That is false and I know it. But, remember, I will never give one inch! Never!" And here the papers said Lizzie had held up the tip of her little finger for emphasis, showing her sister just how little she would budge, then defiantly turned her back to Emma for the rest of her visit.

Exactly what secrets Emma had "given away," the papers never so much as hinted at. Nevertheless, Lizzie's words were so tantalizingly close to a confession that the argument became a sensation. Finally, the public feasted on just the sort of brash dramatics it had been craving from the stoic Bordens. No one could get enough of it.

Matron Reagan promptly denied the entire tale, just as the *Globe* had cleverly predicted. "If approached I have no doubt she would absolutely refuse to talk," Porter's anonymous informant had warned, "and, perhaps, in self protection, would deny the story. But it is true."

"Naturally it was denied," the *New Bedford Evening Standard* retorted with unmistakable sarcasm. "Everything is denied just now, and it is somewhat doubtful if a murder has been committed."

The next day the newspapers were in a frenzy. At the close of Bridget Sullivan's testimony on August 26, a cadre of reporters approached the defense table in hopes of questioning Lizzie Borden herself about the quarrel. Lawyer Jennings became indignant at the very idea. Was he supposed to let them at Lizzie every time the press churned out another ridiculous story? Some of the newspapermen bristled at Jennings's tone. Their papers had already denounced the tale entirely, and they would not be lumped together with the *Globe*'s scandal-mongering—not when they had been specifically sent to find out if there was any truth to the story.

By now Lizzie's friends had joined the fray, and their comments about the press were no more complimentary than Jennings's. The only way to end the nonsense was with a sworn statement from Matron Reagan. Lawyer Jennings quickly drew up an official denial for the matron to sign.

What happened next is a matter of some confusion. According to Edwin Porter, author of the original article on the quarrel, "Mrs. Reagan refused, saying that she would have to consult with the marshal." Others said she was willing to sign until a Providence police detective interfered with advice to ask the marshal's permission before committing her name to the document. What is certain is that things heated up in a hurry.

Reverend Buck accompanied the matron to Marshal Hilliard's office. A reporter from the *New York Recorder* managed to squeeze into the room unnoticed and watched the marshal's face cloud as he read the document. "If you sign this," the reporter heard Hilliard say to Matron Reagan, "you do it against my order."

"Then he turned around and saw me," the *Recorder* man reported, "and nearly had a fit. 'This is a private office!' he shouted." Hilliard ordered the press out of the room, but not before some of the newspapermen heard him tell Matron Reagan that if she had anything to say about any of it, she could do so on the witness stand.

Jennings was incensed. The marshal's conduct was an outrage, he shouted, and every newspaper should publish it.

The scene was edging dangerously close to a riot. Police officers stepped closer as Lizzie's friends continued to attack the article. "The man that wrote it should be driven out of town!" they cried.

Remarkably, the man that wrote it spoke up. "If you want affidavits," Edwin Porter said, "you'd better take mine. I know what Mrs. Reagan told me, and I am willing to swear to it."

In the end, no one budged. Porter would not back down, and neither would Lizzie's supporters. Only Hannah Reagan could break the stalemate, and by order of the city marshal, her side of the story must wait until the trial.

"MY HEART ALMOST STOOD STILL WITH ANXIETY"

The room lay deadly silent as Professor Edward Stickney Wood of Harvard University stepped up to the witness stand on Tuesday, August 30. This was the chemist whose tests had delayed the hearing—the man entrusted with examining Mr. and Mrs. Borden's stomachs, as well as the hatchets, axes, and clothing collected from the crime scene. If there were any telltale traces of poison or blood, he would be the one to find them.

"It was doubtful," the *New Bedford Evening Standard* said, "that the old court-room ever saw so many people before." Women stood on the seats at the back, so tall and still they looked like Greek columns holding up the ceiling. "My heart," Lawyer Jennings later admitted, "almost stood still with anxiety."

Knowlton asked Professor Wood to begin with his examination of the Bordens' stomachs, no doubt in hopes of introducing forensic proof to link two critical pieces of circumstantial evidence: the Bordens' violent illness of August 2, and druggist Eli Bence's claim that it was Lizzie who tried to buy a deadly dose of prussic acid on August 3. "I found that both stomachs were perfectly natural in appearance," Wood told the court. "They were in the condition of apparent perfect health."

"Did you find any trace of any poison in either stomach?" Knowlton asked.

"There was no evidence of any irritant poison having been in the stomach at all," Wood said. The spectators turned to each other in stunned silence. No poison?

Next came the hatchet. From the lurid descriptions of the battered corpses, the crowd was braced for a fearsome weapon. Instead, the *Boston Advertiser* said, Professor Wood "pulled out an innocent-looking hatchet from a medium sized valise." It was the claw-headed hatchet—the one with the hair and red stains on the blade.

Without any dramatics or fanfare he informed the court, "The hatchet contained quite a number of suspicious-looking spots which looked like blood spots on the head of the hatchet, and also on the handle. These were examined very carefully and thoroughly, but there was no blood spot upon the hatchet whatever, no trace of blood."

The only speck of blood Wood could find was on Lizzie Borden's white underskirt—a single spot right at the front, about six inches from the bottom and no bigger around than a grain of rice. This, Lizzie had already admitted at the inquest, was likely from "flea bites." ("Fleas" was a peculiar euphemism, possibly unique to Fall River, for a woman's menstrual period.) There was nothing on her blue skirt or waist, nothing on her shoes or stockings, nothing on the cover from the dining room lounge.

It was bewildering.

At last Wood had compared the hair samples from Mr. and Mrs. Borden with the hair found on the hatchet.

"The hair taken from the hatchet was about one inch long, and under the microscope was seen to have a red brown color, and contained both the root and the point. In other words, it was hair like that from a cow, or an animal, and was not a human hair."

A tremor went through the listening crowd. Shocked newspapermen dropped their pencils. No poison. No blood. Not even so much as a hair.

Only one portion of Professor Wood's testimony proved troublesome for Lizzie Borden's case. By examining the contents of the Bordens' stomachs, Wood estimated that at the time of his murder, Mr. Borden's digestion had been in process for three and a half to four and a half hours. Mrs. Borden's stomach, however, had likely been churning her breakfast for only two to three hours. Given that the two had eaten the same breakfast at the same time, Wood's observations strongly suggested that Mrs. Borden had died first—possibly as much as two hours before her husband. (Abby Borden had last been seen alive at nine o'clock, ruling out a two-and-a-half-hour difference.) Wood's testimony allowed the authorities to target a ninety-minute window for Mrs. Borden's death, somewhere between nine o'clock and ten-thirty, by calculating all the varying scenarios, such as working backward from the discovery of Mr. Borden's body or forward from breakfast.

The timing fit perfectly within both Bridget's and Uncle Morse's recollections of the morning of August 4. Wood's conclusions also aligned with the time of death Medical Examiner Dolan had deduced based on the bodies' differing temperatures and coagulation of blood.

Expert and lay witnesses agreed: between nine o'clock and ten-thirty, someone had murdered Abby Borden. By her own admission, Lizzie Borden had been in the house the entire time.

"GOD GRANT YOUR HONOR WISDOM TO DECIDE"

On Thursday, September 1, day seven, Lizzie came into court as she always did, on the arm of Reverend Buck. But this time was different. One look at her eyes told everything—Lizzie Borden had been crying, and anyone could guess the reason why. Today Judge Blaisdell would decide whether to send her home to Second Street or return her to Taunton Jail. All the testimony was in. Even her inquest testimony had been read into the official record. Only the attorneys' closing arguments remained.

The audience on this most pivotal day was especially lively. Most of the area's lawyers had taken the day off to hear the arguments. The women had brought boxes of candy and crimped their children's hair, and chattered as though they were waiting to watch a matinee.

Lawyer Jennings stepped forward first. Carefully, he laid out the timing of Mr. Borden's errands in town, his arrival home, and the subsequent sounding of the alarm barely thirty minutes later. Suddenly, Jennings shouted, "Lizzie Borden did not do this crime! It was the work of an insane man or of a person whose heart was black as hell itself."

Every reporter in the room noticed Lizzie Borden's reaction. "Her form was convulsed," Edwin Porter of the *Globe* remembered, "her lips were trembling, and she shaded her eyes with her hands in order to partially conceal the tears, which were freely flowing."

Those terrible, bone-crushing wounds, Jennings continued, spoke for themselves. Every blow was distinct and parallel, the work of a strong and experienced hand. Yet the weapon had not been found, and the motive remained unaccounted for.

"Evidently," the *Evening Standard* observed, "Mr. Jennings feels in his innermost conscience the weight which is pressing on his client." It was impossible to miss. Jennings paced and shouted as he drove each point home, his plea fueled by a passionate energy. He paused only to refresh himself with a sip of ice water or a nip from a stick of licorice. (Knowlton, meanwhile, sat at his desk with the morning papers as though nothing of the least interest were going on.)

The house and barn had been burgled on three separate occasions, Jennings said, proving that someone could get on and off the property undetected. And there was the matter of strangers seen lurking about the place.

"Why have not the police found these suspicious-looking characters outside the house?" Jennings demanded, pointing to Marshal Hilliard and District Attorney Knowlton. "Why, because they have made up their minds the murderer was inside, and are not looking outside."

"That brings it down to Lizzie and Bridget." And who would be more likely to murder a man, Jennings pondered aloud, his servant or his youngest daughter? The woman who swept up after him or "the pet of the family; the one whose fingers were last clasped by the dead father, and the one whose head last rested against his breast"?

Again Lizzie's composure crumbled. Jennings himself was almost in tears.

"Understand me, I don't believe that Bridget Sullivan did that deed any more than I believe Lizzie Borden did it," Jennings assured the court. His point was only that from the outset Bridget had been treated with far less suspicion than Lizzie. "Was Bridget Sullivan compelled to tell how many dishes she washed, where she put them and how she laid them away?" he asked.

"Here is Lizzie Borden," he continued, "who has been taking prescriptions to cause her to sleep, and because she cannot tell the minutest details she is supposed to be the guilty party."

At last he cried, "I demand her release! Don't, Your Honor, when they don't show an incriminating circumstance, don't put the stigma of guilt upon this woman, reared as she has been and with a past character beyond reproach. Don't let it go out in the world as the decision of a just judge that she is probably guilty. God grant Your Honor wisdom to decide."

The room was awash. Colonel Adams wept right along with Lizzie's friends. The mayor and the medical examiner stepped forward to shake Jennings's hand as first a timid pattering and then a thunder of applause broke over the room.

It was an almost impossible act for Knowlton to follow. Not only was there still no direct evidence, not one tangible link between Lizzie and the crime, but Jennings's emotional plea had forced the district attorney to take on the role of a villain to do his duty as prosecutor.

Where Jennings had struck hotly with emotion, Knowlton turned his aim toward cool, impartial logic. Hands in his pockets, he spoke "in a most impassive manner." The district attorney also had a singular advantage: all he had to do was make Lizzie Borden appear *probably* guilty. Proving it beyond a reasonable doubt could wait until the trial.

He began with his own assessment of the wounds. "They are not such blows as a strong man would strike," Knowlton contended, "but those of a weak, irresolute, imperfect feminine hand, not striking to kill the first time, but striking and striking and striking until death was apparent."

"Who would be benefitted by this murder?" Knowlton asked.

That led him to an unpleasant fact: Lizzie Borden had renounced the name of Mother from the only mother she had ever known. It did not seem cause enough for murder, Knowlton acknowledged, but the "stubborn fact" remained that Lizzie was the only person in the world with whom Mrs. Borden had any discord.

Unfamiliar people were indeed seen outside the house, but not, Knowlton emphasized, entering or leaving it. Further, the defense had provided no explanation for how anyone could have gotten into a house so thoroughly locked up, both inside and out. It only stood to reason that those inside were immediately suspected.

"Next comes the servant girl. Now, I am a lover of fair play, and in my eyes one class of people is no different from another," Knowlton said. "Let us assume that Bridget Sullivan told all the truth," he proposed. Both times Bridget had left Lizzie alone with one of her parents—first at 9:30 to wash windows and then at 10:55 to go nap—one of them had ended up dead.

As for Lizzie's story of idling in the barn while someone

chopped up her father? Too convenient, as far as Knowlton was concerned. "She could have but one alibi," he said. There was only one place on the Borden property where she could not see someone leave the house, Knowlton pointed out, making it clear that he believed Lizzie had deliberately chosen the barn for her cover story.

And of course, there was the matter of Lizzie's implacable reserve. "While everybody is dazed there is but one person who, throughout the whole business, has not been seen to express emotion," Knowlton claimed—in bald contradiction of Lizzie's most recent bursts of tearfulness.

As much as her coolness had disturbed Officer Harrington and Assistant Marshal Fleet, Knowlton had found a way to make Lizzie's behavior both incriminating and unexpectedly reassuring. Better for a murderess to be outwardly cool and cunning than disguised behind a delicate, feminine veneer. "This somewhat removes from our minds the horror of the thing," he said. It was an inspired approach. Reluctant as most people were to suspect a woman of such a crime, no one wanted to contemplate the more terrifying possibility that their own sweet-tempered daughters might be capable of murder.

If Judge Blaisdell sided with the earnest, passionate Jennings and the clamor of spontaneous applause his argument had sparked, Knowlton said, "we would all be proud of it, and would be pleased to hear him say: 'We will let this woman go.' But that would be but temporary satisfaction," Knowlton concluded. "We are constrained to find that she has been dealing in poisonous things; that her story is absurd, and that hers and hers alone has been the opportunity for the commission of the crime. Yielding to clamor is not to be compared to that only and greatest satisfaction: that of a duty well done."

Deathly silence.

"THERE IS ONLY ONE THING TO DO"

There was no lively chatter now, no rustling of peppermint wrappers. Only Judge Blaisdell's voice, husky and indistinct, as though he did not want to hear his own words.

"The long examination is now concluded," he said, "and there remains but for the magistrate to perform what he believes to be his duty. It would be a pleasure for him, and he would doubtless receive much sympathy if he could say 'Lizzie, I judge you probably not guilty. You may go home.'" But sympathy must be laid aside in view of the evidence, Blaisdell continued. Imagine a man standing before the court under the same circumstances, offering the same alibi, he proposed. There would be no question as to what should be done with such a man.

"So there is only one thing to do, painful as it may be." Judge Blaisdell paused, turning aside to wipe his cheeks. "The judgment of the Court is that you are probably guilty," he said, "and you are ordered committed to await the action of the Superior Court."

A sound rose from the spectators, something between an excited hum and a groan. Lizzie Borden sat stone still. Stunned or indifferent, no one could tell; it was as though the news had not penetrated her. Her lower lip slid silently into her mouth.

"Lizzie A. Borden stand up," Clerk Leonard commanded.

But Lizzie could not—her whole body was shaking now. Reverend Buck and Lawyer Jennings rushed to help her. As soon as she was on her feet, the trembling ceased. "Don't be afraid," she told Reverend Buck, motioning for him to release her arm. "I am all right."

"The judgment of this court is that you are probably guilty of the offense charged against you," Clerk Leonard read, "and it is therefore the order of this court that you be committed to the

Taunton Jail, there to await the action of the Grand Jury, which meets the first Monday of November next."

Lizzie sank wearily into her seat. Reverend Buck leaned over to console her, but Lizzie interrupted. "It is for the best, I think. It is better that I should get my exoneration in a higher court, for then it will be complete."

Nevertheless, Lizzie Borden wept as she was led away to the matron's room.

THE WAITING TIME

"FLAP-DOODLE, GUSH, IDIOTIC DRIVEL"

There was nothing to do but wait. Just over two months stood between Lizzie Borden and the grand jury. Sixty-six days of wondering whether the twenty-one-man jury would send her to trial or set her free.

The newspapers could hardly bear it. With little actual news to print about the case, they squabbled over Lizzie's treatment in jail. Some sneered at what they believed were her many privileges; others had her "shivering in the chilliness of her temporary tomb, wrapped in shawls for comfort."

Only one of the stories had any possible basis in fact. All along, reporters had begged for interviews at Taunton Jail, and Lizzie refused every one of them—until a letter came from Mrs. Kate McGuirk, an old acquaintance in her charity work.

Would Miss Borden grant an interview for the *New York Recorder*? she wanted to know. Lizzie agreed.

I was anxious to see if this girl, with whom I was associated several years ago in the work of the Fall River Fruit and Flower Mission, Mrs. McGuirk wrote in her article, *had changed her character and become a monster since the days when she used to load up the plates of vigorous young newsboys and poor children at the annual turkey dinner provided during the holidays for them and take delight in their healthy appetites.*

"How do you get along here, Miss Borden?" Mrs. McGuirk began her interview.

"To tell the truth, I am afraid it is beginning to tell on my health," Lizzie said. She missed fresh air and exercise. "I cannot sleep nights now, and nothing they give me will produce sleep."

Without her friends standing by her, Lizzie emphasized again and again, she would have fallen apart. Their loyalty made it bearable. "The hardest thing for me to stand here is the night, when there is no light," Lizzie confessed. Lights-out began at seven-thirty, and no exceptions. "They will not allow me to have even a candle to read by, and to sit in the dark all the evening is very hard; but I do not want any favors that are against the rules."

Seen through Mrs. McGuirk's eyes, Lizzie's stoicism bloomed into something meek and admirable. Lizzie had either been grossly misrepresented by the press, or she and Mrs. McGuirk were putting a masterful spin on her personality. Likely a measure of both was coming into play.

SECOND STREET FROM ANOTHER ANGLE

The house on Second Street had not been fitted out with all the latest conveniences, Mrs. McGuirk's interview explained, because there was talk in the family "of moving up 'on the hill.'" Mr. Borden was as satisfied with the old place as ever, but if his daughters wanted to move, then he wanted to please them. Even so, Andrew Borden was not inclined to spend any more than necessary to do it—for the last year, a real estate agent had been hunting for a bargain for him. In the meantime, McGuirk claimed, it was not Andrew Borden who resisted updating their current residence. "When Mr. Borden wanted to put in modern improvements, the wife and daughters said they preferred to stand it than have the house torn up for piping."

"There is one thing that hurts me very much," Lizzie said. "They say I don't show any grief. Certainly I don't in public. I never did reveal my feelings, and I cannot change my nature now. They say I don't cry. They should see me when I am alone, or sometimes with my friends. It hurts me to think people say so about me. I have tried hard to be brave and womanly through it all." She spoke slowly, Mrs. McGuirk wrote, and her eyes filled with tears that did not fall before they were wiped away. "I know I am innocent, and I have made up my mind that, no matter what happens, I will try to bear it bravely and make the best of it."

The accusation that she was unwilling to have her room searched also stung. "Why, I had seen so many different men that first day, and had been questioned about everything till my head was confused and in such a whirl that I could not think," Lizzie said. Dr. Bowen was just preparing something for her headache when Fleet rapped at the door. That was the only reason they had not let the assistant marshal in immediately, she explained.

"As to our not putting on mourning, of which people spoke unfavorably," Lizzie continued, "there was not a moment when I could think of such a thing as a hat or a dress. Somebody was talking to me, it seemed, all the time about the murder and asking me questions, and I could not think of anything else." And besides, she explained, their father had never approved of the custom.

"If people would only do me justice that is all I ask, but it seems as if every word I have uttered has been distorted and such a false construction placed on it that I am bewildered. I can't understand it."

There was not a trace of anger in her tones, Mrs. McGuirk concluded—*simply a pitiful expression.*

"Petticoat propaganda," the *Fall River Globe* branded it. Newsman Edwin Porter pronounced it "a magnificent 'fake.'" Perhaps it was. Or perhaps the *Globe* was envious of Mrs. McGuirk's scoop. While no one has yet proven the McGuirk interview inauthentic, nonsense was indeed running rampant in most newspapers'

Borden coverage in the early fall of 1892—and it was just getting started.

"LIZZIE BORDEN TOOK AN AXE"

Every editor in New England salivated at the sight of the *Boston Globe*'s front page on October 10, 1892:

LIZZIE BORDEN'S SECRET

MR. BORDEN DISCOVERED IT

AND HOT WORDS FOLLOWED

It was an explosive story, more dramatic than the alleged jailhouse quarrel between Lizzie and Emma. Twenty-five new witnesses had stepped forward, each with evidence more stunning than the last, and there was only one place to read it. Column after column, the *Globe* laid out its exclusive revelations:

While pushing her baby carriage down Second Street on August 4, a Mrs. Gustave F. Ronald had heard "a terrible cry or groan." Looking up to the Bordens' window, she spied a woman in a rubber hood or cap. Just then, Peter Mahany of 103 Pleasant Street walked up and confirmed that the hooded woman who glared down at them before slamming the window was none other than Lizzie Borden. Yet another man, Augustus Gunning, also saw the whole thing from his rented room at Mrs. Churchill's house.

Mr. and Mrs. Frederick Chase, along with their daughter Abigail, witnessed the motive when they'd knocked at the Bordens' back door the night before the murder. From inside the dining room, they heard Mr. Borden's voice:

"You can make your own choice and do it to-night. Either let us know what his name is or take the door on Saturday, and when you go fishing, fish for some other place to live, as I will never listen to you again. I will know the name of the man who got you into trouble" ("trouble" being a delicate way of referring to the pregnancy of an unmarried woman).

Despite the fact that no will had yet been found, Mr. George J. Sisson of 180 Rock Street confided to the *Globe* that Mr. Borden had indeed made a will, leaving his daughters only $25,000 apiece; moreover, Dr. Dolan had uncovered evidence that generous bequests were made to Bertie Whitehead and other members of Mrs. Borden's family.

Bridget Sullivan, the story continued, had heard Uncle Morse talking to Lizzie about the will late on the night before the murder. "Quarreling will not fix the thing," Morse said. "Something else has got to be done and I will do all I can." Worse, Bridget had learned from Mrs. Borden that the father of Lizzie's child was none other than Uncle Morse. "Keep your tongue still and don't talk to these officers and you can have all the money you want," Lizzie had promised Bridget the evening of the murders.

If that were not incriminating enough, a former Fall River lawyer, Frank Burroughs, claimed Lizzie had been inquiring about wills and property inheritance for months, showing particular interest in the case of a stepmother dying before her husband.

The *Globe*'s revelations spanned fourteen columns.

The whole thing was, of course, a spectacular hoax. Anyone with a lick of sense ought to have known it was too deliciously sordid to be true—an illicitly pregnant Lizzie Borden hacking up her stepmother in plain view of the neighborhood and buying the maid's silence?

But the *Boston Globe*, fearful that its archrival, the *Boston Herald*, would get hold of its monumental scoop, had printed the story without verifying the most basic facts. Within ten hours the *Globe* realized it was all a dreadful mistake. By then it was too late—the whole thing was on the verge of detonating into the biggest Borden scandal yet.

A $500 FAKE, the *Boston Herald* headlines trumpeted that evening. ASSAULT ON MISS BORDEN'S HONOR IS PURELY A MYTH.

The Fall River city directory, Lawyer Jennings had discovered, contained no Frederick Chase, no George Sisson. Not only that, but their supposed addresses did not exist at all. None of them did.

Incest. Murder. Bribery. The story had besmirched Lizzie Borden from every possible angle without a shred of proof. John Morse telegrammed threatening a libel suit.

How had a paper as prominent and respected as the *Boston Globe* gotten itself into such a fix?

It turned out that a young *Globe* reporter by the unfortunate name of Henry Trickey had purchased the entire fraudulent story from private detective Edwin McHenry for $500. Trickey had no reason to doubt Detective McHenry. The two had done business before, and after all, McHenry was temporarily on the Fall River Police Department's payroll and likely to have inside information.

Unbeknownst to Trickey, Edwin McHenry was himself a phony—he'd established his own detective agency under false pretenses and had already been involved in three cases of fraud. McHenry tried to wiggle clear of the scandal, claiming the next day that of course some of the particulars had been changed to protect the witnesses' identities. But the Boston paper was above such shenanigans. One day of uproar and investigation was enough to convince the *Globe* that it had been swindled. On October 12, the *Boston Globe* completely retracted the entire story and printed a boxed front-page apology to both Lizzie Borden and John Morse.

The apology was sincere, and the whole episode won Lizzie the support of both Boston's *Globe* and *Herald*. But the damage to

Lizzie Borden's reputation would never be completely undone. Sometime that fall, in the midst of all the stories and scandals, the children of Fall River began to sing:

> *Lizzie Borden took an axe,*
> *Gave her mother forty whacks.*
> *When she saw what she had done,*
> *She gave her father forty-one.*

"THEY'LL HANG HER, SURE"

Just under a month after the *Boston Globe* fiasco died down, Lizzie Borden's case came before a grand jury of the Superior Court of Massachusetts. Their decision marked the point of no return. Based on the evidence they heard, the grand jurors could either drop the case and set Lizzie free or indict her for murder and send her to trial for her life.

Like Lizzie's inquest testimony, this vital piece of the Borden case has been lost. The entire transcript—every word of it. And because grand jury sessions are always closed to the public, there are no newspaper accounts to reconstruct it from.

Only these facts are available: the twenty-one-man jury convened on Monday, November 7. For the next two weeks they heard evidence from a number of cases, including Lizzie Borden's. On Monday, November 21, they adjourned without taking any action on the Borden case—no indictment, no release of the prisoner.

More evidence was coming, the papers assured a puzzled public.

It did. On Thursday, December 1, 1892, the grand jury reconvened. One of the witnesses had asked to be recalled: Miss Alice Russell.

She had not wanted to say any more than she had to. When first examined before the Grand Jury, Alice had not mentioned that Lizzie burned a dress on the morning of Sunday, August 8. Conveniently, District Attorney Knowlton had not known to ask. But through the middle of November, Alice's conscience plagued her so fiercely that she could not sleep nights. The oath she had taken was to tell the truth, *the whole truth,* and nothing but the truth. Finally, she consulted an attorney to see whether there was any legal way around divulging what she knew. There was not.

The day after Alice testified, Lizzie Andrew Borden was indicted on a vote of twenty to one for the murders of Andrew and Abby Borden. The jurors had deliberated for just ten minutes.

"They'll hang her, sure," one of them said.

Alice's conscience was relieved, but her troubles were far from over. It was her revelation that had "clinched" the grand jury's decision to indict her friend of nearly a dozen years for murder.

Now it was in all the papers. They had it partly wrong, of course—some said the dress had been burned the very morning of the murder, before the police arrived. Others said Saturday, before the police searched the house from the ridgepole to the cellar.

It did not matter that her name was not in the early reports of the indictment. Lizzie and Emma would know. There was no one else who could have told about that dress. It would be an astonishment if either of them spoke to her again. Emma Borden was confined to her bed; Lizzie, though she reportedly took the news with "the same stolid demeanor," was said to be "much distressed" by the following week. How much of their suffering was due to the indictment itself and how much to Alice's confession was impossible for Alice—or anyone else—to gauge.

"I HAVE SCARCELY EXPECTED A VERDICT OF GUILTY"

Alice Russell was not the only one losing sleep over the Borden case as winter closed in. Lawyer Jennings also "lay awake half of the night thinking about it and arranging matters in his head," the *New Bedford Evening Standard* reported.

By February, Jennings had recruited the Honorable George Dexter Robinson to Lizzie's defense team—not just to assist but to lead—for the reported fee of $25,000. His prestige alone warranted a hefty sum. According to the *Boston Globe,* Robinson had been "a prominent figure in Massachusetts political and legal circles for so long that his name is almost a household word." Not only had the fifty-nine-year-old Robinson served as governor of Massachusetts, but during that time he had appointed one of the three judges who would preside over the Borden trial. Lizzie, it was later said, adored Governor Robinson from their first meeting, when he patted her arm and promised, "It's all right, little girl."

The defense was not alone in fortifying itself. Sometime in late March, the state attorney general appointed young William Henry Moody to join District Attorney Knowlton for the prosecution. A graduate of Harvard, the forty-year-old Moody was also a district attorney in his own right, in Essex County, and was considered "one of the most skillful and successful pleaders of the Essex bar." Although the Borden case would be his first murder trial, in time he would become Secretary of the Navy and a justice of the United States Supreme Court.

And yet District Attorney Knowlton's mind was no more at ease than Lawyer Jennings's. In the first place, he had not expected to be the one to try Lizzie Borden at all. Usually, the state attorney general took responsibility of capital trials. But he had demurred on his doctor's advice. So he said. Despite recurring newspaper reports of ill health, some wondered if the attorney general had deliberately dodged the Borden case. It was growing clear that whoever prosecuted Lizzie Borden was going to become very unpopular among some large cross-sections of voters—not just Fall River society, but religious conservatives and women's rights champions all across Massachusetts and beyond who were outraged at the very idea of a woman facing the death penalty—and the attorney general had his eye on the Republican nomination for governor. No one with such aspirations wanted to open his mailbox and find spiteful postcards like Knowlton had received:

> *One thing is sure and that is you will never be*
> *District Attorney again.*

> *The people of Bristol Co will attend to that next Nov.*

> *After the mean underhanded part you have taken in the*
> *Borden case you deserve to be kicked out.*

> *Respectfully yours*
> *Voter.*

SUPPORT FOR LIZZIE

Immediately following her arrest, a number of respected organizations came out publicly in support of Lizzie Borden's innocence.

On Monday, August 15, Lizzie received a message in Taunton Jail:

We, the members of the Young People's Society of Christian Endeavor, desire to extend to our fellow member, Miss Lizzie A. Borden, our sincere sympathy with her in her present hour of trial, and our confident belief that she will soon be restored to her place of usefulness among us.

The message was also released to the press.

That same day, the local chapter of the Women's Christian Temperance Union convened a special meeting to publicly declare their sympathy, support, and "unshaken faith" in Lizzie Borden. By the next afternoon, the Women's Auxiliary of the YMCA was praying for her, too.

As interest in the Borden case spread, Lizzie's advocates multiplied. At a Boston meeting just three days after Lizzie was judged probably guilty at the preliminary hearing in September, the president of the Massachusetts Women's Christian Temperance Union read aloud a petition asking the governor to release Lizzie Borden on bail. All but 40 or 50 of the 2,500 members in attendance stood to show their support.

But it was more than politics troubling Knowlton. The district attorney had begun to believe that the whole trial was a lost cause.

"Personally I would like very much to get rid of the trial of the case," Knowlton wrote to the attorney general in late April 1893, "and fear that my own feelings in that direction may have influenced my better judgement." Exactly what those feelings were, Knowlton did not say. It hardly mattered. Once the grand jury had indicted Lizzie Borden for murder, there was virtually no legal way of backing out. "[I]t does not seem to me that we ought to take the responsibility of discharging her without trial, even though there is every reasonable expectation of a verdict of not guilty," Knowlton wrote. They had even investigated the possibility of insanity to spare the time and cost of trying Lizzie, to no avail.

"The situation is this," Knowlton summed up, "nothing has developed which satisfies either of us that she is innocent, neither of us can escape the conclusion that she must have had some knowledge of the occurrence."

The prosecution had no choice but to forge ahead with what Knowlton believed to be a doomed effort.

"I TRY TO FILL UP THE WAITING TIME AS WELL AS I CAN"

While the two legal teams squared off, Lizzie waited in jail. Unable to go outdoors, Lizzie was permitted to tend to a row of little pots lined up in a windowsill: geraniums and ivy, and strawberry plants sent by strangers as well as friends. Her sole form of exercise was tramping up and down the corridor outside the women's cells. On days without visitors, there was only the prison cat, a lazy yellow and white tom named Daisy, for company.

Weeks passed, then months, with no trial date in sight. All the while she was keenly aware of the changing seasons outside her window—the blasts of autumn wind, winter sleigh bells jingling, the scent of spring.

In one way, at least, seclusion was good for Lizzie. Since Alice Russell's revelation about the burned dress had crisscrossed the nation, public opinion was swerving back toward guilty. Once again, suspicion began to find a foothold in the popular mind, and the newspapers were happy to oblige with their own fanciful concoctions.

Even the state attorney general was getting fed up with them. "[I]t is singular that newspapers cannot tell the truth, even when it is put before them and they know it is the truth," he complained to District Attorney Knowlton after the press mangled yet another of their official statements.

Knowlton did not have to open the papers to see the latest stories. Letters from all manner of people crammed his mailbox, showering him with theories, tips, rumors, and clues. Maybe she'd done the killing with a flatiron rather than an axe, a Boston man proposed. A Brooklyn woman suggested Lizzie had worn a rubber cloak and sponged off the blood afterward. And most scintillating of all: could a young woman with such "wonderful nerve" have stripped herself naked to commit the crime and then burned the paint-stained dress as a decoy?

More than a few had something to say about Lizzie's personality. Not one of them had met her, but all were certain what kind of a person she was. For one thing, her reaction to the murder was not natural. That was sure. In exactly what way, they could not agree.

"No sudden, frantic scream when she finds her murdered father—no rushing to his side—no examination to find a spark of life—no calling for the mother whom she had heard come in—nor to the neighbors!" admonished one.

Another asked, "[W]hy did she not rush, terror stricken, from that house as far as she could go—just as any other woman would have done under the circumstances of finding her father murdered?"

There was no winning—whether Lizzie rushed toward her father's body or away from it, she was branded unnatural. Nothing about her was deemed genuine. "Her religious pretences are only cloaks to hide her real nature," one critic declared.

Glimmers of that real nature, someone else insisted to Knowlton, had been apparent even before Andrew and Abby Borden turned up dead: "A MAN NAMED RODMAN OF BOSTON HAD A SISTER WHO WAS SICK ABED WITH A COLD. SHE HAD HEART DISEASE AND THE DOCTOR SAID SHE MIGHT DIE ANYTIME OF HEART DISEASE. LIZZIE BORDEN WAS HER FRIEND AND WAS ALONE WITH HER WHEN SHE DIED— AFTER HER DEATH BLACK MARKS WERE FOUND ON HER NECK AND HER JEWELRY WAS GONE."

How much of the public sentiment might have reached Lizzie is difficult to know. At the very least, she realized what was at the core of the feelings against her. "What would they have me do?" she asked one visitor. "Howl? Go into hysterics? I am wrongly accused of two horrible crimes. I know it is useless to cry out in indignation at the outrage, so I am trying hard to keep calm and self-controlled until I shall be proved innocent."

Whatever the cause, Lizzie's mood was plainly suffering. She had not been keeping up with her correspondence since mid-January. "My head troubles me so much," she apologized in a letter to her friend Mrs. Annie Lindsey of Dorchester. "I think soon they can take me up the road, to the insane asylum." She never failed to appreciate her friends' small kindnesses—books and flowers and boxes of candy—but their optimism seemed to be wearing on her. "Do you know I cannot for the life of me see how you and the rest of my friends can be so full of hope over the case," Lizzie continued. She'd known for months that her lawyers held out little promise of an acquittal, and nothing encouraging had happened in the meantime. "To <u>me,</u> I see nothing but the densest shadows."

Finally, the date was settled. Her trial would open on Monday, June 5, in New Bedford.

By mid-May, Lizzie's morale had slumped lower than ever. She had been arraigned before the Superior Court, then almost immediately laid up with bronchitis. "My spirits are at ebb tide," she confided to Annie.

> *I see no ray of light amid the gloom. I try to fill up the waiting time as well as I can, but every day is longer and longer.*
>
> *I began to think the tangled threads will <u>never</u> be smoothed out. My friend—do not make any plans for me at Christmas. I do not expect to be free—and if I am, I could not join in any merry making. I don't know that I ever could again, certainly not at present. You know my life can never be the same again if I ever come home.*

ANOTHER MURDER IN FALL RIVER

On the morning of May 31, 1893, twelve-year-old Freddy Manchester returned home from delivering milk with his father to find his sister, twenty-two-year-old Bertha, splayed facedown before the kitchen stove. Pools and smears of blood stained the floor, her face, her arms. It matted her long brown hair and dripped through the floorboards to the cellar below. Her neck was slashed, the top of her skull "crushed to a jelly," and five of her teeth had been knocked from her mouth. The scene, the *Evening Standard* said, was "fully as revolting as the appearance of either victim in the Borden tragedy." A bloodied axe was found in plain sight on the woodpile.

Despite the obvious parallels, Marshal Hilliard insisted there was no similarity between Bertha's murder and the Bordens'. The motive in this case, the marshal said, was obvious: Bertha's watch and money had been stolen, and her position on the floor indicated that she had "struggled for her honor and her life," though she had not been raped.

Following the trail of Bertha's missing property, police soon accumulated enough evidence to arrest a Portuguese immigrant named Jose Correa deMello, who had recently been fired from the Manchester farm without pay.

Jose Correa deMello first pled not guilty, then, most likely in hopes of escaping the death sentence, switched his plea to guilty of second-degree murder. On January 8, 1894, he was convicted and sentenced to the state prison for life.

To the Borden jurors, who were already sequestered before word of the deMello arrest hit the newsstands, it must have appeared that an axe-wielding murderer was still on the loose. Surely they wondered—could it have been the same killer? A coincidence? Or was it what we would now call a copycat crime?

One thing was undeniable: it could not have been Lizzie Borden.

But could Jose Correa deMello have killed the Bordens? At the time of his arrest in May 1893, he had been in the United States for less than a year—possibly as little as two months. Depending on exactly when he arrived, Correa may not have been in the country on August 4, 1892.

Here is something else the Borden jurors could not take into account: two decades after the murder of Bertha Manchester, Jose Correa deMello was pardoned and instructed to go home to the Azores, never to return to the United States again. Why? No one, not even the most exhaustive Borden references, offers an explanation.

TRIAL OF THE CENTURY

DAY ONE

Monday, June 5, 1893

From behind the New Bedford courthouse came the hum and click of a dozen trembling telegraph instruments. The entire country panted for news, and so the horse shed had been converted into headquarters for the telegraph operators. There was a floor now, and partitions to make three small rooms: one for the Postal Telegraph-Cable Company, one for Western Union, and one shared by the *Evening Standard* and the Associated Press.

Inside the courthouse, twenty-five reporters bent like schoolboys over their notepads. Sheriff Wright had personally numbered each seat in the press box and presented tickets to select newspapers. Twelve went to the Fall River and New Bedford dailies, two to nearby Attleboro and Taunton, and four to the Associated Press. The rest went to Boston's five most prominent papers. At the last minute, the prisoner's dock had been hastily divided in half to squeeze in six more reporters from the New York papers. Every other member of the press would have to vie for a seat in the spectators' benches, like anyone else.

But today no spectators had been admitted. There was no room. One hundred fifty men had been called as potential jurors, and they filled every seat. Not one of them was from Fall River.

The only glimpses within the New Bedford courthouse that first day would come via the newspapermen, and they were determined not to let their readers miss a thing. Even before the proceedings opened, the telegraphs clattered with descriptions of the room itself: the drab walls trimmed with white, the carpeted floor liberally scattered with spittoons, the scent of wisteria and magnolia seeping in through the windows along with the sound of a cow mooing loudly in a nearby field. Two bunches of carnations, one pink and one red, sat on the judges' bench before the three white-bearded justices: Chief Justice Albert Mason and his associates, Caleb Blodgett and Justin Dewey. Between them, the three men had amassed a total of ninety-nine years' experience with the law.

At eleven o'clock on the dot, in came the accused.

"Those who saw Miss Borden for the first time were very much astonished," the *Boston Globe* noted. "Her newspaper portraits have done her no justice at all."

They had expected a monster, a virtual Medusa with hair of serpents and a gaze of stone. Instead, a shockingly ordinary New England spinster walked across the room and sat down in the prisoner's dock, seemingly unaffected by the hundreds of stares that greeted her.

Even the most seasoned journalists were surprised. "It has been said again and again that this maiden prisoner is a great strong woman, capable of extraordinary physical exertion," said the famous Julian Ralph of the *New York Sun*. "It is not so. She is very little, if anything, above average stature of women. She is not of large build; she does not look to weigh more than 135 pounds at the outside, and if her arms, which cannot be seen in her puffed sleeves, are large and muscular, they assuredly terminate in very small and ladylike hands."

"Some have made her out a hard and hideous fright," the *Globe* observed, "and others have flattered her." Suddenly, it did not matter how many times she had been described before. Hardly a reporter in the room could resist the opportunity to do it yet again.

They assessed every inch of her, from the blue feather in her black hat right down to her "common sense, broad-toed, brand new shoe," noting when she wiped the perspiration from her face or bit nervously at her fan. And yet with the woman sitting before them, with nothing to do but look her over while the lawyers consumed the entire day selecting a jury, the papers still could not fully agree on Lizzie Borden's appearance.

Her dress was black, trimmed with bands of velvet ribbon at the hem and cuffs, but whether it was brocade, mohair, or merino, "cut in the latest style" or "of a very old fashion," depended entirely on whether the information came out of Boston or New Bedford. A large enamel pin in the shape of a pansy nestled at her throat. One reporter thought it "modest," another "rather loud." The *Boston Globe*, still feeling the sting of the Trickey-McHenry debacle, tended to be complimentary whenever possible. "Her dress fitted her as perfectly as if she had been measured for it in Paris," it said. (She had been measured not in Paris but in Taunton Jail. Ten months with little exercise to counteract the many boxes of sweets sent from well-meaning friends meant that a seamstress had to be called in to let out some of Lizzie's dresses for the trial.)

Other papers were not inclined to be so courteous. They discussed her face as though they were measuring it for wallpaper, with talk of perpendicular lines dropped from this point to that, the distance between the bridge and the tip of the nose, whether her forehead protruded more than her chin. That chin was "obstinate and stubborn," proclaimed Joe Howard of the *Boston Globe*, one of the most famous journalists of the day. The lips were too thick, the eyes set too wide apart, the cheekbones too high, yet the cheeks themselves too full and heavy.

The problem was simple: those who believed her guilty wanted—needed—Lizzie Borden to look the part of a coarse and brutish killer. Those who favored her innocence required a dainty, delicate lady. Lizzie Borden was neither. She was only herself, and as everyone had come to expect, her outward appearance gave little indication of the personality within.

DAY TWO

Tuesday, June 6, 1893

Mr. Moody, the young district attorney from Essex County, rose from the prosecutor's table and approached the rail of the jury box. Twelve grave-faced men looked back at him. With his blond hair, bright blue eyes, and trim mustache, Moody looked like a boy compared with the dozen bearded, balding jurors. This was William Moody's first murder case, and it had fallen to him to open the trial of the century.

THE JURY

George Potter, farmer, age 54, Westport

William F. Dean, farmer, age 54, Taunton

John Wilbur, farmer, housewright, and surveyor, age
    60, Somerset

Frederick C. Wilbur, cabinetmaker, age 36,
    Raynham

Lemuel K. Wilbur, farmer, age 56, Easton

William Westcot, farmer, age 48, Seekonk

Lewis B. Hodges, iron moulder, age 59, Taunton

Augustus Swift, manufacturer, age 42, New Bedford

Francis G. Cole, jeweler, age 49, Attleboro

John C. Finn, painter, age 35, Taunton

Charles I. Richards, real estate and town assessor, age
    64, North Attleboro (elected foreman)

Allen H. Wordell, agricultural retailer, age 45,
    Dartmouth

The moment he began to speak, Lizzie's eyes snapped toward him. Lizzie Borden, who had spent her courtroom hours staring fixedly at the carpet, or the corner of a desk, suddenly followed Mr. Moody with as much interest as any of the hundred-odd spectators behind her.

He spoke, as he promised the jury, "in the plainest, simplest and most direct manner," doing his best not to overburden them with details that were bound to come out in the evidence. Even so, Moody took the better part of two hours to outline the government's case.

Much of what he told the jurors was old news to anyone who had been following the case: the indications of an unkindly feeling between Lizzie and Abby Borden, the Bordens' Tuesday-night illness, Mrs. Borden's fears of poisoning, Eli Bence's claim that Lizzie had tried to buy prussic acid Wednesday morning, and Lizzie's worrisome Wednesday-night visit with Alice Russell. He guided them through the layout of the house and the movements of the family from the locking of the doors Wednesday night to the discovery of the bodies Thursday morning. He covered Lizzie's wavering alibi, the note from Mrs. Borden's sick friend that had never materialized, and the confounding results of Professor Wood's examinations.

Meanwhile, the mercury climbed steadily toward 93 degrees, until even the judges had trouble keeping their eyes open.

Then Moody said, "On the morning of Sunday Miss Russell came into the kitchen," and the courtroom perked up with interest. At last, the burning of the dress. "It was a dress which the prisoner had purchased in the spring of that year, a cotton dress and not a silk dress like this." Moody held up a dark blue dress for the jury to see, then tossed it down to the table. As he did, a flutter of tissue paper at the top of a nearby handbag caught

Lizzie Borden's eye. Beneath it she glimpsed the crowns of her parents' bald, bleached skulls. Up went her big black fan, hiding her flushed face from the court, and there it stayed while Moody riveted the court with Alice Russell's revelation and then an exhibition of the handleless hatchet.

"The Commonwealth will prove that there was an unkindly feeling between the prisoner and her step-mother," Moody declared as he drew to a close, "that upon Wednesday, August 3, she was dwelling upon murder and preparing herself with a weapon which had no innocent use; that upon the evening of Wednesday, August 3, she was predicting disaster and cataloguing defences." No one but the prisoner, Moody said, was in the house from the time Mrs. Borden went upstairs to change the pillow slips until Lizzie came down stairs an hour later. No other human being could have done it, Moody told the jury, because it could not be done without intimate knowledge of the inside of that house and the habits of that family.

"We shall prove that this prisoner made contradictory statements about her whereabouts, and, above all, gave a statement vitally different upon the manner in which she discovered these homicides. We shall prove beyond all reasonable doubt that this death of Mrs. Borden's was a prior death. Then we shall ask you to say, if say you can, whether any other reasonable hypothesis except that of the guilt of this prisoner can account for the sad occurrences which happened upon the morning of August fourth."

Moody was done. There was no applause, just a patient wondering—what would come next? No one could have guessed.

For two days Lizzie Borden had sat, the *Boston Globe* said, "like a graven image," hardly moving except to wave her Japanese fan or rest her head on the rail behind her.

Now, someone noticed, "the fan and the arm that held it up

dropped upon the prisoner's lap. Her head was back against the rail, her eyes were shut, her mouth was open, and her breast heaved with very long breaths. 'Lizzie Borden's asleep,' was the whisper that galloped through the court room."

The sheriff gently shook her arm. "He might as well have shaken a pump handle," the *Globe* remarked. Her head lolled, her face went purplish.

Lizzie Borden was not asleep—she was unconscious.

The hot and drowsy courtroom sprang to life. Someone sat her up. Reverend Jubb fanned her; the deputy sheriff brought a glass of water. Lizzie seemed to half come to, and Reverend Jubb demanded her smelling salts. "Her hand went into her pocket mechanically and came out with a little cut glass bottle in it. Then she put both hands on the arm of her chair and fell back against the railing, not half over her faint."

Finally, she had done what a woman under intense strain was supposed to do: "Lizzie Borden, the sphinx of coolness, who has so often been accused of never manifesting a feminine feeling, had fainted," marveled the *Fall River Globe*.

DAY THREE
Wednesday, June 7, 1893

Overnight, Lizzie Borden had become human. "Since her fainting yesterday she is regarded as being full of startling possibilities," said the *Rochester Democrat & Chronicle*. Women of all ages, from society matrons to work girls in calico, abandoned their children and their jobs for the day to come watch her. "Valentines and daisies," the press soon dubbed the female spectators.

To many, the third day felt like the first real day of the trial.

Today there would be nothing but testimony. The mood in court was high. A northeast wind had broken the oppressive heat. Even Lizzie Borden seemed in high spirits. "To-day she held her head up, looking at everything out of bright eyes, moved her chair about and shifted herself in it quite like any one else."

But a courtroom, as the valentines and daisies soon found out, is a mostly boring place.

The first witness, surveyor Thomas Kieran, sounded like a talking yardstick as he answered question after question about the measurements and blueprints he had made of the Borden house and its vicinity. Even the judges were bored.

Then came Lawyer Jennings's turn with Kieran. "At the time you were making measurements of the closets on the lower floor of the Borden house, was your attention called particularly to the size of the closet in the front hall?"

"It was."

"Did you see at that time any experiment performed as to whether a person could or could not go in there and have the door completely shut?"

Jennings knew perfectly well what the answer would be. He himself had stepped into that closet and shut the door behind him. Finding that he fit, Jennings stepped out, put his assistant inside, and called Kieran's attention to the experiment. Even with the door slightly ajar, Kieran told the jury, he had failed to see anyone standing inside. If a lawyer could hide in there, the jurors had no choice but to assume, a murderer could, too.

Jennings had landed his first punch for the defense—and with one of the prosecution's own witnesses. Nor was he finished.

Upstairs, Kieran's assistant had lain down on the floor where Mrs. Borden was found. Kieran discovered he could not see any part of the man's body from Lizzie Borden's doorway, even though his assistant was so much taller than Mrs. Borden that his feet stuck out beyond the end of the bed. (Mrs. Brigham and Uncle Morse had performed an identical experiment, with identical results, the jury later learned. The bed made it impossible to see the body, even from the guest-room doorway.) Only when Kieran paused at the center of a certain step with his eyes level with the floor could he see anyone lying there. As soon as his head rose above the bottom of the bed, the body became undetectable.

Knowlton followed with his star witness: Bridget Sullivan. Just twenty-six years old. Irish. She had spent the last seven years doing nothing more interesting than cooking other people's dinners, sweeping their floors, and washing their clothes. Under any other circumstances, no one would have taken the slightest notice of her life. Now the mere mention of her name, the sight of her in a maroon dress, feathered hat, and black kid gloves, caused a sensation in the courtroom. No one knows a family better than its maid, and everyone, down to Lizzie Borden herself, wanted to hear what this girl who had refused to set foot in the Borden house since the first day of the inquest now had to say about them.

Mr. Moody questioned her carefully, politely. There were no secrets or dark revelations to pry out of her. All he needed was a straightforward account of the morning of August 4. As she had done at the inquest and preliminary hearing, Bridget delivered. She spoke so softly, yet her answers were firm. No one could or would give so many details about that morning. Bridget knew who had gotten up when, what they had eaten, where Mr. Borden had dumped his slop pail. It was Bridget who vouched for nearly every time the screen door was hooked or unhooked.

BREAKFAST WITH THE BORDENS

Cold boiled mutton, warmed-over mutton broth, bread and butter, johnnycakes, sugar cookies, bananas, pears, and coffee—people have been wrinkling their noses and cracking jokes at Andrew and Abby Borden's last breakfast for over a century. Even at a time when dishes like pie and pork steak were commonplace on the breakfast table, the Bordens' menu struck many as peculiar, particularly for a well-to-do household.

"A smile played about the lips of Miss Sullivan whenever any reference was made to the component parts of the meals served at the Borden house," wrote Fall River's *Herald* on June 8. "She laughed at the mutton and cold mutton, and mutton broth, just as others have laughed at the same thing. Lizzie laughed, too, at the mutton."

One of the most enduring Borden myths is that rotting leftover mutton caused the family's sickness before the murder. Impossible—the infamous mutton did not debut until Wednesday noon—the day *after* Mr. and Mrs. Borden endured a miserable night of vomiting. The culprit was more likely the fried swordfish they'd eaten for dinner and supper Tuesday.

Aside from her headache, everything about that morning had been perfectly normal: starting the fire, unlocking the door, taking in the milk, putting out the pan for the iceman, getting the breakfast.

The Bordens did nothing out of the ordinary, either. Mr. and Mrs. Borden sat down to breakfast with Mr. Morse by 7:15. Lizzie slept in. When they finished, they rang the bell and went into the sitting room. Bridget sat down in Mr. Borden's chair and had her own breakfast, then cleared away. Next thing she noticed, Mr. Morse was leaving. Bridget saw him go, and heard Mr. Borden invite him back to dinner.

Five minutes or so later, Bridget couldn't say for sure, Lizzie appeared in the kitchen. "I asked her what did she want for her breakfast," Bridget testified. "She said she didn't want any breakfast but she felt as if she should have something, she guessed she would have some coffee and cookies."

Just then, Bridget's breakfast rebelled. Out she went to be sick in the yard. She could not say how long she stayed there—ten or fifteen minutes, perhaps? By the time she returned to her sink full of dishes, Lizzie was gone. There was no sign of Mr. Borden, either. Bridget finished her dishes and carried them into the dining room, where she found Mrs. Borden busy with the feather duster. "She said she wanted the windows washed. I asked her how, and she said 'inside and outside both, they are awful dirty.'" Near as Bridget could figure, it was around nine o'clock. That was the last time she saw Mrs. Borden alive.

As Bridget headed out the screen door with her pail and brush, Lizzie appeared in the entry and asked Bridget if she was going to wash windows.

"Yes," Bridget said. "You needn't lock the door; I will be out around here, but you can lock it if you want to; I can get the water in the barn."

Lizzie did not hook the door behind her.

Bridget went all the way around to the opposite side of the house to begin with the sitting room windows. First she stopped and chatted over the fence with the neighbor's maid; then with her long-handled brush she washed her way around three sides of the house, going back and forth to the spigot in the barn about half a dozen times to refill her pail. In between the washing and the rinsing, she popped into the kitchen for a dipper to fling clean water onto the soapy panes.

During all that time—probably while Mrs. Borden was being murdered—she'd seen nothing out of the ordinary in the yard, barn, or kitchen. She noticed no one on the other side of the sitting or dining room windows. Moody did not specifically ask whether she'd seen anyone through the parlor windows. In fact, Moody had never asked if she actually could see *through* any of the windows.

Whether this was an intentional sleight of hand on Mr. Moody's part did not matter once Governor Robinson began his cross-examination. He was brilliant at it, the *Rochester Democrat & Chronicle* noted: "With his queer spectacles, which have only half a glass for each eye, poised on the end of his nose, he seems so fatherly, and he has such a friendly and sympathetic air that there is no withstanding him. But, whenever he and a witness are getting along swimmingly, let that witness look out. In two jerks, the ex-governor will make him tell what he does not want to."

Often he did it by wording his questions as if he were thinking aloud. "On the outside of the parlor you say the blinds were closed when you went around there?" he asked Bridget.

"I know they was closed on the front part any way."

"But you can't tell us at all whether the parlor curtains or shutters on the inside were closed?"

"I can't remember how they were."

Then came the question he'd been intending to ask all along: "Whether anybody was in that room you can't tell?"

"No, sir, I couldn't."

He did it again with the dining room windows, chatting amiably about their height and position until he came to the pertinent point:

"Can't see in, can you?"

"I can't see," Bridget admitted, rather as if the thought had not occurred to her before—not unless someone stood right up against the panes, she guessed.

Once inside, Bridget had washed just half of one sitting room window before she heard Mr. Borden's key rattling uselessly at the front door. She let Mr. Borden in, spluttering at the infernal bolts and locks, and returned to her work without another word. The last Bridget saw of Mr. Borden, he was reading the paper in a rocking chair in the sitting room. As she finished up the dining room windows, Lizzie came in and set up the little ironing board on the table to press her hankies.

"Maggie," Lizzie said, using her nickname for Bridget, "are you going out this afternoon?"

"I don't know; I might and I might not; I don't feel very well."

"If you go out, be sure and lock the door, for Mrs. Borden has gone out on a sick call, and I might go out, too."

"Miss Lizzie, who is sick?"

"I don't know; she had a note this morning; it must be in town."

There was still an hour yet before dinner. Bridget went up to her attic room and lay down. Three, maybe four minutes later, the city hall clock tolled eleven times. No more than fifteen minutes after that, Bridget said, the cry came up the stairs:

"Maggie, come down!"

DAY FOUR
Thursday, June 8, 1893

At the calling of Alice Russell's name, Lizzie's face went livid. She straightened up in her chair and watched the door. One paper said Alice looked everywhere but at Lizzie as she walked in;

another reported that her pale blue eyes blazed at the sight of her old friend in the prisoner's dock.

"[E]xtremely trim in her manner," the bombastic columnist Joe Howard told his readers, Miss Russell "holds her mouth as though *prisms* and *prunes* were its most frequent utterances." As she testified, he noted that "with crossed arms, she emphasizes her replies with little taps with a bombazine fan."

Moody began with Lizzie's Wednesday-night visit to Alice's house. Alice, who at the preliminary hearing had been asked by a frustrated Knowlton, "Do you remember anything that took place at all?" now recalled enough of Lizzie's forebodings to cover five pages of stenographer's notepaper. Her memory of the day of the murder had not improved, however: "I cannot tell it in order, for it is very disconnected," she said. "I remember very little of it." But Alice distinctly remembered Lizzie standing by the stove Sunday morning, tearing up a dress. It was a cheap cotton dress, a light blue Bedford cord with a small dark figure printed on it. The hem was soiled—Lizzie had held the edge up for Alice to see—and what she saw of it was not bloodstained. Alice Russell was emphatic on that point. Alice also made it clear that she had not actually seen Lizzie burn the dress. She heard Lizzie say that she was going to do it, saw her tearing a portion of it up, and saw another piece of it on the shelf in the cupboard. That was all.

Nevertheless, the implication was obvious: Lizzie Borden had not turned over the right dress to the police. That Bedford cord, the prosecution alleged, was the reason no one, from Bridget to the neighbors to the police, had seen one speck of blood on Lizzie Borden from the instant the crime was discovered. She'd somehow managed to keep it hidden during the searches, then burned it Sunday morning—in plain view of the officers standing guard in the yard outside.

Could Lizzie Borden have pulled off something so brazen with such a crucial piece of evidence? Was that blue Bedford cord, in fact, the same dress she had worn Thursday morning?

Hard to tell. The dress Lizzie provided to the police apparently has not survived. Only a handful of people had seen what Lizzie was wearing before she changed into her pink-and-white striped wrapper, and since none of them realized at the time that it would become a vital piece of evidence, their attempts to describe it ten months later do not paint a vivid—much less consistent—picture.

DESCRIBING LIZZIE'S DRESS

BRIDGET SULLIVAN:
"I couldn't tell what dress the girl had on."

MRS. CHURCHILL:
"It looked like a light blue and white ground work; it seemed like calico or cambric, and it had a light blue and white ground work with a dark navy blue diamond printed on it."

ALICE RUSSELL:
"[I]t was loose here (indicating some part of the bosom) when I started to unloosen them. That is the only thing about the dress I notice[d]."

DR. BOWEN:
"It was an ordinary, unattractive, common dress that I did not notice specially."

CHARLES SAWYER:
"I couldn't tell you the colors, as I know of."

> INSPECTOR PATRICK DOHERTY:
> "I thought she had a light blue dress with a bosom in the waist, or something like a bosom. . . . I thought there was a small figure on the dress, a little spot like."

Mrs. Churchill's description was far and away the most specific, but her credibility eroded under Governor Robinson's cross-examination, when she guessed that Bridget was wearing a light calico dress. Bridget Sullivan's dress that day had been a dark indigo blue with a white clover leaf. Alice Russell's dress was a complete blank to her.

Bridget's dress also brought Inspector Doherty's powers of observation into question when he called it "kind of a brown." That was easy enough to explain—Patrick Doherty was color-blind. At the preliminary hearing, when asked to point out a garment or object the same shade of blue as Lizzie Borden's dress, Doherty had selected a white necktie.

Dr. Bowen's wife had been there, too, but her recollections were a mess. At one of the earlier proceedings, she'd apparently testified to "[a] white dress with a waist with blue material, a white spray running right through it." At the trial it became a dark dress with a round figure or flower on the waist.

Realizing the discrepancy, Knowlton asked, "It is not a spray that is on the dress?"

"I should say not," Mrs. Bowen answered. "I did not mean a dress with any white," she said, "but dark blue, the dress with a blouse, that had the figure in it." She was not sure whether the print was a figure or a spray.

BLOUSES, WAISTS, AND WRAPPERS

The garment called a *waist* had nothing to do with a woman's waistline. It was short for "shirtwaist"—the bodice of a two-piece dress. A loose bodice was called a *blouse waist*, or a *bosom*, while a tight-fitting one was known as a *basque*.

Wrappers, though they sound for all the world like bathrobes, were simple form-fitting house dresses with a front closure and a ribbon or sash to cinch the waistline.

Lizzie herself had said nothing about a print, describing the dress only as "navy blue, sort of a bengaline or India silk skirt, with a navy blue blouse."

Each time a witness was called, the evidence swung from one side to the other. It did not help that Lizzie Borden owned no less than eight blue dresses, nor that the attorneys doing the questioning were three-quarters inept when it came to the style and terminology of ladies' fashions. Every woman in court laughed at Moody's and Knowlton's attempt to properly lay out Lizzie's bengaline silk for the witnesses to examine, for the two men could not find the waistline.

But even the ladies were occasionally at a loss. Mrs. Churchill was unfamiliar with Bedford cord material, so she could not say whether the dress she remembered from Thursday morning was made of Bedford cord or not. "I thought it was a cotton dress of some kind," she said, not realizing that Lizzie's Bedford cord *was* cotton. Yet Alice Russell testified that she had seen the Bedford cord exactly twice: first when it was new, then the Sunday after the homicide, and never again in between.

BENGALINE SILK AND BEDFORD CORD

One sounds like silk, the other corduroy. Neither is quite what it seems. Bengaline offers the look of silk for a fraction of the cost, by weaving fine silk threads around strands of wool, cotton, or, in Lizzie Borden's case, linen. The combination results in a ribbed fabric with a silky sheen.

Bedford cord is also ribbed and relatively inexpensive but lacks both the sheen of bengaline and the velvety texture of corduroy.

Out of seven witnesses, only Mrs. Bowen recognized the navy blue bengaline silk displayed by the prosecution as the one Lizzie had worn Thursday morning.

It was a jury's nightmare.

Regardless of what Lizzie's dress looked like, the question of how could she have kept the police from finding it remained. The prosecution called Assistant Marshal John Fleet to the stand to answer to that.

It would be unfair to say the initial search on Thursday, August 4, had been cursory. Mr. Moody's questioning showed that Fleet and his fellow officers had been all over the Borden property during the course of that first day, and they looked everywhere. The very first policeman dispatched to 92 Second Street on August 4, Officer George Allen, had opened the kitchen cupboard where Alice Russell eventually saw the Bedford cord before he returned to the station for backup. The issue was a matter of focus. The officers were making a broad sweep of the house, looking for the weapon, the criminal—items so glaring they couldn't be called clues.

So when Fleet asked Lizzie to unlock the clothes press upstairs, he had no expectation of finding anything, and no intention of pausing to examine every garment right then and there. The assistant marshal was only covering his bases, and he was up-front about it on the witness stand.

"How much of an inspection or search did you make in that room at that time?" Mr. Moody asked.

"We just looked over the clothing, looked round the floor, and up on the shelf. We did not search very closely."

It was not an unreasonable approach, but to hear Governor Robinson's cross-examination, it sounded as though the police had done no more than look under the beds for the bogeyman. A whole new side of Robinson emerged to deal with the assistant marshal. The fatherly gentleman made himself irritable, stern, and impatient, and within five minutes he was under Fleet's skin.

Governor Robinson treaded a delicate line, though. He needed to show it was possible for the police to have overlooked the Bedford cord, but he needed to do it in exactly the right way. Make the police appear incompetent, and Robinson risked leaving room for the jury to believe Lizzie could have successfully hidden the dress from the officers. Fleet made it almost too easy.

Q. Would you have seen any paint the way you looked?

A. I don't think that I should.

Q. Would you have seen any blood the way you looked?

A. Not without it was on the outside, right before my eyes. I didn't look at them close enough to notice.

Robinson did not bother with Fleet about the search he'd conducted of the clothes press with State Officer Seaver on Saturday,
August 6. He would wait until Seaver himself took the stand two
days later to fully demolish the prosecution's allegation that the
Bedford cord had never been in the clothes press.

By the time the ex-governor was done, it did not matter that
Seaver had answered *no* when Mr. Moody asked point-blank,
"Did you see a light blue dress, diamond spots upon it, and paint
around the bottom of the dress and on its front?" Robinson made
it painfully clear that the policemen had been so focused on looking specifically for blood, they noticed almost nothing else about
the dresses themselves.

Officer Seaver could not tell whether he had seen a dress made
of challie, delaine, or alpaca, much less a Bedford cord. If he had,
he wouldn't have known, because he did not recognize the different fabrics. By now Lizzie Borden's pink-and-white striped wrapper was known the world over, yet he could not say whether he
had seen a pink dress. According to Emma Borden's inventory,
she and her sister owned ten blue dresses between them, but
Seaver also could not say whether there were any blue dresses. All
he remembered for certain were one or two black ones in wool
or silk. (And here Lizzie Borden shook her head and whispered to
her lawyers she had no black silk.) For a moment, he even thought
maybe Lizzie was wearing the blue Bedford cord the day of the
search, then changed his mind.

"Was you actually looking after that blue dress at all?" Robinson asked.

"No, sir," Officer Seaver admitted.

DAY FIVE

Friday, June 9, 1893

Assistant Marshal Fleet's credibility was on the line. The day before, Fleet caused a mild sensation with the revelation that he had run across the handleless hatchet the very day of the murders. So far as the public knew, it had not been discovered until Monday, August 8, by Officer Medley. Fleet had said nothing about all this at the preliminary hearing, but at the trial he stood in the witness box claiming to be the first to have seen the alleged murder weapon. Not only that, he gave conflicting testimony regarding the handle's stump—the afternoon before, he had sworn to Mr. Moody that the broken part was coated with ashes like the blade. A tiny detail, but one the defense was eager to seize—if that break was as dusty as the blade, then the hatchet could not have been broken by the murderer. But on the morning of day five, when Governor Robinson tried to confirm the fact, Fleet reversed his story.

"I didn't notice any ashes, on the new break," he told Robinson.

Into this quagmire stepped Officer Mullaly. Michael Mullaly was the officer Bridget had led to that box of tools—by all accounts, the first policeman to lay eyes on the box itself. According to Fleet, Mullaly had been there when he discovered the handleless hatchet lying in the bottom, and Mullaly had seen him put it back into the box. If anyone could clear things up, Michael Mullaly was the man to do it.

"He did not look like a powder magazine on the point of exploding, but that is what he proved to be," the *Rochester Democrat & Chronicle* wrote.

Without any fuss, Mullaly verified for the court that he had indeed directed Fleet to the box where the first two hatchets had been found.

"What did you do after you showed him the box?" Mr. Moody asked.

"He took a hatchet out of there."

Mullaly described the hatchet head just as Fleet had done: smaller than the rest, both sides of the blade covered in ashes, its handle freshly broken. The ashes, Mullaly said, "looked so as though it was rubbed on there, wiped on, would be my way of expressing it," but he'd noticed no ashes on the broken handle.

"What did Mr. Fleet do with it after each of you had observed it?" Moody asked.

"I believe he put it back."

That ought to have settled it. Then came Governor Robinson's turn with Mullaly.

"Do you know anything of what became of the box?" Robinson asked.

"No, sir."

"Nothing else was taken out of it while you were there?"

"Nothing but the hatchet and parts of the handle," Mullaly said.

"Well, parts," Robinson said dismissively. He indicated the little stump of wood that had been removed from the eye of the hatchet at Harvard's chemistry lab. "That piece?"

"That piece, yes," Mullaly said.

"Well, that was in the eye, wasn't it?"

"Yes; then there was another piece."

"Another piece of what?"

And then Mullaly dropped his thunderbolt.

"Handle."

Governor Robinson gasped. District Attorney Knowlton and Mr. Moody sat rigid in their seats, dumbstruck. Since the opening arguments the prosecution had been steering the jury toward the conclusion that this handleless hatchet was the murder weapon, its blade clumsily masked with ashes and the bloodstained handle broken off and tossed into the stove. With one word, the state's own witness had blown the theory to shreds. If the handle had been there all along, clean, dry, and bloodless, that hatchet could not have been used to kill the Bordens.

The defense was no less astounded. The courtroom reeled in silent shock as Robinson continued, rapid-fire.

"Well, did you take it out of the box?"

"I did not."

"Did you see it taken out?"

"I did."

"Who took it out?"

"Mr. Fleet took it out."

"Mr. Fleet took it out?"

"Yes, sir."

"You were there?"

"I was there."

"Anybody else?"

"Not as I know of."

"Did Mr. Fleet put that back too?"

"He did."

Robinson glared at the prosecution's table. "Have you that handle here, gentlemen?"

"No," Knowlton said.

"You haven't it in your possession, may I ask?"

"Never had it."

"The government does not know where it is?"

Knowlton sounded like another man entirely. "I don't know where it is," he said. "This is the first time I ever heard of it."

—•—

Minutes later, Assistant Marshal Fleet was back on the stand. Officer Mullaly had been sent to an anteroom to ensure the two officers could not discuss their conflicting testimony. Robinson asked Fleet to restate what he had found in the box.

"I found a hatchet head, the handle broken off, together with some other tools in there and the iron that was inside there."

The governor held up the handleless hatchet head.

"Was this what you found?"

"Yes, sir."

"Did you find anything else, except old tools?"

"No, sir."

"Sure about that?"

"Yes, sir."

As he'd done with Mullaly, Robinson indicated the wooden stub. "Now, if I understand you," he continued, "this piece was in the eye of the hatchet?"

"Yes, sir," Fleet answered.

"That has been driven out since?"

"By somebody."

"Yes, not by you. And taking these two together, that was all you found in the box, except some old tools which you did not take out at all. Is that right?"

"That is all we found in connection with that hatchet."

"You did not find the handle, the broken piece, not at all?"

"No, sir."

According to Fleet, Mullaly had not removed any handle from the box. So far as Fleet knew, there was no handle to remove.

"You looked in so that you could have seen it if it was in there?"

"Yes, sir."

"You have no doubt about that, have you at all?"

"What?"

"That you did not find the other piece of the handle that fitted on there?"

"No, sir."

"You would have seen it if it had been, wouldn't you?"

"Yes, sir, it seems to me I should."

The courtroom shivered with excitement as John Fleet stepped down. How could the two officers' testimony be so drastically different?

DAY SIX
Saturday, June 10, 1893

By Saturday, the carnations on the judges' bench were finally wilting. Or rather, half of them were. According to the *Boston Herald,* the vase of red blossoms, symbolizing bloody guilt, hung their heads. If the flowers were any indication, the prosecution needed to revive its case. The task fell to Inspector William Medley.

Medley testified to arriving at the Borden house just a little after 11:40. He'd circled the perimeter and tried the cellar door (locked) before going in and speaking to Lizzie Borden upstairs. Something she said about being up in the barn gave Medley an idea, and he went outside.

Policemen were all about the house and the yard, but the barn door was shut, fastened with a hasp and an iron pin. Medley pulled the pin and went in. He headed straight for the stairs.

Three or four steps from the top, Medley paused in the stairwell and looked around the loft. Nothing seemed to have been disturbed, not even the dust on the floor. He stooped down level with the floorboards and peered across them. If Lizzie Borden had just been walking across that floor, Inspector Medley reasoned, shouldn't there be some marks in the dust?

"I didn't see any," Medley said, "and I reached out my hand to see if I could make an impression on the floor of the barn, and I did by putting my hand down so fashion, and found that I made an impression on the barn floor."

"How distinctly could you see the marks which you made with your hand?" Mr. Moody asked.

"I could see them quite distinctly when I looked for them," Medley answered.

"Go on and describe anything else which you did?" Moody prompted, perhaps twiddling his coattails in anticipation. Those who watched Moody carefully had noticed his habit of rolling or bundling up his coattails when his questioning went well.

"Then I stepped up on the top and took four or five steps on the outer edge of the barn floor, the edge nearest the stairs, then came up to see if I could discern those, and I did." When he stooped back down level with the floor, his footprints were plainly visible.

"Did you see any other footsteps in that dust than those which you made yourself?" Moody asked.

"No, sir."

Governor Robinson did not dwell much on Inspector Medley's troubling information about the barn. Instead, he focused most of his questions on the handleless hatchet. In his usual genial way, Robinson gathered as many details about the hatchet as he could. After all, Medley was the officer who'd first recognized the hatchet head as potentially important.

Little in Medley's cross-examination seemed significant, except for his opinion that the ashes on the hatchet head were coarse. That was new. All the other officers said they were fine.

"And you didn't look to see whether the other contents of the box were about in the same condition?" Robinson asked.

"I did not. In fact, I didn't go back there after showing it to the Captain," Medley said.

He and Captain Desmond examined it, and then, Medley said, he wrapped it up in a piece of brown paper and carried it straight down to Marshal Hilliard's office.

"You wrapped it up in a paper and folded it up," Robinson repeated. Heaven only knows what prompted him to suggest, "Perhaps you will illustrate how you folded it up in the paper."

Medley took a piece of brown paper from Robinson and folded the hatchet head into it. "I am not very tidy at such things," he apologized, handing the little parcel to Robinson. "Now that, as near as I can think, is about how I did it."

"And then you put it in your pocket?"

"I put it in my pocket."

By now, the bulk of the police's testimony was bordering on redundant. With the exception of Mullaly's sensation about the hatchet handle, it sounded as if the officers had all memorized the same basic script. Captain Dennis Desmond, at first, was no different.

He agreed with Inspector Medley about the coarseness of the dust on the hatchet head. "It was all dirty," he told Mr. Moody, "that is, it was covered with a dust which was not of a fine nature, that is, it was too coarse to be called a fine—what I mean is, it wasn't any sediment that might have collected on it from standing there any length of time: it was a loose, rough matter, which might be readily pushed off or moved by pushing your finger on it." It was not really dust, he said, but dirt.

That was a minor quibble, considering that everything he

said about the box was the same: fourteen or fifteen inches long, maybe four inches wide, filled with dusty cast-off tools and bolts and nails. Coarse or fine; ash, dust, or dirt; the key point for the prosecution was that the dust inside the box did not match the dust on the hatchet head, and Captain Desmond was positive about that.

But what he said next about Inspector Medley taking the hatchet down to the police station stopped Mr. Moody's questioning cold. "I gave it to him wrapped up in a newspaper."

Desmond had no way of knowing he'd just contradicted Officer Mullaly, and so Governor Robinson did not pounce and risk putting his witness on guard. Gradually, he worked his way toward the hatchet with questions about the search Desmond had led on August 6.

Was he certain he had done the wrapping? Robinson wanted to know.

"Positive," Captain Desmond said. "I got the paper from the water-closet there to do it up with."

Robinson handed him the hatchet head and a piece of brown paper, just as he'd offered Inspector Medley. "Well, won't you wrap it up in about as large a piece of paper?"

"I shall have to get a full-sized newspaper to do it," Desmond said, "much larger than that, sir."

Desmond settled for a *Boston Globe,* though that was still not big enough, he said. Then the entire court watched in bemused awe as Captain Dennis Desmond solemnly demonstrated how he'd rolled up the very same hatchet Inspector Medley had sworn to wrapping in brown paper.

It might have been less ridiculous if the two policemen's parcels resembled each other even slightly. But Medley's brown paper packet had looked like a wedge of pie, while the Sunday *Boston Herald* called Desmond's "a great newspaper bundle big enough to conceal a pair of longshoreman's shoes."

First the hatchet handle, now this. By the next day, the Fall River Police Department was the laughingstock of all the papers.

"The handleless hatchet, now generally known as the 'hoodoo hatchet,' continued its demonish pranks in the trial of Lizzie Borden for her life today," the Sunday *Boston Herald* ribbed in a special dispatch. "It chopped another great hole in the case of which it is the most important feature."

DAY SEVEN
Monday, June 12, 1893

After a week of testimony, there was still no greater evidence in the case against Lizzie Borden than her own inquest testimony. As he had done at the preliminary hearing, District Attorney Knowlton wanted to read that mass of inconsistencies into the record, to let the jury hear for themselves how Lizzie Borden had wavered and hesitated and changed her story.

But that testimony, the defense argued, was not admissible. The issue hinged on whether Lizzie's statements at the inquest had been made voluntarily—a question the three justices had to decide.

And so, shortly after nine o'clock, the jury was sent from the room, while for two hours Governor Robinson and Mr. Moody presented their arguments.

According to Robinson, although Lizzie willingly obeyed the summons to appear at the inquest, the crucial fact was that she had testified unaware that she was already under arrest in all but name. Police surrounded her house day and night almost from the instant the crime was discovered; the mayor himself had instructed her to stay inside. Worst of all was the secret warrant, waiting in Marshal Hilliard's pocket throughout the inquest. The very existence of that warrant proved that the authorities already believed Lizzie guilty, and yet they called her to testify. Her lawyer was not present, nor had she been informed of her right not to testify. Rather, Robinson said, "the City Marshal stood at her shoulder, authorized and directed to lay his hand upon her at any instant and make her a prisoner." After Knowlton had gotten all the information he could from her, Lizzie was not allowed to go free but was held in the matron's room until a new warrant was drawn and her arrest made official.

"If that is freedom," Robinson thundered, "God save the Commonwealth of Massachusetts!" And if anything said by a defendant under those circumstances was termed voluntary, he proclaimed, then the very meaning of the word must be changed.

The way the authorities had deliberately dodged the Constitution, Governor Robinson admonished, was "[w]orse than burning a dress."

"May it please Your Honors: I have very little to offer in reply," Mr. Moody began. Governor Robinson's argument, he acknowledged, "is magnificent, but it is not law."

Given the circumstances of the murders, Moody believed, the court had done nothing but its duty. Lizzie Borden had been summoned in the usual way, and she had appeared. Lawyer Jennings's request to be present had been declined, Moody said, "because the law expressly gives [the courts] the power to decline it."

As far as being informed of her right not to incriminate herself, Moody also acknowledged that she was not cautioned in the courtroom before Judge Blaisdell. However, Lizzie had been permitted to consult with Lawyer Jennings before testifying. "And Your Honors can have no doubt that the reason why the caution was omitted at the beginning of this testimony was because that subject had been thoroughly talked over between counsel and client, and she knew and understood her rights." It would be an insult to Lawyer Jennings to presume otherwise.

Further, Robinson's argument assumed that the only motive for the inquest was to wrench a confession from Lizzie Borden. Why, Moody asked, didn't anyone assume that the inquest gave Lizzie Borden as much chance to clear her own name as it had given Bridget Sullivan? Similarly, Moody argued, the police surrounded the house as much to observe Bridget Sullivan and John Morse as Lizzie Borden. That was their duty.

"There was nothing in that warrant in Mr. Hilliard's pocket which changed her legal position or her legal liabilities one iota," Moody said. If the question was whether Lizzie had testified voluntarily, how could a warrant she did not even know about affect her willingness to take the stand?

When Moody finished, the three justices withdrew, and for an hour and a half the court waited for an answer. Lizzie Borden leaned forward as they filed back onto the bench.

"From the agreed facts and the facts otherwise in evidence," Chief Justice Mason said, "it is plain that the prisoner at the time of her testimony was, so far as relates to this question, as effectually in custody as if the formal precept had been served." There was more to his explanation, but only the last four words mattered to the hushed spectators: "[T]he evidence is excluded."

It was a triumph for the defense. The pears, the sinkers, the upstairs-downstairs absurdities—not one word of it would reach the jury. Lawyer Jennings and Colonel Adams beamed. Governor

Robinson's face was one giant *I told you so*. Opinions and emotions erupted throughout the courtroom until the sheriff pounded the gavel for order.

And what of Lizzie Borden?

For a moment, nothing. Then the realization flashed upon her. One bright instant of exultation lit her face, and Lizzie Borden burst into tears. She pressed her handkerchief into her eyes and buried her face in her fan, but there was no hiding it. Her whole body shook with the force of her relief.

DAY EIGHT
Tuesday, June 13, 1893

Things were getting gruesome. The pillow shams and bedspread speckled with Mrs. Borden's blood had been draped over the rail of the jury box the day before. Crime-scene photographs, stained pieces of woodwork, dresser-top marble, and blood-stiffened carpeting all made vivid appearances.

It was literally sickening. Governor Robison had had to fan Lizzie as Medical Examiner Dolan gave his painstaking recital of each blood spatter and wound, showing on a pair of plaster heads where each whack of the hatchet had fallen.

The heat did not help. A quick smattering of rain on the eighth morning brought no relief, leaving the air moist as breath as Dr. Dolan continued his grisly testimony.

It boiled down to these four points:

The blows to both victims could have been inflicted by a woman of ordinary strength, using a sharp cutting instrument with the leverage of a handle.

Furthermore, Dr. Dolan believed the assailant had stood over and astride Mrs. Borden—that is, with one foot on either side of her body. (The significance is all but lost to us now, but in 1892, the thought of a woman standing this way was ludicrous. Women did not even part their knees to ride horseback. Only a man, it was thought, would straddle his victim.) Mr. Borden's assailant had likely stood behind him, at the head of the sofa, and chopped downward.

The slashes on the Bordens' skulls ranged from half an inch to five inches long, making it impossible for Dolan to single out any of the hatchets found on the Borden property as the murder weapon.

Although the chipped edges of some of the cuts in Mr. Borden's skull suggested the blows had fallen from left to right—indicating a left-handed murderer—Dolan decided that the angled position of Mr. Borden's head was the true cause of the left-to-right beveling, and the blows were most likely struck straight on.

It was almost too much for one juror. Shortly after Dr. Dolan pantomimed the blow to Mrs. Borden's back on one of the stenographers, fifty-nine-year-old Lewis Hodges grew faint. His distress earned the jury a five-minute recess.

The horror show had only just begun. Dr. Frank Draper, medical examiner of Suffolk County, was still to testify. At first it was all the same: measurements, skin flaps, bone chips.

And then District Attorney Knowlton asked whether there was anything in the nature or character of the wounds that would help the doctor determine the size of the weapon.

There was, Dr. Draper said, on the head of Mr. Borden.

"Would the skull itself be of assistance in pointing out such things as occur to you to be important?"

"It would."

"Then in that case, although I regret very much the necessity of doing it," Knowlton said, "I shall have to ask Dr. Dolan to produce it." The attorneys and justices conferred for a moment; then Justice Mason quietly announced that Lizzie Borden would be excused from the room during the display.

The *New York Tribune* considered it an act of genuine mercy. All morning long Lizzie Borden "sat with red eyes and trembling lips and with deep marks in her pale face, looking as long as she could, listening as much as she could, and finally retreating in grief and tears behind her fan."

Then in came the skull of Andrew J. Borden, "done up in a white handkerchief," one reporter wrote, "and looked like a bouquet, such as a man carries to his sweetheart."

The murder weapon's blade, Dr. Draper believed, measured three and one-half inches—exactly the size of the hoodoo hatchet.

"Will you tell us what it is that leads you to that conclusion?"

Draper produced a little plate of tin cut to three and a half inches and fitted it into first one, then another of the fatal gashes on Mr. Borden's skull.

"Are you able to say whether that hatchet head," Knowlton said, displaying the hoodoo hatchet, "is capable of making those wounds?"

"I believe it is."

"Have you attempted to fit that in the wounds?"

"I have seen the attempt made."

"Will you do it yourself?"

"I will try." Dr. Draper lowered the little blade straight down into Mr. Borden's skull.

It fit.

"The handleless hatchet is not an uncommon instrument, is it?" Colonel Adams asked on cross-examination.

"No, sir," Dr. Draper said.

"It has a very general circulation?"

"I think so."

Adams produced a brand-new hatchet, its blade still glinting with gilt. "Is there anything about that which is out of the ordinary?"

"Nothing that I perceive at present, sir."

"Won't you see if you can cut that into the injury or the scar in the skull?" Adams asked. His intent was clear: if that ordinary hatchet fit Mr. Borden's skull, so might any other hatchet from any other cellar or hardware store.

The doctor touched the metal to the bone. "It does not fit the wound," he announced. The blade had not been ground down enough, Draper explained. The corners were too blunt to penetrate the skull.

There was just one problem with Dr. Draper's dramatic demonstration: there was no blood on the hoodoo hatchet. Not one microscopic speck.

Professor Wood had tested scrapings from the blade to make sure no blood was mixed with the iron rust. He had pried the wooden handle stub from the iron eye and soaked it for days in a solution of potassium iodide to determine whether any blood had seeped into the crevice between the handle and the head. The solution remained clean.

The wooden stump, Wood said, had been free of dust when he received it. Whether the sediment on the blade was ash he could not say, but in spite of all the handling and rubbing in his laboratory and the courtroom, traces of the peculiar white dust remained embedded in the hoodoo hatchet's rusty cavities. The material might adhere that way, Wood guessed, if the hatchet had been wet when it came into contact with the stuff.

If that hatchet had inflicted such wounds as were found on Mr. and Mrs. Borden's skulls, District Attorney Knowlton wanted to know, could it be washed clean?

Colonel Adams objected.

"He may answer," Justice Mason ruled.

"Before the handle was broken, not after," Wood said.

"Why do you make that difference, Professor?" Knowlton asked while Adams continued to object, to no avail.

"Because it would be very hard to wash blood off that broken end," Professor Wood said.

"A little louder," Knowlton prodded.

"It would be almost impossible to quickly wash blood out of that broken end. It might have been done by thorough cleansing, but that would also stain the fracture."

It could be done. But could Lizzie Borden—could anyone—have washed that hatchet so thoroughly and so quickly?

DAY NINE
Wednesday, June 14, 1893

District Attorney Knowlton's case was closing in on Lizzie Borden. Marshal Hilliard and Mayor Coughlin told the jury of Lizzie's surprising response to being informed she was a suspect: *I am ready to go at any time.* Cloakmaker Hannah Gifford swore she had heard Lizzie refer to Mrs. Borden as "a mean, good for nothing thing," now adding the detail that she had inadvertently triggered Lizzie's outburst by referring to Mrs. Borden as "mother."

Then the prosecution called a set of six witnesses to eliminate possible escape routes from the scene of the crime.

Next door to the north, Mrs. Churchill's boarder, Thomas Bowles, was washing a carriage at the end of the driveway, where he could look across Mrs. Churchill's yard and see the Bordens' well house.

Directly behind the Churchill lot, a young French girl named Lucy Collette spent an hour sitting out in front of Dr. Chagnon's house, at the northeast end of the doctor's big double lot. To her right lay the Chagnon orchard, which bordered the back of the Bordens' property.

The Chagnons' neighbor to the north, Mrs. Aruba Kirby, was at work in her kitchen all morning, where she had a view of the passage leading into Dr. Chagnon's barn. She remembered looking out the window around 11:30.

South of Chagnon's orchard, in the Crowe yard kitty-corner to the Bordens, two laborers—Joseph DeRosier and John Denny—worked all morning long sawing wood and cutting stone. Sometime between 10:10 and 10:30, a third laborer, named Patrick McGowan, climbed a sawhorse in Crowe's yard and leaned right up over the Bordens' fence to snatch a few ripe pears from their tree.

Not one of them saw anybody enter or leave the Borden property, or anyone cutting through the adjoining yards.

Oddly enough, that was good news for Lizzie Borden. Deputy Sheriff Francis Wixon had climbed the Borden lumber pile and gotten himself up onto the top rail of the six-foot barbed-wire-topped fence at the back of the Bordens' yard between 11:45 and noon that day. He'd shimmied along the whole length of the fence rail before jumping down onto Crowe's lumber pile, completely unnoticed until he spoke to DeRosier. Escaping over the fence would be a gamble for any killer, not knowing who was nearby and which way they might be looking. But if Deputy Wixon had done it, couldn't a murderer?

No one had forgotten the newspaper story of the quarrel Matron Reagan had overheard between Lizzie and Emma Borden, and all the hullaballoo that had followed—how the matron at first contradicted the papers, then refused, by order of the city marshal, to sign her name to an official denial. If she had anything to say about it, Marshal Hilliard had ordered her, the witness stand was the place for it.

Now Matron Hannah Reagan stood in that witness box, ready to testify for the government. "Now will you go on and describe in your own way what occurred after Miss Emma came," Mr. Moody asked, "the time that elapsed, and all that was said and done?"

With noticeable zeal and encyclopedic detail, Matron Reagan recited the whole story—from the moment Emma arrived in Lizzie's cell at 8:40 until Lawyer Jennings came in over two hours later—just as the papers had printed it.

Lawyer Jennings rose to cross-examine her—Lawyer Jennings, whose arrival that day had supposedly interrupted the sisters' stony silence following their quarrel.

"Did Miss Emma come again that day?" Jennings asked.

"In the afternoon, sir."

"What time did she come in the afternoon?"

"I never kept the time of when she came. She came at all hours of the day."

She could not have left Jennings a better opening. "You say she came at just twenty minutes of nine that morning, and now when I ask you what time she came in the afternoon you say you didn't keep the time?"

Matron Reagan's testimony began to quake beneath her. She could not say what time Emma had come that afternoon, or who else had been there—only that there had been lots of visitors. Reverend Buck was one, she said.

"Are you sure he came that same afternoon?" Jennings asked.

"Well, I know we had visitors that afternoon and I think Mr. Buck came."

"Well, how sure are you of that?"

"Well, he came every day," she explained. "There wasn't a day while Miss Borden was there that he hadn't come to the central police station."

"How do you know he didn't come in the morning?"

"No, he didn't come that time in the morning."

"Are you sure he came in the afternoon?"

Perhaps Jennings was only bluffing. If he was, it paid off.

"I couldn't say about it," Matron Reagan said.

"Have you any recollection about it?"

"No," she said, "I was taken away with this trouble so much that it upset me, Mr. Jennings." The sisters' quarrel so disturbed her, she claimed, that she could not remember at all what happened in the afternoon.

"Now let me go a little further and see if I can refresh your recollection," Jennings offered. "Don't you remember that Mrs. Holmes was there that afternoon and you had some conversation about an egg?"

She did indeed. Matron Reagan told all about the afternoon with the egg, the whole amusing conversation, right down to who was sitting where.

"Had quite a pleasant time all the afternoon, didn't you?" Jennings remarked.

"The day of the breaking of the egg we did, laughed and talked," the matron said.

"Well, the afternoon of the breaking of the egg you weren't very much disturbed, were you?"

"No, sir."

He had set a trap, and the matron had fallen in. She knew it, and she could not hide it.

Jennings could not resist driving the point further yet. "Had quite a pleasant afternoon that afternoon, didn't you?"

"Well, I don't know as it was very pleasant," she retorted, "not to me."

Matron Reagan had backed herself into an awful corner. If Jennings undermined her credibility enough to make it appear that she had lied to the papers about that quarrel, she would likely lose her job. But if by changing her story she perjured herself before the Superior Court of Bristol County, she would fare no better.

"Wasn't that afternoon of the egg episode about as pleasant an afternoon as you had had while Miss Lizzie was there?" Jennings pressed.

"I can't answer that," Matron Reagan said. As far as the defense was concerned, she already had.

Lizzie Borden sat forward in her chair and glared at Eli Bence as he took the stand. The directness of her gaze so unnerved the young druggist that he blushed and stammered, "I do," before the clerk of the court finished reciting the oath.

Mr. Bence answered only eight questions before Governor Robinson interrupted. The defense had no intention of letting the druggist tell the jury about the woman who attempted to buy poison from him on August 3. They would not even be allowed to hear the lawyers argue the point, and were sent from the room before the words "prussic acid" were uttered.

Without a prescription, Mr. Moody contended, there was no practical use for prussic acid. Anyone asking for it over the counter must have a sinister purpose in mind, and Eli Bence's testimony would prove that Lizzie Borden had made just such an attempt.

"You propose to bring evidence upon attempts, but not success?" Governor Robinson asked.

"Yes, sir," Knowlton said.

Robinson balked. "She is charged in this indictment with slaying or killing these two people with a sharp instrument; committing the murder with an axe, for instance. Nothing else." Poison had nothing to do with Andrew and Abby Borden's deaths; Professor Wood's testimony had proven that. A failed attempt to buy prussic acid was lean evidence, as far as Robinson was concerned.

Moody argued it showed premeditation, proving that Lizzie Borden was in a murderous state of mind on the third of August. "I can conceive of no more significant act," he concluded, "nothing which tends to show more the purpose of doing mischief to some one than the attempt . . . to obtain one of the most deadly poisons that is known to human kind at the present time."

Governor Robinson insisted that the simple act of asking a druggist for prussic acid proved nothing, especially when Lizzie Borden had shown no prior indication of violence toward her parents—toward anyone at all, for that matter. A statement of intent, Robinson argued, was a critical element in the cases Moody had cited. "But here there is nothing of that," Robinson pointed out. "It is entirely absent." As for the poison itself, Robinson shrugged it off as of little consequence. "Well, people buy prussic acid to kill animals—it may be the cat. That is innocent. It is not a crime, at any rate."

The court agreed. Eli Bence's testimony was excluded.

DAY TEN
Thursday, June 15, 1893

With that, the prosecution rested. Eli Bence's testimony was supposed to be Knowlton's climax. Without it, he had nothing left, and his case closed with a "dull thud" instead of a bang.

The time had come for Lizzie Borden's lawyers, the best legal team money could buy, to have their say.

Already their actions had said plenty. The defense, the *New York Tribune* noted, appeared to have deliberately allowed the prosecution considerable leeway. Robinson, Jennings, and Adams rarely raised objections, resisted interrupting or trying to confuse the government's witnesses, and for the most part sat passively by while Moody and Knowlton coached their witnesses with leading questions. Although the defense's tactic was considered old-fashioned even then, it nevertheless conveyed an air of confidence, silently suggesting that Lizzie Borden had nothing to hide, nothing to fear from the prosecution's evidence. It worked so well that a rumor was circulating that the defense would turn the case over to the jury without another word.

Robinson, Jennings, and Adams were not quite that bold, but they were brief—the defense would take only two days to present Lizzie's case.

As he had done at the preliminary hearing, Lawyer Jennings opened by appealing first to emotion rather than reason, explaining to the jury his lifelong personal connection with the Borden family. "I want to say right here and now, if I manifest more feeling than perhaps you think necessary in making an opening statement for the defence in this case, you will ascribe it to that cause. The counsel, Mr. Foreman and gentlemen, does not cease to be a man when he becomes a lawyer."

Jennings focused on the contrast between the brutality of the murder and Lizzie Borden herself. "We shall show you that this young woman, as I have said, had apparently led an honorable, spotless life; she was a member of the church; she was interested in church matters; she was connected with various organizations for charitable work; she was ever ready to help in any good thing, in any good deed; and yet for some reason or other the government in its investigation seemed to fasten the crime upon her." The only thing more shocking than the crime itself, he asserted, was the fact that such a woman stood accused of it.

"I say this is a mysterious case," Jennings acknowledged. "Everybody, every thinking man, must say the same." But, he reminded them, their task was *not* to solve the mystery. "The issue is a simple and direct one. The Commonwealth here has charged that Lizzie Andrew Borden, in a certain way, at a certain time, killed Andrew Jackson Borden and Abby Durfee Borden with malice aforethought. And that, and that alone, is the question that you are to answer: did she on that day commit that deed? [D]id she commit it in the way alleged?"

The evidence the prosecution had presented, he stressed, was purely circumstantial. "There is not a spot of blood, there is not a weapon that they have connected with her in any way, shape, or fashion. They have not had her hand touch it or her eye see it or her ear hear of it."

At best, there was also only half a motive. All along the government's case had pointed to a single murderer, yet regardless of how Lizzie felt about her stepmother, they had not attempted to show a reason for her to murder her father.

Nor had Knowlton produced the murder weapon. Once Professor Wood's preliminary hearing testimony ruled out the claw-headed hatchet, Jennings noted with perceptible sarcasm, they had quietly substituted the hoodoo hatchet in its place. But they had not connected any of them to Lizzie Borden.

Then came the question of exclusive opportunity. Jennings reminded the jury that the prosecution had failed to rule out the possibility of a murderer escaping from the house. In addition, Jennings said, "there has not been a living soul put on the stand here to testify that they saw Andrew J. Borden come down street from his house. From his house to the Union Savings Bank he has been absolutely invisible. Was it any easier for him to be [unseen] than it would be for somebody escaping from this house if they walked quietly away?" Not only that, but other strange people had been seen in the vicinity—"people who have not been located or identified."

Everything else, Jennings promised—Miss Lizzie's visit to the barn, Officer Medley's failure to find her footprints, the Bedford cord—could and would be explained.

In view of that and of all that had come before, Jennings concluded, "[W]e shall ask you to say, Mr. Foreman and gentlemen, whether the government have satisfied you beyond a reasonable doubt that she did kill not only her stepmother, Abby Durfee Borden, but her loved and loving father, Andrew Jackson Borden on the fourth day of August last."

Lizzie Borden was in tears. After nine days of suspicion and scrutiny, Lawyer Jennings's earnest, eloquent voice pleading on her behalf for an hour straight had undone her. "She had learned to brace herself against adversity and unkindness," the *Boston Herald* sympathized, "but mercy and active friendliness were so new that she broke down before them."

From the moment the prosecution rested, the whole tone of the trial changed. Outside, the pavement was still hot enough to vaporize a splash of water, but something like a breath of fresh air had found its way into the courtroom. Witnesses testified for minutes rather than hours at a time. People laughed—spectators and attorneys on both sides alike—rendering poor Sheriff Wright indignant. Lizzie Borden stopped looking silently into her lap and talked brightly with her lawyers, the conversation "punctured with smiles and ripples of laughter that she silenced in her handkerchief."

Lawyer Jennings struck first with a series of witnesses who had all seen suspicious characters in the vicinity of the Borden house on August 3 and 4.

Late on the night before the murder, Miss Martha Chagnon and her stepmother had been frightened by a noise—something that sounded like footsteps or pounding on wood—coming from the direction of the Borden fence. It lasted for five minutes, on and off.

At about the same time, their neighbors to the north came across a stranger, senseless and unresponsive but apparently not intoxicated, sprawled on the steps leading from the sidewalk in front of the Kirby house. Mr. Kirby hollered at the fellow and tried to shake him awake, with no luck.

Around 9:45 or 9:50 the next morning, Mrs. Delia Manley and her sister noticed a young man they had never seen before loitering at the Bordens' north gate, leaning his arm on the gatepost. The way he watched and listened to what was going on in the street made the sisters think he was nosy or uneasy.

Then there was the uncommonly pale young man Dr. Handy had seen walking slowly up Second Street with his eyes fixed on the sidewalk between 10:20 and 10:40. Everything about him—his pallor, agitation, and gait, combined with an expression so intense he seemed utterly oblivious to his surroundings—made the doctor slow his carriage and turn to watch. Later, it seemed to Dr. Handy that he had seen that man once before—on Second Street.

District Attorney Knowlton hardly needed to roll up his sleeves to discredit a good deal of that testimony.

The Chagnons' windows were shut, Knowlton discovered, and the women did not investigate the source of the sound. For all they knew, he pointed out, it might have come from the nearby icehouse, with its wooden carts and wooden floors. Whatever the noise was, it did not disturb their big Newfoundland dog enough to rouse him from the porch.

Knowlton barely trifled with the young man leaning on the Borden gatepost, except to make it clear that he was standing right out in the open, making no attempt to conceal his face or hands or anything else about himself. He was so unremarkable that the sisters who saw him nearly walked right by without noticing him at all. Nor could they describe him other than to say that he was about thirty, dressed in light-colored clothing.

Dr. Handy had it worst of all. From the moment he learned of the murder, he was convinced the pale stranger he'd seen was "just nerving himself up to go in and commit the crime." But Handy's reaction amounted to a gut feeling, next to impossible to express in a concrete way.

"He was moving very slowly," Handy tried to explain, "and I imagined that he was—"

"I beg your pardon," Knowlton interrupted. "I didn't ask you what you imagined."

It all seemed so flimsy by the time Knowlton was done.

Next came the matter of the locks: three on the front door, a hook on the back screen, and keys to nearly every door on the inside. How could any of those suspicious characters get into what Knowlton had called "the most uniquely locked house in Fall River"?

According to Lawyer Jennings's next witness, Andrew Borden's cousin, Jerome C. Borden, it could be done without even trying. At two o'clock in the afternoon on the day after the murders, with a police officer leaning on the front fence, Jerome walked right up to the front door and let himself in.

"Did you ring before you opened the door?" Jennings asked.

"I did not."

"What did you do? Tell us exactly what you did."

"I walked up the steps, and took hold of the door-knob, and turned it, and pushed the door open."

The court would not allow Jerome to tell whether anyone inside was surprised to see him walk in, but the very fact that Lawyer Jennings attempted to ask the question had likely given away the answer.

The problem turned out to be the spring lock. If the door was not slammed hard, the lock would not catch. John Morse had noticed it, as had Mrs. Brigham. "I found that unless the bolt was used that the spring lock was not sure," she said on the witness stand. "Unless the door was shut with a bang you could not depend upon the spring lock working."

"What is your name?" Jennings asked his next witness.

"Hymon Lubinsky," the young man answered, and everyone knew at once that he was a foreigner. Only eighteen or nineteen years old, he'd been born in Russia and now peddled ice cream in Fall River.

Every morning at ten-thirty he fetched his team from Gardner's stable on Second Street and drove downstreet to Mr. Wilkinson's confectionary to load up his wagon. But on August 4, he'd been running late. His horse was still eating when he arrived, and Lubinsky had to wait. It was a little after eleven by the time he left.

"Well," Jennings asked, "when you got to the Borden house did you see anybody on the premises?"

"Yes, sir."

"Whom did you see?"

"I saw a lady come out the way from the barn right to the

stairs back of the house—the north side stairs, from the back of the house."

Lubinsky's English was not entirely clear. "Right side of what?" Lawyer Jennings asked.

"I saw a lady come out the way from the barn right to the stairs from the back of the house."

"Can you tell how she was dressed?"

"She had on a dark colored dress."

A woman in a dark dress walking from the barn to the house a few minutes past eleven o'clock. Could it have been Lizzie Borden, just as she'd said all along? Could it have been anyone else?

"Had you ever seen the servant who worked in that house?" Jennings asked.

"Yes, sir," Lubinsky answered.

"Had you ever delivered any ice cream to her?"

"Yes, sir."

"How long before this?"

"Oh, two or three weeks before the murder."

"Was the woman you saw the servant?" Jennings asked.

Again Lubinsky's command of English obscured his answer. "I saw the servant and the woman too."

"Was the woman you saw the day of the murder the same woman as the servant?" Jennings asked.

"No, sir."

"Are you sure about that?"

"I am sure about it."

Knowlton came at Lubinsky like an angry bear, bewildering him with a merciless barrage of questions. "You ask too fast," Lubinsky finally protested, "I can't understand what you mean." Yet Knowlton could not shake the young peddler's story. Even if Lubinsky could not always express himself clearly, his confidence was evident, insisting he'd left the stable—just two blocks up from the Borden house—by 11:05 or 11:10.

Knowlton did eventually score a small victory: he clarified that Lubinsky had seen the woman coming from the direction of the barn, as opposed to actually witnessing her leave the barn itself. No matter how Knowlton pushed, Lubinsky remained adamant about everything else he had seen. "What has a person got eyes for," he said, "but to look with?"

Next Jennings called Thomas Barlow and Everett Brown—just two teenage boys, who happened to be fooling around on Second Street on the most legendary morning in Fall River's history.

"When you arrived near the Borden house did you see any person leave the yard?" Lawyer Jennings asked Thomas.

"Yes, sir." It was Inspector Doherty, headed toward Spring Street at a run. That had gotten their attention.

"What did you do then?"

"We went in the side gate."

"You say 'we.' Who?"

"Me and Brownie."

"Well, tell us what you did now?"

"We went up to Mr. Sawyer, he was on the back steps, and asked him to let us go in the house, and he wouldn't let us in, so we went in the barn."

Once they worked up the nerve to go inside, Thomas and Brownie dared each other to go up into the loft, where they spent about five minutes hunting for murderers in the hay and looking out the windows. Then they came down, pulled the door closed, and put the pin back in the hasp where they'd found it.

THE HEAT

"How was the heat up in the barn compared with it out in the sun?" Lawyer Jennings asked Thomas Barlow.

"It was cooler up in the barn that it was out doors," the boy answered.

Eyebrows must have raised on both sides of the courtroom. Anyone with a barn or attic of their own knew perfectly well how uncomfortable the upper story of a building gets on a summer's day, and for many, that alone was enough to throw Lizzie's alibi into doubt.

Every one of the police officers said that barn was hot. *Extremely hot. Close. Stifling.* Assistant Marshal Fleet thought it was one of the hottest days they'd had that summer. Even the peddler Lubinsky agreed it was a hot day, and who would know better than an ice cream man? Since the preliminary hearing in September, District Attorney Knowlton had been saying that the fourth of August was one of the hottest days of the year, and the defense had never contradicted him.

Someone should have, because it simply was not so. It was not even the hottest day in August. According to the United States Signal Service, the highest temperature recorded in Fall River, Massachusetts, on August 4, 1892, was a pleasant 83 degrees—at two p.m.

Midmorning it had been a tad cooler. The *Fall River Evening News* reported 79 degrees at eleven a.m., and two tiny details prove that the members of the Borden household found the weather far from sweltering: Before Andrew Borden settled down on the sofa for his fatal nap, he'd put on his reefer—a cardigan-like jacket. Minutes later, Bridget Sullivan grabbed a shawl when she ran out to fetch Dr. Bowen.

"Do you know Officer Medley?" Jennings asked.

"No, sir," Thomas answered.

"Was there any Officer there at the side gate when you went in?"

"No, sir."

"Any on the walk?"

"No, sir."

"Any on the steps?"

"No, sir."

The court was delighted, so amused by the boys' responses that the sheriff had to rap several times for order. District Attorney Knowlton did not share in the merriment. "Me and Brownie" had left Inspector Medley's claim of finding no footprints in the loft quite literally in the dust. Again and again, he pressed both of them to state what time they'd entered the barn. To his relief, neither boy could.

As it turned out, stating the time wasn't necessary. The events Thomas and Brownie witnessed were enough to single out the minutes between 11:37 and 11:40—just in time to see Inspector Doherty take off to telephone the marshal, and moments before Officer Allen returned with backup.

It also did not matter that neither of the boys had noticed Inspector Medley's arrival. Brownie had virtually guaranteed they'd arrived first when he told Jennings, "I seen Officer Fleet when he was coming up the walk." By that time the boys were back down in the yard, with the barn door fastened behind them. Medley had testified that he was on the Borden lot only "a minute or two" before Fleet arrived, and there was no way Medley could have gotten in and out of the barn in that scant two minutes without running smack into the boys. Medley himself had ruled out that possibility when he said that he spent eight to ten minutes in the yard and house before heading out to the barn. That meant that by his own estimation, Inspector Medley entered the barn a good five minutes after Thomas and Brownie left.

If that was so, how had he missed their footprints?

THE CROWE BARN HATCHET

"I'VE FOUND LIZZIE BORDEN'S HATCHET!"

The cry came from the roof of John Crowe's barn, just behind the Bordens' yard, on the evening of June 15. A boy trying to retrieve a lost ball had discovered it—the handle weathered, the three-and-three-quarter-inch blade spotted with rust. But beneath the rust, a glint of gilt, indicating the hatchet had been new when it was lost.

Almost no one would realize the significance of that detail until 1989, when District Attorney Knowlton's papers were donated to the Fall River Historical Society. Among his correspondence was a letter from Medical Examiner Frank W. Draper dated May 31, 1893, which revealed an extraordinary fact never brought to light during the trial:

"[O]n one of the cuts in Mrs. Borden's skull, near the right ear, there is a very small but unmistakable deposit of the gilt metal with which hatchets are ornamented when they leave the factory; this deposit (Dr. Cheever confirmed this observation fully) means that the hatchet used in killing Mrs. Borden was a <u>new</u> hatchet, not long out of the store."

The Crowe barn hatchet remains missing to this day.

DAY ELEVEN
Friday, June 16, 1893

The heat had broken, stilling the constant flutter of paper fans. Governor Robinson sported a new pair of trousers for the second day in a row. His associates had proclaimed them lucky and insisted he wear them until the end of the trial.

Most of that eleventh morning had been devoted to beating the Matron Reagan fiasco into the ground, with four different witnesses swearing under oath that the matron had privately denied the story of the sisters' argument to each of them. Inspector Medley's footprint testimony—now dubbed Medley's cake walk by the defense—had also been trampled by a *Fall River Globe* reporter who'd explored the barn even before Thomas and Brownie.

In the spectators' seats, however, interest in these details was growing stale. The people had come for what they hoped would be the defense's grand finale: Miss Emma Borden, sister of the accused.

From the blue feather in her hat to the tips of her patent-leather boots, Emma was her sister's double. But her frame was more delicate, her chin less prominent than Lizzie's. One look at her seemed enough to conclude that Emma was the milder of the two sisters. The heartbreak of the last ten months was so plain upon her face that no matter what people thought of Lizzie, they felt for Emma.

Emma began by reading the balances of Lizzie's four bank accounts at the time of the murder, totaling $2,811 (almost $70,000 today). There were stocks in a local bank and mill as well. She did not have to say it outright—the figures spoke for themselves. Lizzie Borden was no millionaire, but she had no need of money.

Next Emma touched ever-so-lightly on the affection between Lizzie and their father, speaking of a ring belonging to Mr. Borden—the only article of jewelry he'd worn for the last ten or fifteen years. Lizzie had given it to him, Emma told the jury, and he'd worn it so constantly ever since that he had been buried with it.

Finally, the subject everyone was waiting for: the Bedford cord. Everything Emma said about it aligned with Alice Russell's testimony—when it was made, the style and cut, the color and fabric, the paint stains.

"Now where was that dress, if you know, on Saturday, the day of the search?" Lawyer Jennings asked.

"I saw it hanging in the clothes press over the front entry," Emma said.

"At what time?"

"I don't know exactly; I think about nine o'clock in the evening."

"How came you to see it at that time?"

"I went in to hang up the dress that I had been wearing during the day," Emma explained, "and there was no vacant nail, and I searched round to find a nail, and I noticed this dress."

Had she said anything to Lizzie about that? Jennings wanted to know.

"I said, 'You have not destroyed that old dress yet; why don't you?'"

It was like something out of a novel—Lizzie's steadfast sister, the only remaining member of her immediate family, shouldering the blame for Lizzie's most incriminating act. Could it be true? No one who knew Miss Emma Borden would dream of doubting her word. But some of the jurors must have wondered, if only for an instant: did Emma's loyalty run so deep that she would lie under oath to save her baby sister from the gallows?

Underneath her placid exterior, Emma Borden had as much of the Borden mettle as her sister, and it appeared the instant the district attorney confronted her. "[U]pon Mr. Knowlton she turned a cold, steely eye, a set mouth and a proudly erect head," wrote the *Rochester Democrat & Chronicle*. "She nerved herself for him at the start, and she never relaxed her bold, calm demeanor for an instant."

Both Emma and the district attorney knew this was Knowlton's last chance to prove one of his most vital points. No one but Emma was left to testify about the relationship between Lizzie and Mrs. Borden.

Always, it came down to the rift over Bertie Whitehead's house.

"And do you say that the relations were entirely cordial between Lizzie and your stepmother after that event?" Knowlton asked.

"Yes, I do," Emma answered.

"Have you ever said differently?"

"I think not."

"Did your sister change the form of address to her mother at that time?"

"I can't tell you whether it was at that time or not."

"She formerly called her 'Mother,' didn't she?"

"Yes, sir."

"She ceased to call her 'Mother,' didn't she, practically?"

"Yes, sir."

"And wasn't it about at that time that she ceased to call her 'Mother'?"

"I don't remember," Emma said.

Knowlton poked and prodded, but Emma would not admit to any link between the two events.

"And don't you recall that was sometime in connection with the transaction in relation to the house?" Knowlton persisted.

"No, sir," Emma declared, "I do not know when it was."

Nor would she accept the notion that she herself had been the first to ask Lizzie what she was doing with the Bedford cord on Sunday morning. "Wasn't the first thing said by anybody, 'Lizzie, what are you going to do with that dress?'" Knowlton asked.

"No sir," said Emma, "I don't remember it so."

If he could just get Emma to admit to asking that one question, it would compromise her own claim that she had told Lizzie to destroy the dress the night before.

"Why doesn't it seem so to you, if I may ask you?"

"Why, because, the first I knew about it, my sister spoke to me."

"That is what I thought you would say," Knowlton remarked. He could only push so far. Emma Borden was easily the most tragic figure in the whole affair—the motherless little girl who had grown up to see her father murdered and her sister tried for the crime. Knowlton could not afford to badger her in front of the jury. And Emma Borden would not give one inch.

DAY TWELVE

Monday, June 19, 1893

The evidence was in. All that stood between Lizzie Borden and the jury were Governor Robinson and District Attorney Knowlton's closing arguments. It promised to be the greatest courtroom battle the state had ever seen, a contest between Robinson's smooth tongue and Knowlton's incisive mind. The prize: Lizzie Borden's life.

All the surprises and contradictions and exclusions had left Knowlton's case weaker than anyone—including the district attorney himself—could have anticipated. Governor Robinson had practically been handed the opportunity to pulverize the prosecution, yet he did not seize it.

Perhaps it was because the governor knew Lizzie Borden's greatest danger no longer came from within the courtroom. "You will need at the outset, gentlemen," he told the jury, "to dismiss from your minds entirely—entirely—entirely—everything that the press ever said about this case, anything that your neighbors have ever said about it, anything that you have ever heard about it except in this Court room at this time. Every rumor that has run about, every idle tale or every true tale that has been told, you must banish from your minds absolutely and forever. . . .

"I have no right to tell you that I believe so and so about this case," Robinson continued in the same vein. "I may believe all I want to, but my duty is to keep it inside of me, that is all."

It was good legal theory, but for a man as persuasive and engaging as Governor Robinson, it was a disappointment. Robinson's strength was never in the words he chose but in the way he said them. Always, the rise and fall of his voice, his movements, his personality, drove his points home. Yet at this critical hour, he chose to hold his personal feelings for the case in check.

Not that he wasn't expressive. He was by turns earnest, sarcastic, forceful. But something was missing. Robinson's argument "never reached into the heart," the *Evening Standard* lamented, never sounded "a note of triumph," never once boldly declared Lizzie's innocence.

For four hours, he explained and justified Lizzie's actions, when really there was no need. As Robinson himself said, the Commonwealth had not proven one single thing Mr. Moody had promised in his opening remarks. They had failed to show that Lizzie hated her stepmother, that she was plotting murder, or that she had made contradictory statements about her whereabouts during the crime. The prosecution had not proven motive or exclusive opportunity, had not even produced the weapon. Why, no matter which hatchet the police put forward, Robinson mocked, Professor Wood exonerated it. They never would have resorted to the dusty, broken hoodoo hatchet at all if the others hadn't been ruled out. They would have convicted her on rust and a cow's hair.

Nor would it do to judge her by the emotions she had or had not expressed throughout her ordeal, Robinson said. Lizzie Borden was innocent because the prosecution had not proven her otherwise. That was the law.

"Gentlemen," he pleaded, "with great weariness on your part, but with abundant patience and intelligence and care you have listened to what I have had to offer. So far as you are concerned it is the last word of the defendant to you. Take it; take care of her as you have and give us promptly your verdict 'not guilty' that she may go home and be Lizzie Andrew Borden of Fall River in that blood stained and wrecked home where she has passed her life so many years."

Robinson sat down and put his head into his hands. Beside him, Lizzie Borden silently reached out and touched his arm.

—•—

With the exclusion of Eli Bence's and Lizzie's inquest testimony, two out of three legs had been kicked out from under the district attorney's case. Time and again the police officers had contradicted themselves, causing yet more evidence to disintegrate before his eyes. And so, having proved almost nothing, Hosea Knowlton relied almost entirely on what he believed.

The effect was unmistakable. Even those outside the courtroom were struck by the tremendous vigor of his argument as it rumbled through the open windows.

"You couldn't see the gestures, you couldn't see the gleam of the eye, but you could stand in the shade of the wide spreading trees and hear the rise and fall of the tones and then it was easy to imagine the severe words they represented," marveled the *Boston Globe*.

"Murder is the work of stealth and craft," Knowlton reminded the jury, "in which there are not only no witnesses, but the traces are attempted to be obliterated." No one would ever know precisely what had gone on behind those tightly locked doors—whether in the years before or the moments after the murder.

But circumstantial evidence could be every bit as satisfying as direct evidence, Knowlton argued, and he provided a startlingly conspicuous example: "Nobody that has told of it has seen Lizzie Andrew Borden burn that Bedford cord dress. There is not a witness to it." And yet nobody, not even the defense, ever tried to claim that dress had not been burned.

From there, Knowlton plunged forward, creating an image of Lizzie Borden that would last over a century—a cunning, savage Lizzie Borden, seething with unexpressed hatred. There had been only tiny glimpses of it before, he said, but one August morning that pent-up rage had finally driven Lizzie to climb the stairs and smash her stepmother to pieces.

"But Lizzie Andrew Borden, the daughter of Andrew Jackson Borden, never came down those stairs," Knowlton proclaimed. "It was not Lizzie Andrew Borden, the daughter of Andrew J. Borden, that came down those stairs, but a murderess, transformed from all the thirty-three years of an honest life, transformed from the daughter, transformed from the ties of affection, to the most consummate criminal we have read of in all our history or works of fiction."

It was an ingenious approach. No one doubted Lizzie's remarkable self-control. The jurors had seen it with their own eyes. And they had also seen it suddenly desert her, when she fainted during the prosecution's opening remarks. It was almost impossible to keep from wondering if Knowlton could be right.

Lizzie herself seemed riveted by Knowlton's argument. During Governor Robinson's closing, she had bent her fan around her face and stared into her lap. Now she kept her gaze fixed straight on the district attorney as he spun his tale, staking his entire case on a missing piece of evidence: the note.

As far as Knowlton was concerned, the fact that no note calling Mrs. Borden to the bedside of a sick friend had ever appeared, that neither the woman who had written it nor the boy who delivered it had ever come forward, proved that Lizzie had lied about her stepmother's whereabouts. And there was no reason for her to invent that note unless she had murdered Mrs. Borden.

Lizzie Borden had killed her stepmother in a fit of passion, Knowlton declared, without any thought of how she would answer to her father for what she had done. The imaginary note bought her time, time in which to conceive what Knowlton called "a wicked and dreadful necessity"—the murder of her father.

The risk and the strategy of Knowlton's argument were astounding. He had transformed his case's greatest weakness into the backbone of a chilling, compelling scenario. Where Robinson claimed that the lack of evidence proved Lizzie Borden innocent, Knowlton used it to pronounce her guilt.

Only the jury could decide.

DAY THIRTEEN
Tuesday, June 20, 1893

"Lizzie Andrew Borden," said Chief Justice Mason, "although you have now been fully heard by counsel, it is your privilege to add any word which you may desire to say in person to the jury. You now have that opportunity."

Lizzie stood and spoke just thirteen words: "I am innocent," she said. "I leave it to my counsel to speak for me."

Then the jury stood for its charge from Justice Dewey. He explained all the usual legalities: the prisoner was to be presumed innocent unless the prosecution had proven otherwise. No evidence from the inquest or preliminary hearing could be considered, nor anything Lizzie Borden had said or done since her arrest. Certainly nothing the newspapers said held any weight. He defined reasonable doubt and affirmed the validity of circumstantial evidence.

But that was far from all.

Straying well outside the customary bounds, Justice Dewey cautioned the jury against stretching the testimony that Lizzie had once called her stepmother a mean, good-for-nothing thing in order to fit the government's theory of motive. One rude and careless remark, Dewey obviously believed, should not outweigh what he called "the general tenor of their lives." He undermined the crux of Knowlton's closing argument, suggesting that it made no sense for Lizzie to invent an imaginary note she could not account for instead of simply telling her father Mrs. Borden had gone out. Without ever mentioning it specifically, he discounted Lizzie's infamous remark to Assistant Marshal Fleet, reminding the jurors to consider whether she had ever obstructed any searches or refused to answer any questions. And of course, the dress. Could they, he asked, fit all the witnesses' various descriptions together into a single, identifiable dress?

Justice Dewey spoke for almost an hour and a half. It was all worded as neutrally as possible, framed in questions and suggestions, yet there was no doubt. Justice Dewey expected—virtually requested—a verdict of not guilty.

After all that, could those twelve men possibly find her otherwise? "There is so little absolute evidence that everybody can interpret the probabilities and the circumstantial indications to suit himself," the *New York Times* pointed out, "and much will depend upon his general view of human nature and its capabilities."

At 3:24, the jurors marched out and the wait began.

Not long after, a square parcel arrived for Miss Lizzie Borden. She opened the lid and her face brightened. Inside lay a large bouquet of cut flowers. Such a small kindness in such a dark hour, but it was enough to make her smile.

Barely an hour later, the reporters' seats suddenly began to fill.

Lizzie Borden went white, then flushed. Within two minutes, judges and jury were back in their places.

"Lizzie Andrew Borden, stand up," said the clerk. She was so pale she might have been made of marble, if only marble could quiver. "Gentlemen of the jury, have you agreed upon your verdict?"

The soft fluttering of paper fans seemed to crackle and snap in the momentous quiet.

"We have," said Foreman Richards.

"Lizzie Andrew Borden, hold up your right hand," the clerk commanded. Lizzie detached her hand from the rail of the prisoner's dock. She had been clutching it as though she were the only thing holding it up. "Mr. Foreman, look upon the prisoner; prisoner, look upon the foreman."

The jurors did an about-face and gazed as one on Lizzie Borden. Everyone in the courtroom knew from their faces what the verdict would be. But Lizzie could not make herself look. Her eyes would not obey. They lolled in a great dread-filled circle, seeing nothing.

"What say you, Mr. Foreman—"

"Not guilty," the foreman interrupted.

Lizzie Borden dropped as though she'd been shot. A reporter twelve feet away felt the walnut rail shake beneath him as she crashed down onto it, her face buried in her arms. And then the tears, all the tears she had held so tight within herself through all those ten long months, burst free.

Cheers rattled the courthouse and tumbled out into the streets of New Bedford. Handkerchiefs waved like little lace-edged banners. Tears shone in the judges' eyes, and in the sheriff's. "Thank God!" Lawyer Jennings exclaimed, his voice breaking as he squeezed Colonel Adams's hand. The colonel could not say a word. Governor Robinson beamed upon the jury like a proud new father. Trembling with relief, Jennings pushed his way to the dock and tried to lift Lizzie's head from the rail. It was more than either of them could manage. Only one small bare hand emerged to clasp his.

Ever the gentleman, District Attorney Knowlton crossed the room to shake hands with his opponent, never betraying a trace of disappointment at the verdict. Then, wrote the *Rochester Democrat & Chronicle*, "Mr. Robinson dodged under the rail of the bar and pushed by the now useless deputy who guarded the prisoner. He stooped down and put his face against hers. Presently his left arm slipped round her waist and, like the father he has been to her, he raised her up."

At the sight of her tearstained face and waving handkerchief, a jubilant crowd swarmed so thickly around Lizzie Borden, it blocked Emma's path to her sister. Mrs. Holmes and Reverend Buck reached Lizzie first. Close behind came Colonel Adams, reaching for her with both hands. And then the jury, marching one by one to shake her hand. "She gave them a wealth of glad smiles, greeting each of them with a fresh sparkle of her eyes, a warm grasp of hand and a look so grateful and kindly that the heart of every man among them must have been touched."

His arm still around her, Governor Robinson led Lizzie to a small anteroom, where Lawyer Jennings barred the door from all but her most intimate friends. There at last Lizzie sank into her sister's arms. "I want to go home," she told Emma, "take me straight home tonight."

"Tonight?"

"Yes, tonight," Lizzie said. "I want to see the old place and settle down at once."

The crowds outside the courthouse in New Bedford cheered for ten minutes, pushing and shoving around her carriage for the chance to shake her hand. Her wreath of smiles, her excited flush, made Lizzie seem a different woman. As she waved her handkerchief to the well-wishers, it looked for all the world as though she were bidding the last of her troubles goodbye.

But the mood in Fall River was something else altogether. Three of every four people believed Lizzie Borden was guilty, and her friends feared rudeness, even violence, awaited her at home. At the very least a crowd—if not a mob—would be gathered around Number 92.

So instead of taking the train and proceeding back to Second Street as expected, Lizzie and Emma went by carriage to the brightly lit Holmes residence on Pine Street, where the Bowens, Reverend Jubb and his family, Lawyer Jennings, and other close friends waited to celebrate. For those few hours, she reveled in her acquittal, proclaiming herself "the happiest woman in the world," while over on Second Street a band played "Auld Lang Syne" to appease the two thousand people waiting to see her.

Lizzie Borden could not escape the public's curiosity for much more than an evening. When the neighbors noticed her moving from room to room inside her own house in the days that followed, they told the papers. For days, people gathered on the sidewalks of Second Street or peered over the fences, hoping to spy the woman they believed had gotten away with murder.

They could not stop looking, any more than the papers could stop talking. The most mundane incidents carried headlines that sounded like the case had been cracked.

IT WASN'T MISS BORDEN, announced the *New Bedford Evening Journal* when a woman resembling Lizzie caused a stir on State Street in Boston.

IN JAIL! trumpeted the *Fall River Globe* when Lizzie boarded a train to Taunton to thank the sheriff and his wife for the care and consideration they'd shown her.

NOT AT CHURCH, the *Boston Globe* scolded the first Sunday after her acquittal. They did not know that Lizzie had managed to slip away from Fall River's prying eyes to the seaside town of

Newport, Rhode Island, to recuperate privately from her long ordeal.

Time did nothing to quell the public's interest. When the real Lizzie Borden was at last spotted in downtown Fall River weeks later, shops and offices emptied into the street to gawk. Heads popped out of second story windows. Hoodlums and urchins trailed behind her. Even the sight of a trunk bearing the label *L. Borden, Fall River*—whether it belonged to her or not—brought gawkers running.

She could draw the curtains on her carriage tight, do her shopping discreetly in Providence, Boston, and Washington, D.C., but it made little difference. Until the end of her days, no matter where Lizzie Borden went, headlines followed.

Fall River Evening News,
August 4, 1892.

Collection of Fall River
Historical Society.

FALL RIVER EVENING NEWS, THURSDAY, AUGUST 4, 1892.

MURDER MOST FOUL.

Andrew J. Borden and His Wife

Horribly Butchered at Their Home.

A Double Murder in the Heart of the City.

NO CLUE TO THEIR ASSAILANT.

But a Portuguese Who Has Been in Mr. Borden's Employ Suspected of the Crime.

Their Youngest Daughter Makes the Horrible Discovery.

A Servant Girl in the Upper Part of the House Knew Nothing of the Crime.

DELAY IN NOTIFYING THE POLICE.

A Decoy Postal.

During the morning Mrs. Borden received a postal card informing her that a friend was ill, and asking her to call. This postal has since been thought to have been a decoy to get her out of the house, but it has not yet been followed up. She did not go, and was in the house when Mr. Borden returned.

Mr. Borden sat down in a rocking chair in the sitting room when he came in and began to read a paper. This sitting room is very pleasantly located on the ground floor and faces the south. In the rear of this room is the kitchen. Mrs. Borden had gone upstairs to her room on the second floor, in the northwest corner of the building. The servant girl, Bridget Sullivan, was downstairs with Mr. Borden shortly after he came in, when he said something about not being well, and taking off his frock coat he put on a short reefer, or house coat. His frock coat he placed on the head of the sofa and arranging a pillow he stretched himself out on the sofa. It is presumed that he fell asleep.

The servant went upstairs to wash the windows in her bedroom in the third story and knew nothing more of what occurred until called by Mr. Borden's daughter, Elizabeth. The daughter was about down stairs when her father came in and went out into the yard in the rear and was engaged there and in the barn. From this point the details have to be taken from what has been found since the discovery.

Mrs. Borden the First Victim.

The theory most generally accepted by the police and others who have been investigating is that the murderer was concealed somewhere about the house when Mr. Borden came in, as no one saw him enter.

The most probable hiding place was in the cellar. As soon as it became quiet in the rooms above he is thought to have come up stairs with the intention of murdering Mr. Borden. Before he could accomplish his purpose Mrs. Borden's attention was probably attracted, or she saw her com...

left eye was forced out and the face and skull about the left temple completely crushed.

The wound inflicted by the hatchet head was four inches long and two inches wide. It is from this wound that the physicians judged more than anything else the nature of the weapon.

Mr. Borden must have been instantly killed, as he was found lying in an easy position on the sofa, with his legs extended and his feet on the floor.

A Daughter's Horrible Find.

The first to discover the crime was the daughter, Miss Elizabeth Borden. While in the yard she heard groans, or sounds that resembled groans. Hurrying into the house, she discovered her father lying on the sofa, with blood flowing from wounds on his face. She ran to the foot of the back stairs crying, "Murder! Murder!" and calling up to the servant, Bridget, exclaimed, "My God! Father is dead."

The servant hurried down stairs and Miss Elizabeth alarmed the neighbors living in the house to the north and one of them ran across the street to call Dr. Bowen. He was not in and efforts were made to telephone to other physicians and later the central police station.

The neighbors who were first alarmed were much confused, and while attempts were being made to get physicians and ascertain the nature of the injuries, the police were not thought of. The message that at length reached the central station was that Andrew J. Borden had been hurt, and there were no particulars.

Later Police Notification.

It was 10:40 o'clock when a woman ran across the street for Dr. Bowen, and it was after 11 o'clock before an officer could be sent from the station. Officer Doherty was first sent, and Officer Mullaly followed.

Officer Doherty was the first member of the force to learn that a murder had been committed. The news did not spread very...

Abby Borden's body, photographed on the afternoon of August 4, 1892.

Collection of Fall River Historical Society.

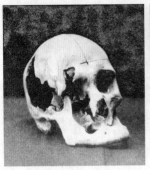

Skulls of Andrew Borden (left) and Abby Borden (right).

Collection of Fall River Historical Society.

The receiving vault at Oak Grove Cemetery, where Andrew and Abby Borden's bodies were held following the funeral service on August 6, 1892.

Collection of the author.

Crowds gathered outside the central police station, awaiting news of the Borden affair.

From The Fall River Tragedy; *collection of the author.*

Fall River Police Department arrest book, detailing Lizzie Borden's arrest on August 11, 1892. • "Height: 5'4"; Complexion: Light; Hair: Light; Eyes: Gray."

JUGGLING WITH A WOMAN'S LIFE.

Brave(?) Fall River Police in Their Great Hatchet Throwing Feat to Convict Lizzie Borden of Murder.

"Juggling with a Woman's Life." Newspaper cartoon denouncing Lizzie Borden's treatment at the hands of Hosea Knowlton and the Fall River Police Department.

Taunton Jail. Lizzie Borden spent ten months in cell No. 3, awaiting trial.

From The Fall River Tragedy; *collection of the author.*

New Bedford courthouse.

From The Fall River Tragedy; *collection of the author.*

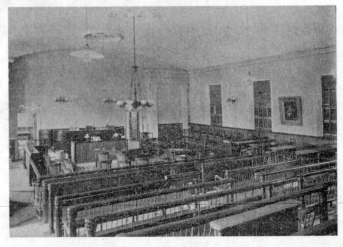

The courtroom where Lizzie Borden was tried for murder.

From The Fall River Tragedy; *collection of the author.*

The "hoodoo hatchet."

Collection of Fall River Historical Society.

Front page of the *Boston Daily Globe,* June 14, 1893, depicting Dr. Draper as he matches the blade of the hoodoo hatchet to a wound on the skull of Andrew Borden.

Boston Public Library.

Lizzie Borden and Governor Robinson before the verdict. *Frank Leslie's Illustrated Weekly*, June 29, 1893.

Library of Congress.

The jury. The "jolly crowd" of twelve men sat for this portrait and presented it to Lizzie in July of 1893. "[A]lways shall I think of you all as my faithful friends," Lizzie wrote in response.

From The Fall River Tragedy; *collection of the author.*

A snapshot of Lizzie Borden on a friend's piazza in Newport,
Rhode Island, possibly taken within days of her trial.
The significance of the ring on her left hand is unknown.

Collection of Fall River Historical Society.

Lizzie's beloved Maplecroft, as it looked in 1899.

Collection of the author.

Miss Lizbeth Borden of Maplecroft, around
the time Emma departed French Street.

Collection of Fall River Historical Society.

The Borden family monument at Oak Grove Cemetery, commissioned by Emma and Lizzie in 1895 at a cost of $2,124.

Collection of the author.

Lizzie Borden's headstone. Visitors often leave pennies, flowers, or other tokens of remembrance.

Collection of the author.

AFTERMATH

"THE 'THING' THAT BUTCHERED
THE BORDENS STILL AT LARGE"

"Never," Emma Borden had said as she sat waiting for the verdict, "never had girls such faithful friends as we have had during our troubles."

Now that the troubles were over, the damage the ten-month ordeal had silently inflicted on those relationships began making itself felt. On Sunday, July 23, Lizzie returned to the Central Congregational Church for the first time since the murders. Accompanied by Dr. Bowen and Mr. Holmes, Lizzie made her way up the side aisle to her usual pew, number 22.

Without a word, parishioners in the surrounding rows left their seats, silently detaching themselves from Lizzie Borden. These were not simply their accustomed pews—they were reserved and paid for, sometimes occupied by generations of the same families. The snub could hardly have been more deliberate, or more cutting.

Lizzie was prepared for such treatment. "[I]f any of my old friends sees fit to ignore me," she'd told columnist Joe Howard, "I shall, I suppose, be compelled to drop them." But the situation was beyond her control. Lizzie Borden had become a spectacle. Anything or anyone connected with her was fair game, as far as the newspapers were concerned, and few people were willing to abide that kind of attention, even secondhand. Those who bravely insisted on associating with Lizzie found themselves shunned within their own circles. Even the faithful Mrs. Brigham could not withstand the pressure, and gradually stopped visiting.

Beneath these superficial snubs, an entirely different kind of unease gnawed at the citizens of Fall River. The jury had declared Lizzie Borden not guilty of the crime, yet to many who found themselves living alongside her, the distinction between *not guilty* and *innocent* must have become uncomfortable to contemplate—especially when the police abandoned further investigation of the crime. "THE 'THING' That Butchered the Bordens Still at Large," the *Fall River Globe* put it. If not Lizzie, then who?

With no other suspect to blame, rumors ran rampant, intensifying in blatant disregard of Lizzie's acquittal. One of them was said to have originated from a woman having her nails done in Boston. She'd overheard a manicurist named Titia telling a story she'd heard from a friend, who in turn had heard it from a friend of Lizzie Borden. This unnamed lady had been frightened by a cat jumping into her lap, and Lizzie had taken it away. A few minutes later Lizzie returned, announcing, "That cat won't ever bother you again!" When asked why, Lizzie replied, "I've chopped its head off!"

The stories of her pilfering from the dead resurfaced, too, spread by a prominent Massachusetts clergyman. Over the years, those rumors would further morph into the ghoulish notion that the Scrooge-like Andrew Borden chopped the feet off his clients to fit them into smaller, cheaper coffins.

The more discerning minds of Fall River could doubtless dismiss such outlandish gossip for what it was. But one thing remained that no one could dismiss: Lizzie's inquest testimony.

Lizzie had wept for joy when the judges excluded it from the jury. Unwilling to see the information withheld from the public at large, District Attorney Knowlton furnished the press with a full transcript that very same day. "Lizzie's Story," printed verbatim in the *New Bedford Evening Standard*, hit newsstands on Monday, June 12. Reading it was enough to challenge anyone—even her friends—to maintain a belief in Lizzie Borden's innocence.

———

Whatever people thought of them, there was business to attend to, personal business that, like everything else, the Borden sisters were helpless to keep from the papers. In one such instance, the publicity was both accurate and favorable. The *New York Times* gossip column was exactly right in noting that Emma and Lizzie had "voluntarily" transferred their dead stepmother's property to her next of kin.

Because Mrs. Borden had died first, and without a will, all her property had become her husband's—for an hour or so, anyway. Likewise, the moment Andrew Borden died, everything he owned reverted to his surviving heirs: Emma and Lizzie. As far as anyone knows, he'd made no will specifying otherwise. (Contrary to persistent assumptions, Lizzie and Emma would *not* have been left penniless if the situation had been reversed. By law, only one-third of Mr. Borden's fortune would have gone to Abby Borden and her heirs if she had even momentarily survived her husband.) But all the medical experts had agreed: Mrs. Borden died first. Legally speaking, Emma and Lizzie did not have to part with one penny of their stepmother's $4,000 estate.

And yet they did—nearly every cent of it. Abby Borden's two sisters, Bertie and Priscilla, each received $788 in cash from Mrs. Borden's bank accounts. The deed to Bertie Whitehead's house on Fourth Street, which had caused so much irritation in the Borden family, they transferred to Bertie and Priscilla for a single dollar.

One very sensitive issue, at least, Lizzie and Emma did manage to resolve with utmost secrecy. On July 14, 1893, Medical Examiner Dolan received a letter from District Attorney Knowlton:

> *Dear Sir,*
>
> *Mr. Jennings insists that the skulls of Andrew*
> *and Abbie Borden be returned to his clients. As*
> *there is no pending case and they were held for*
> *evidence only, I see no reason why they should not*
> *be returned.*

So far as we know, Dolan complied, and the skulls were returned. They've never turned up elsewhere, that's certain. How
or when they were laid to rest remains mostly a mystery. Although no record of their burial exists, radar scans of the Borden
plot conducted in 1992 by James Starrs, a forensic professor from
George Washington University, revealed small irregularities in
the soil over Mr. and Mrs. Borden's coffins. Professor Starrs believes these disturbances, about thirty-six inches above Andrew
and Abby Borden's feet, mark the place where the Borden sisters
privately reunited their parents' skulls with the bodies.

Try as she might to bury it, Lizzie Borden's past was no longer entirely her own. Her trial was a matter of public record, making it
inevitable that someone would try to cash in on the Borden fascination. The only surprise was how quickly. *The Fall River Tragedy:
A History of the Borden Murders* arrived in readers' hands less than
two months after the verdict. Its author was twenty-nine-year-old
Edwin Porter, the very same *Fall River Globe* reporter who was
behind the story of the Borden sisters' jailhouse quarrel.

Lizzie, everyone knew, immediately tried to suppress the publication. That can't be denied, but as is so often the case where
the Borden murders are concerned, the circumstances are more
complicated than they appear.

Word about Porter's intent to publish a book on the crime had broken while Lizzie Borden was still in jail. Fearful that it would ruin his client's chances for a fair trial, Lawyer Jennings contacted Edwin Porter in late January of 1893:

"You are therefore hereby notified that you will be held directly accountable for all statements published in such book or pamphlet, and for any false statements or colorful descriptions you will be promptly prosecuted," he warned. The notice went on to forbid Porter from printing any likeness—or pretended likeness—of Andrew, Emma, or Lizzie Borden, John Morse, or Jennings himself. (It seems no one minded if Porter printed photos of Abby Borden.)

Within a week, Jennings learned from Porter that the book would not go to press until after the trial. The two men also reached an apparent compromise about photographs: no living members of the Borden family were pictured in *The Fall River Tragedy*—only Mr. and Mrs. Borden. Jennings pursued the matter no further.

In reality, Lizzie had little to fear from Edwin Porter. *The Fall River Tragedy* was in essence a thinly veiled compilation of his *Globe* articles. If the people of Fall River were hoping for shocking new revelations, or perhaps even a solution to the mystery, Porter was a complete disappointment.

THE FALL RIVER TRAGEDY

Victoria Lincoln, who was born in Fall River in 1904 and grew up just down the block from Lizzie Borden, offered a different explanation for the scarcity of Porter's book, and it is hers that has taken root in the popular imagination. "[L]ike most of Fall River, I had always wanted to read Edwin H. Porter's *The Fall River*

Tragedy," she wrote in her 1967 biography of Lizzie Borden. "However, Lizzie bought off the printer, a local, and the books were destroyed before they hit the shop."

Over the years the "fact" that Lizzie Borden burned all but four copies of *The Fall River Tragedy* sprouted out of Lincoln's story, despite the absence of any evidence supporting her claim. On the contrary, a 1933 *New Yorker* article reported that Porter's book failed to sell well, leaving a portion of the original print run to gather dust in the loft of an old barn.

It may be true, however, that the majority of copies never found their way onto bookshop shelves, for *The Fall River Tragedy* was sold at least in part by subscription rather than in stores. After browsing the forty-eight-page sample, subscribers could reserve a copy for $1.50 and have it delivered directly to their door. Subscribers included Mrs. Brigham, Lawyer Jennings, and Lizzie's cousin, Anna.

Yet the irresistible image of a frantic Lizzie Borden snatching up all those incriminating books with her dead father's money endures. That myth, combined with the book's meager print run—some say only five hundred copies were printed; others estimate a thousand—was enough to make the world believe there was something between the covers of Porter's unpopular green hardback that Lizzie Borden was desperate to hide.

"CAN'T ANYBODY FRIGHTEN HER OUT OF DOING WHAT SHE WANTS TO"

Though she refused to indulge gawkers or journalists with photographs or comments, Lizzie Borden also would not permit Fall River's blend of ostracism and intrusiveness to impose upon the life she intended to lead. "[C]an't anybody frighten her out of doing what she wants to," as one astute observer had predicted the day before Lizzie's acquittal.

So if neighbors thought the sight of moving vans pulling up to the curb of 92 Second Street on September 6, 1893, signaled Lizzie and Emma's departure from Fall River, they were sorely mistaken.

"A good many persons have talked to me as if they thought I would go and live somewhere else when my trial was over," Lizzie told a columnist at the close of the trial. "I don't know what possesses them. I am going home and I am going to stay there. I never thought of doing anything else."

For three days, wagonloads of the Borden sisters' possessions passed by the clusters of onlookers and made their way up to the Hill. The vans stopped at Number 7 French Street, an elegant Queen Anne–style residence, only four years old, perched on an expanse of green lawn and fitted up with the latest conveniences: electricity, a powder room downstairs, and a full bath upstairs. The lower half was painted a dull bronze green, the upper story buff. A spindled front porch wound lazily around one corner of the house. Above it, a sideways-facing dormer window with a funny little peak like a witch's hat jutted toward the sky.

A parlor, dining room, breakfast room, and kitchen comprised the first floor. Upstairs were two bedrooms (eventually, Lizzie added a third summer bedroom for herself), and a sitting room with french doors leading into a well-stocked library. Lizzie occupied the front bedroom, complete with fireplace and a window seat under the little dormer window. The third floor housed the servants: a housekeeper, two maids, and a coachman, who later became chauffeur for Lizzie's handsome black Packard Phaeton automobile.

The interior of the Borden sisters' French Street house has rarely been seen or photographed, but over the years, the details of some of its finer appointments have leaked out: carved mantelpieces, parquet floors, stained-glass windows, Tiffany wall sconces, gold-leaf woodwork, linen-covered ceilings, floral-painted bathtubs. For those who suspected that Lizzie had committed murder for her father's fortune, no further evidence was necessary.

Yet considering that Lizzie and Emma had recently come into hundreds of thousands of dollars, the French Street house was not a tremendous splurge. At around $13,000, its cost was just over half of what the Borden sisters reportedly paid Governor Robinson to save Lizzie from the gallows. Nor was the Borden sisters' new home a great deal larger, though its wide porch, gabled peaks, and bulging bay windows make it seem so. At the time they purchased it, Number 7 French Street was a little more than five hundred square feet bigger than their old home. And besides, did anyone truly expect them to remain in what the papers had long ago dubbed "the house of horrors"?

Lizzie christened their new home Maplecroft. She seemed to revel in the place, delighting in marking it as her own. A brass letter "B" adorned the double front doors; another was etched into the frosted glass of the back door. She and Emma ate from monogrammed silverware. Lizzie had little green foil stickers printed—"B" stamped in gold above a small maple leaf, surmounted by the word "Maplecroft"—to seal her letters and fix to the flyleaves of her books. When she remodeled the front porch,

"Maplecroft" was carved into the top riser of the new granite steps, leaving no doubt about her intent to remain in Fall River.

"When the truth comes out about this murder," Lizzie said, "I want to be living here so I can walk down town and meet those of my old friends who have been cutting me all these years."

Fall River's grudge against Lizzie Borden was never entirely personal. Few, if any, hoped to deliberately wound her by turning their collective back on her. More than anything, the citizens wanted to move beyond the Borden affair, to wipe the woman who lived at 7 French Street entirely from public consciousness. Lizzie seemed to share the sentiment. She did not want to be renowned as the murderer any more than Fall River wanted to be famous as the scene of the crime. When articles about the killing appeared in the papers, Lizzie withdrew, cloistering herself within the sanctuary of Maplecroft. As local fascination faded, the city and its most notorious citizen settled into an implicit truce. So long as Lizzie did not draw attention to herself, Fall River did its best to take as little notice of her as possible.

THE HIP BATH COLLECTION

Chief among those who did not wish to recall the Borden trial was Andrew Jennings. He never spoke of the case again, even within the privacy of his own home. Unbeknownst to his family, Lawyer Jennings also bundled up the many documents and pieces of physical evidence he'd collected during the ten-month trial and deposited them in an empty tin bathtub in his attic.

Decades later, Jennings's children stumbled across

this unconventional treasure chest while clearing out his estate. The hip bath collection, as it quickly became known, contained a stunning array of Borden artifacts, including the hoodoo hatchet, the bedspread and pillow shams stained with Abby Borden's blood, and the only known transcript of the preliminary hearing testimony.

In 1968, Jennings's daughter donated the bulk of the hip bath collection to the Fall River Historical Society, keeping back only two red leather notebooks that contained her father's personal notes on the case. In 2012, Jennings's grandson bequeathed Lawyer Jennings's precious notebooks to the society, where they are currently being prepared for publication.

Nevertheless, every few years a new chapter of the Borden saga flared to life in the newspapers. Some, like Lizzie's eviction of the Young Women's Christian Temperance Union from the A. J. Borden building and her disagreements with neighbors over fence lines and unruly animals, were based in fact. Others—that the case was to be reopened, that Lizzie had confessed or was engaged to be married—were pure fantasy. At least one fell somewhere in between.

On February 16, 1897, *Providence Journal* headlines proclaimed: "LIZZIE BORDEN AGAIN, A Warrant for Her Arrest Issued from a Local Court."

It was not murder this time, but shoplifting. Two paintings were discovered missing from a Rhode Island jewelry store after a visit from Lizzie Borden, the *Journal* said. "Investigation followed and the missing goods were tracked to the present residence of Miss Borden at Fall River."

Another paper's version of the story claimed that the paintings (this time on porcelain rather than marble) were not missed at all until a woman brought one in to Tilden-Thurber to have it framed (or repaired, depending on who tells it). The clerk recognized the artwork and realized that it—and another like it—had disappeared from the shop without anyone noticing. According to the woman, both of the paintings were gifts from none other than Lizzie Borden.

When questioned, Lizzie declared that she had bought the artwork at Tilden-Thurber. But the *Journal* reported that no one at the company had any record or memory of such a sale. The police chief of Providence amplified the suspicion by refusing to make a statement. "He will not deny, however, that a warrant charging Miss Lizzie Borden with larceny from the Tilden-Thurber Company was issued." Yet Lawyer Jennings claimed he knew nothing at all of the incident, and would say nothing except that he did not believe it.

And then, before anyone could decide whether the conflicting details were due to sloppy reporting or an all-out hoax, the story vanished from the papers. Tilden-Thurber said nothing more about it for almost thirty years, until a journalist researching Lizzie Borden inquired into the incident and was informed that the store had no record of it. As far as the company representative could recall, the matter had been "adjusted." The nature of the adjustment is anyone's guess. Settled out of court, perhaps? Or had Tilden-Thurber discovered a mistake and dropped the issue altogether?

Lizzie paid the consequences either way. Henceforth, when she entered Gifford's jewelry store in Fall River, she was watched. Of course she was. The rumors and suspicions were strong enough to warrant caution. She was Lizzie Borden, after all. But nowhere in Gifford's account books is there any record of Lizzie actually stealing. For that matter, no evidence of Lizzie Borden shoplifting from anyone has ever come to light.

KLEPTOMANIA

As with so many things connected with Lizzie, the few facts of the Tilden-Thurber incident dwindled through the decades, allowing the bones of the story to grow entirely new flesh. This episode seems to have spiraled backward, spawning a legend that when Andrew Borden was alive, he'd given instructions to the local shopkeepers to quietly bill him for anything Lizzie stole. The logic was warped—would such a stern old skinflint really fund his daughter's petty thievery? Why not buy her the little luxuries she wanted and spare his family the shame? After she'd inherited her father's savings, the notion made still less sense. And so the legend expanded to answer that, too: Lizzie became a kleptomaniac, compelled to steal no matter how much finery she could afford.

"I DID NOT GO UNTIL CONDITIONS BECAME ABSOLUTELY UNBEARABLE"

Through it all, Emma stood by her sister. Their mother's death, their father's remarriage, the murders, the trial, the stigma and isolation that followed—for forty years, Emma's support never wavered.

And then, in June of 1905, the *Boston Sunday Herald* announced, "After repeated disagreements, Lizzie A. Borden and her sister,

Emma Borden, have parted company." More astonishing still, the story was true. "Several days ago Miss Emma packed up her belongings, called a moving wagon and shook the dust of the French street home, where they have lived together ever since the acquittal in the famous murder trial, from her feet."

After so many traumas weathered side by side, it was difficult to imagine what new horror could make Emma suddenly pack up her things. The newspapers had two guesses: an actress, and a coachman.

The actress was Nance O'Neil. Audiences from San Francisco to New Zealand to South Africa were raving over the six-foot beauty at the turn of the century, sometimes applauding so zealously that they split the seams of their gloves. Among them was Lizzie Borden.

Lizzie adored the theater, traveling at least twice a month to Boston, sometimes taking in two performances in a single day. No one knows what role she first saw Nance O'Neil play during the actress's triumphant 1904 tour of New England, but whatever it was entranced her. Lizzie did not even return home before dashing off a fan letter. Her request to meet the actress arrived on hotel stationery, accompanied by a bouquet of flowers.

Nance O'Neil later claimed she had no idea she was agreeing to meet the notorious Lizzie Borden—by that time Lizzie had adopted the name "Lizbeth"—and learning Lizzie's identity did not deter her. On the contrary, Nance O'Neil had made herself famous playing tragic roles. How could she pass up an opportunity to befriend a living, breathing tragedy?

Whatever her motivation, Nance found herself captivated by Lizzie—her refinement and intellect, her kindness and loneliness all aroused Nance's sympathy. That autumn, when Nance O'Neil played Fall River, she and her whole company dined afterward at Maplecroft. Talk in town was of a splendid affair, with catered food, palm trees, and an orchestra. It was also rumored that Lizzie had funded a lavish weeklong party at Nance's country home earlier that summer.

Entertaining a troupe of actors was not exactly scandal-worthy, but it did attract a certain amount of attention—attention Emma did not welcome. She may have retired to her room or left the house entirely, for Nance O'Neil stated years afterward that she'd never met Emma Borden.

No one knows just how intensely Emma disapproved of Lizzie's relationship with Nance, but whatever Emma's feelings, they were not enough to discourage her sister. Early May of 1905 again found Nance enjoying Lizzie's hospitality. A little more than a week later, Emma had left Maplecroft forever.

It could hardly have been a coincidence. But while Nance O'Neil was almost certainly the last straw, she was not the root of the problem. The fact was, Emma had been contemplating parting with Lizzie for at least a year before Nance entered the picture—otherwise, Emma could not have confided her troubles in Reverend Buck before his death in March of 1903. When he'd heard what was going on at Maplecroft, Emma said, Reverend Buck told her "it was imperative that I should make my home elsewhere."

Perhaps Reverend Buck was referring to the coachman. According to the newspapers, Lizzie's coachman, Joseph Tetrault, was "a fine looking young man and reported to be very popular among the ladies." Always generous toward those she valued, Lizzie at some point presented Tetrault with a gold watch chain decorated with an onyx horse's head. But in 1903, he'd been dismissed from Maplecroft, reportedly because of "Miss Emma's dislike of some of [his] doings and position."

That business about him being popular with the ladies is our only clue as to why. Was Tetrault consorting with women, and if so, would he have dared bring them to his quarters at Maplecroft for trysts? Had he and Lizzie become romantically involved? Could he possibly have made unwelcome advances toward Emma? Or maybe the problem with Tetrault was something else entirely. Perhaps it was just another groundless rumor.

Given the timing, it's plausible that after consulting with Reverend Buck, Emma had delivered Lizzie an ultimatum: me or Tetrault. If that was the case, dismissing the coachman was only a temporary solution. Once the talk in town had subsided, Tetrault returned to his former position at Maplecroft, remaining there until 1907. Emma's reaction, or what she endured for the next year and a half, is a matter of speculation. All she said publicly was "I did not go until conditions became absolutely unbearable."

So far as anyone knows, Lizzie and Emma never saw or spoke to one another again.

"GUILTY?–NO! NO!"

The year 1913 marked the twentieth anniversary of the verdict. Two decades of rumors, gossip, and prying. Two decades of insinuation and slander, and neither Lizzie nor Emma Borden had ever acknowledged a single word, much less spoken out against any of it.

All that changed in April, when the *Boston Sunday Herald* ran an article entitled "Lizzie Borden Twenty Years After the Tragedy." The story presented a grim picture of a Lizzie Borden held prisoner by Fall River's suspicion, detested by all but her house pets and servants.

Every old rumor was there, and more—Lizzie's extravagant habits, the shoplifting, lawsuits with neighbors over spite fences, Porter's book, Nance O'Neil, her father's stinginess, and her refusal to call Mrs. Borden "Mother"—everything right down to how liberally she paid her servants.

As always, Lizzie had no interest in responding. "Nothing to say," she calmly told a reporter from a rival paper who called for an interview. "Nothing, absolutely nothing to say," she shouted when he would not take no for an answer, and slammed down the receiver.

To everyone's amazement, it was Emma Borden who agreed to break the family's silence. No one knows for certain what goaded Lizzie's famously reticent sister to speak, though it's conceivable that the *Herald* had struck a nerve with its remark that "[p]robably the most remarkable and unusual event of the past 20 years in the life of Lizzie Borden is the desertion of her by her sister Emma."

The next Sunday, Emma Borden's one and only interview with the press debuted in the *Herald*'s rival, the *Boston Post*.

"The tragedy seems but yesterday, and many times I catch myself wondering whether it is not some frightful dream, after all," Emma began.

"Some persons have stated that for years they considered Lizzie's actions decidedly queer," she admitted. "But what if she did act queerly? Don't we all do something peculiar at some time or other?

"Queer? Yes, Lizzie is queer. But as for her being guilty, I say 'No,' and decidedly 'No.' "

After sitting through Lizzie's trial, testifying for her, and paying half her legal fees, Emma said, she was not going to sit by and watch her sister be cruelly slandered—not after the promise she had made at her mother's deathbed. She would not speak of what had happened between them at Maplecroft. They had agreed that Lizzie could stay there for the rest of her life, but, Emma said, "I do not expect ever to set foot on the place while she lives.

"I did my duty at the time of the trial, and I am still going to do it in defending my sister even though circumstances have separated us," she added. "The vision of my dear mother always is bright in my mind. I want to feel that when Mother and I meet in the hereafter, she will tell me that I was faithful to her trust and that I looked after 'Baby Lizzie' to the best of my ability." After fifty years her childhood vow remained so strong, it brought her to tears.

Emma also stoutly refused to tolerate barbs directed at her father. "Some unkind persons have spread the report that my father, despite his great wealth, was niggardly and that he refused to even give us sufficient to eat," she said, possibly referring to the *Herald*'s claim that the family had nothing but crackers and milk for supper the night before the murder. "That is a wicked lie. He was a plain-mannered man, but his table was always laden with the best that the market could afford.

"Every Memorial Day I carry flowers to father's grave," she said. "And Lizzie does not forget him. But she generally sends her tribute by a florist." With that, Emma ended the interview.

As she accompanied the *Post*'s reporter to the door, he heard her say, as if to herself, "Yes, a jury declared Lizzie to be innocent, but an unkind world unrelentingly persecuted her. I am still the little mother and though we must live as strangers, I will defend 'Baby Lizzie' against merciless tongues."

It was the last word the public would hear from the Borden family.

"SHE CONSTANTLY HOPED THAT BEFORE SHE DIED SHE WOULD BE PROVEN CLEAN-HANDED"

On June 1, 1927, Lizzie Borden died at Maplecroft.

No one, not even her friends, was sorry to see her go. Life, said one of her nearest and dearest, had become a burden to her. Those who knew Lizzie Borden best "were very glad that it had come to an end, and knew she was glad, too."

Only a select few had known she was dying; only the presence of the undertaker's automobile in the drive indicated that it had happened.

To most of Fall River, the news came out of nowhere, but Lizzie's friends had noticed her health faltering for the last two years. The final decline was sharp and swift—six days and it was over. Years ago, the papers had accused her of having no heart at all, but in the end, it was her heart that gave out. The death certificate read myocarditis. She was sixty-six years old.

Her funeral, as she had specified, was "strictly private." Neither the undertaker nor the cemetery would release any information, ensuring that in death, at least, Lizzie Borden would not be hounded by the press or the public. Mrs. Vida Turner, who was summoned to Maplecroft at noon on Saturday, June 4, to sing the single hymn Lizzie had requested, recalled, "The undertaker unlocked the door, let me in, and locked the door immediately. I was ushered into a room, sang the song, and was then ushered out. The undertaker told me, 'Go straight home and don't tell anyone where you have been.'"

The papers made it sound as though Lizzie had no friends, no one but her servants to tend to her last hours and carry her casket to the grave. They did not know that at the close of the ceremony, the cards were removed from the wreaths and baskets of flowers, to keep her friends' names from being exposed to the public.

By her own request, she was buried at her father's feet.

EPILOGUE

For over a century, the public saw her only through a haze of headlines and rumors. But who was the woman behind the stories? How did she view herself? A photograph commissioned by Lizzie Borden herself and known only to her closest friends provides a bounty of clues.

Framed by the spindles and stonework of Maplecroft's back porch, a plump and graying Lizzie sits in a wicker rocking chair. Her lacy white summer gown just brushes the top of her shoe. A half smile plays about her lips, while her eyes, formerly so direct and penetrating, gaze down at the Boston bull terrier perched in her lap. One dainty hand curves around his fat rump.

She looks nothing like most people imagine, yet this is the image she wanted to project. Indeed, this is how her friends and neighbors remember her.

They remember a yard full of birdhouses, and squirrels so tame they climbed her shoulders. For young Russell Lake, who lived across the street, that yard was a haven, a place to escape from the neighborhood bully. Other children were frightened to walk by the place, but Russell knew he had nothing to fear—Miss Borden was always the best customer at his lemonade stand.

To her chauffeur's son and daughter she was "Auntie Borden," the lady who picnicked with them, sent them postcards and birthday wishes by special delivery, and took them on drives to nearby Tiverton, Rhode Island, for ice cream, in the fancy car with a little window seat made specially for her dog. Other youngsters cherished memories of reading or sharing games of cribbage with Auntie Borden beneath the shade of her maple trees. Lizzie's attentions made a profound impression on her surrogate nieces and nephews—one of them never failed to exclaim to her own grandchildren, "Now you remember . . . Lizzie had nothing to do with it," each time they drove past Maplecroft.

Her thoughtfulness extended beyond the city's children. She

sent weekly deliveries of groceries to pensioners and lent her automobile to invalids and shut-ins. Over the years, Laughlin McFarland, owner of a local bookstore, watched her buy hundreds of books for the city's poor. He thought so highly of her that he refused to stock a popular early study of the Borden case. When she died, she left $30,000 of her fortune to Fall River's Animal Rescue League.

Unlike her father, she used her money to bring ease and comfort to herself and others. But money could not buy the one thing Miss Lizbeth wanted most. "I would give every cent I have in the world and beg in the streets," she once told a friend, "if it could only be proved while I live that I did not kill my father and my stepmother."

No one has ever proved or disproved it. Over one hundred years after the crime, the murders of Andrew and Abby Borden remain unsolved. Lizzie Borden had her own suspicions but refused to divulge them. "When I know how easy it is to be accused," she explained, "it ill befits me to accuse in my turn, since I don't know."

> *Lizzie Borden took an axe,*
> *Gave her mother forty whacks.*
> *When she saw what she had done,*
> *She gave her father forty-one.*

Lizzie Borden, like the murders she was accused of, is an enigma—a symbol of either tortured innocence or insensible evil. The simplest solution to the mystery is also the most difficult to stomach, and so with each telling, the morning becomes hotter, the mutton older, the house on Second Street smaller and more cramped. Mr. Borden grows stingier, Mrs. Borden greedier. Lizzie Borden has become something so inhuman, her eyes glow red with hatred.

Despite the grip that legend continues to hold on the popular imagination, almost anyone who studies the Borden trial has no choice but to admit that the jury returned the proper verdict: not guilty. The evidence presented to those twelve men simply was not enough to put her to death.

But was Lizzie Borden truly innocent? We may never know.

ACKNOWLEDGMENTS

I am indebted to Borden scholars Terrence Duniho, Kat and Stefani Koorey, Faye Musselman, and Harry Widdows, whose digital transcriptions of both primary and secondary sources made my research infinitely less cumbersome.

Michael Martins and Dennis Binette, curator and assistant curator of the Fall River Historical Society, devoted an entire afternoon to acquainting me with the museum's Borden artifacts and their own matchless perspective on Lizzie Borden herself. Without their book, *Parallel Lives,* I don't know whether I would have been able to conceive of Lizzie Borden as a human being instead of a Halloween tchotchke. I have aspired to the standards of precision and impartiality set by their work.

Deputy Police Chief Charles J. Cullen photographed original documents from the Fall River Police Department's archive.

Naomi Balmer-Simpson, Helena Belden, and David Finch provided scans of decades-old magazine articles.

Meagan Burns trudged through the snow-clogged city to retrieve newspaper images from the Boston Public Library.

Dr. Tim Newton answered questions regarding morphine dosage and its effects.

Laura Bailey, Candace Fleming, and Kathe Koja read and offered comments on early drafts.

Thanks to Beverly Benczik and Heather VanFleet for the beige rooms, the Lopus Resort for the deck; Pat Jones for the gift that funded my purchase of *Parallel Lives;* and John Bertolini for the hatchet handle (which I broke). And thanks to my parents, who never flinched when I took my antique Underhill Edge Tool Company No. 1 shingling hatchet out to the woodpile for a few practice whacks.

RESEARCHING THE BORDENS

Who murdered Andrew and Abby Borden? After reading all the court documents backward and forward, I remain as baffled regarding the identity of the murderer as I was when I started.

That has been an unexpected advantage. Attempts to solve the mystery have obscured the facts of the crime for decades, for authors who are determined to crack the case have rarely been able to prevent their theories from dictating which points of evidence they emphasize and which they ignore. Mrs. Borden's request that Bridget wash windows on a warm summer day when the maid had already been ill in the yard leads some to believe Bridget committed the crime out of pure spite. Others interpret the murderer's ability to enter the house undetected as proof that the family knew the killer—perhaps Emma Borden secretly caught an early train from Fairhaven and slaughtered her parents, or perhaps the man Mr. Borden argued with that morning was a mentally unstable, illegitimate son threatening blackmail. Similarly, Lizzie Borden herself undergoes constant transformations as her words and reactions are reinterpreted to support one theory after another, such as the claim that she murdered her parents during an epileptic seizure triggered by her menstrual cycle.

It's enough to tantalize anyone into digging deeper, and the deeper I dug, the more incredulous I became. Before long, the discrepancy between the "facts" about Lizzie as reported by the media and the actual Lizzie who began to emerge from my research triggered my moral outrage and pulled me headlong into the story.

My ambition quickly became twofold: to present Lizzie Borden as a human being, and to be scrupulously fair in my presentation of the facts surrounding the murder. That commitment is what prompted me, for example, to describe Lizzie as noticeably fond of pansies rather than to assert that pansies were her favorite flower. More cumbersome, I'll admit, but also truer to the known facts.

So in the interest of accuracy, let me make a few things clear about the underpinnings of this book:

My description of the discovery of Mr. Borden's murder is constructed almost exclusively from the testimony of the first witnesses on the scene: Lizzie Borden, Bridget Sullivan, Adelaide Churchill, Dr. Seabury Bowen, and Alice Russell. Whenever possible, I favored their earliest statements, when the information was at its freshest. Occasionally, when the phrasing was clearer or more direct, I deferred to trial testimony—most often in the case of Bridget Sullivan, whose inquest testimony is lost. (This, incidentally, is why Dr. Bowen and Mrs. Churchill seem nearly absent from the legal proceedings—the bulk of the information their testimony provided was already presented in the narration.)

None of the dialogue in this book is invented. However, it is not all relayed firsthand. For example, because District Attorney Knowlton's questions provided very little opportunity for Lizzie to report her own speech, virtually all of Lizzie Borden's words immediately following the discovery of Mr. Borden's body are quoted from Bridget Sullivan's and Adelaide Churchill's testimonies rather than Lizzie's own.

A few courtroom scenes presented similar difficulties. Transcripts of Lizzie Borden's arraignment and the closing arguments of the preliminary hearing apparently do not exist, forcing me to rely on inconsistent secondary sources. For instance, accounts of Lizzie Borden's arraignment published in the *New York Herald,* the *Fall River Herald,* and Edwin Porter's *The Fall River Tragedy* all contain direct quotations, and all of them vary slightly—despite the fact that all three reporters were present that day. When read side by side, it becomes evident that each reporter, working from notes and memory, reconstructed the dialogue differently. Although all three versions convey essentially the same information, it is impossible to know which (if any) are the precise words spoken in the courtroom that day. Once I realized that, I felt free to cobble together some of these quotes from multiple sources, again choosing the phrasing that was clearest or most vivid.

Newspapers proved the most troublesome sources of all. From the moment the very first report of the crime botched Lizzie's name and address, the papers were loaded with errors, misinformation, and flat-out balderdash. Even the prosecution complained of "garbled and wickedly sensational" reports. How did I tell the difference? Some stories, like the Trickey-McHenry affair, were eventually debunked by the press itself. More often, I relied on my own accumulation of knowledge and intuition to recognize nonsense, such as the claim that Lizzie was so fond of her stepmother that as a grown woman she often sat in Mrs. Borden's lap.

I should also caution those who wish to explore the Borden case further that a few books in my bibliography do not qualify as reliable sources. (Most glaring: Lincoln and Pearson. Robert Sullivan also tends to bend the facts and occasionally misquotes testimony.) However, a story so influenced by rumor and gossip requires more than facts, and even an unreliable source often contains a unique rumor or anecdote that can't be found elsewhere— just as the most reliable has an inevitable blunder or two.

There is no greater authority on the Borden murder than the court documents themselves. Nevertheless, it is wise to keep in mind that even the court transcript does not necessarily reveal what truly happened inside 92 Second Street on the morning of August 4, 1892. It can only record what people *said* happened, what they remembered, ten months after the fact. Memories, it turns out, are not verbatim recordings that allow limitless, identical replays. They are assembled, piece by piece, each time the brain calls up a scene from the past, making our recollections quite literally *re*-collections. Information gleaned from related sources and experiences, such as being questioned by police or reading news reports, can and does influence a witness's memory of an event. The transcript is the official record of what happened, but there are no guarantees.

Those who do read the transcript will discover more evidence supporting Lizzie Borden's guilt, as well as more evidence supporting her innocence. With over 2,500 pages of primary sources, every book and article on the Borden case must leave out something. Among other points, I myself am guilty of glossing over the small inconsistencies in Lizzie's earliest versions of her alibi. (Was she looking for tin, iron, or lead? To mend a screen or to make sinkers?) On the other hand, I also omitted testimony suggesting it was not unusual for Lizzie to burn her worn-out dresses. Likewise, entire witnesses had to be omitted for sake of space; I chose those I believe best illustrate opposing positions on the questions of motive, means, and opportunity to commit the crime. I have not aimed for neutrality in making these choices. Instead, my goal has been *balance,* to allow the prosecution and the defense equal opportunity to present as well as refute their most crucial points of evidence.

Guilty or innocent—whatever verdict you ultimately favor, I will be content if what I've written enables you to hold your mind open to both possibilities. As for me? If I could grant Lizzie Borden's dearest wish, I would. This book, which I hope achieves that delicate balance between fairness and humanity, is the nearest thing I can offer her instead.

NOTES

Page numbers of court documents refer to pagination of the original documents, not electronic or bound reprints.

David Kent's *Lizzie Borden Sourcebook* reproduces a vast scrapbook of Borden newspaper clippings, many undated. In most instances, context provides a probable date. These unconfirmed dates are indicated with a question mark in brackets: [?].

EPIGRAPH

Both of these quotations were inscribed in Lizzie Borden's own hand in a book entitled *Between the Lights: Thoughts for the Quiet Hour*. See Martins and Binette, *Parallel Lives*, 787–789.

LIZZIE BORDEN TOOK AN AXE . . .

Andrew Borden now is dead: Martins and Binette, *Parallel Lives*, 693.
"Miss Borden, don't pay any attention to them": Ibid., 901.
"Auntie Borden": Ibid., 912.
"incarnate fiend in human form": Kent, *Forty Whacks*, 211.

MURDER!

"Somebody has killed Father": Lizzie A. Borden, quoted by Adelaide B. Churchill, *Inquest*, 128; see also *Preliminary Hearing*, 271, 282.
"I did not notice anything else": Lizzie A. Borden, *Inquest*, 78.
"What is the matter?": Lizzie A. Borden, quoted by Bridget Sullivan, *Preliminary Hearing*, 27.
"Go for Dr. Bowen as soon as you can": Lizzie A. Borden, *Inquest*, 78.
"Oh, Maggie, don't go in": Lizzie A. Borden, quoted by Bridget Sullivan, *Trial*, 244.
"rang violently": Phoebe Bowen, *Witness Statements*, 10.
"Miss Lizzie, where was you": Bridget Sullivan, *Trial*, 245.
"Go and get her": Lizzie A. Borden, quoted by Bridget Sullivan, Ibid.
"Lizzie, what is the matter?": Adelaide B. Churchill, *Preliminary Hearing*, 271; see also *Trial*, 358.
"running, and she looked as if she was scared": Adelaide B. Churchill, *Inquest*, 127.
"as if she was in great distress": Ibid., 128.
"O, Mrs. Churchill": Lizzie A. Borden, quoted by Adelaide B. Churchill, *Inquest*, 128; see also *Preliminary Hearing*, 271 & 282.
"pale and frightened": Adelaide B. Churchill, *Preliminary Hearing*, 282.

"O Lizzie, where is your father?": Adelaide B. Churchill, *Inquest*, 128.

"I don't know but what Mr. Borden is dead": Bridget Sullivan, quoted by Alice M. Russell, *Inquest*, 147.

"What is it Bridget? Are they worse?": Alice M. Russell, *Inquest*, 147.

"What is the matter, Lizzie?": Dr. Seabury W. Bowen, *Inquest*, 117; see also *Preliminary Hearing*, 409.

They want you quick over to Mr. Borden's!: Dr. Seabury W. Bowen, *Inquest*, 117.

"Has there been anybody here?": Ibid.

"Like a flash": Ibid.

"Will somebody find Mrs. Borden?": Lizzie A. Borden, quoted by Alice M. Russell, *Inquest*, 147.

"dazed": Alice M. Russell, *Inquest*, 148.

"Sit right down here Lizzie in the kitchen": Ibid., 147.

"Will somebody find Mrs. Borden?": Lizzie A. Borden, quoted by Alice M. Russell, *Inquest*, 147.

"Oh, Lizzie, if I knew where": Bridget Sullivan, *Trial*, 247; see also *Witness Statements*, 22.

"No, I think I heard her come in": Lizzie A. Borden, quoted by Bridget Sullivan, *Witness Statements*, 22.

"I don't know where Mrs. Borden is": Lizzie A. Borden, *Inquest*, 83.

"That is awful": Dr. Seabury W. Bowen, quoted by Adelaide B. Churchill, *Inquest*, 128.

"O, I can't go through that room": Bridget Sullivan, quoted by Alice M. Russell, *Inquest*, 148.

"Get me a sheet, and I will cover Mr. Borden over": Dr. Seabury W. Bowen, quoted by Alice M. Russell, *Inquest*, 148.

"Go and get the police as fast as you can": Dr. Seabury W. Bowen, quoted by Hosea M. Knowlton, *Inquest*, 124.

"Doctor, will you send a telegram": Lizzie A. Borden, quoted by Adelaide B. Churchill, *Inquest*, 129.

"I will do anything for you": Dr. Seabury W. Bowen, quoted by Adelaide B. Churchill, *Inquest*, 129.

"the old lady where Emma was visiting": Adelaide B. Churchill, *Inquest*, 129.

"All right, come right in": Dr. Seabury W. Bowen, quoted by George W. Allen, *Witness Statements*, 1.

"You go down, and tell the marshal all about it": Ibid.

"Go and get the police as fast as you can": Dr. Seabury W. Bowen, quoted by Hosea M. Knowlton, *Inquest*, 124.

"I wish someone would go": Lizzie A. Borden, quoted by Adelaide B. Churchill, *Inquest*, 129.

"O, Mrs. Borden!": Adelaide B. Churchill, quoted by Alice M. Russell, *Inquest*, 148.

"Is there another?": Alice M. Russell, quoted by Adelaide B. Churchill, *Witness Statements*, 12.

"For God's sake, how did this happen?": John V. Morse, *Preliminary Hearing*, 245.

"very much overcome": Alice M. Russell, *Inquest*, 147–8.

"threw herself": Dr. Seabury W. Bowen, *Trial*, 325.

"I am not faint": Lizzie A. Borden, quoted by Alice M. Russell, *Trial*, 382.

half the force: Demakis, 21.

"majority": Ibid.

limited to off-duty patrolmen: Radin, 67.

Did you see anyone around here?: John Fleet, *Witness Statements*, 2.

Is there any Portuguese: Patrick Doherty, *Preliminary Hearing*, 333.

What motive?: Philip Harrington, *Witness Statements*, 5.

"She better go up to her room": Dr. Seabury W. Bowen, *Preliminary Hearing*, 405.

"When it is necessary for an undertaker": Lizzie A. Borden, quoted by Alice M. Russell, *Trial*, 383.

"We knew the state she was in": Alice M. Russell, *Inquest*, 149.

"wanted to get into a respectable appearance": Ibid., 155.

"When one was out, another made a point": Ibid., 149.

"apt to open it": Marianna Holmes, *Trial*, 1500.

"a thought that was most revolting": Philip Harrington, *Witness Statements*, 6.

"Has your father or mother": Koorey, Stefani, "Fleet's Notes," *Hatchet* 7, no. 2 (2012): 41; see also John Fleet, *Trial*, 464.

Lizzie stood by the foot of the bed: Philip Harrington, *Witness Statements*, 5–6.

THE BORDENS

"She is very strong willed": Hiram C. Harrington, *Witness Statements*, 11.

597,850,000 yards of cloth: Earl, 4.

83,000 people: Rebello, 61.

"uterine congestion, 4 mos": Rebello, 6 (footnote).

"I had never been to her as a mother": Lizzie A. Borden, *Inquest*, 52.

"watch over baby Lizzie": "Guilty—No! No!" *Boston Sunday Post*, April 13, 1913.

Lizzie's gaze: see "Strange Look in Her Eyes," *Boston Daily Globe*, August 30, 1892; "No Trial," *Boston Globe*, September 3, 1892; "Selected," *Boston Daily Globe*, June 6, 1893.

"shut his teeth and walked away": Martins and Binette, *Parallel Lives*, 20.

"A great deal is said about her coolness now": "Stand By Her," *Boston Daily Globe*, August 15, 1892.

"subject to varying moods": "Says She Is Innocent," undated *Woonsocket (RI) Call* article, in Kent, *Sourcebook*, 171.

"This girl Lizzie Borden": Martins and Binette, *Knowlton Papers*, 105.

"Lizzie is known to be ugly": Ibid.

"repellent disposition": Martins and Binette, *Parallel Lives*, 42.

"Mrs. Morse the mother of Lizzie Borden": Martins and Binette, *Knowlton Papers*, 102.

"a monument of straightforwardness": "Stand By Her," *Boston Daily Globe*, August 15, 1892.

"shocking bad hats": "Twelve Cuts," *Boston Daily Globe*, August 5, 1892.

"said that she had lost in Mrs. Borden": "Thursday's Affray," *Fall River (MA) Daily Herald*, August 5, 1892, in Kent, *Sourcebook*, 10.

"Sit right down": Ibid., in Kent, *Sourcebook*, 8.

more, perhaps, than her own husband and his children: see Emma L. Borden, *Inquest*, 112: "well, we felt that she was not interested in us"

"I don't know just how to put it": Alice M. Russell, *Inquest*, 151.

"not at all affectionate": "Awaiting Monday," *Fall River (MA) Daily Herald*, August 20, 1892, in Kent, *Sourcebook*, 137.

"never spoke or acted unkindly": "A Talk With Lizzie Borden," *Woman's Journal*, May 27, 1893: 163.

"outsiders": Lizzie A. Borden, *Inquest*, 86.

"[W]hat he did for her people": Ibid.

"persuaded": Ibid.

"A very close mouthed woman": Jane Gray, *Witness Statements*, 17.

"He was close in money matters": "A Talk With Lizzie Borden," *Woman's Journal*, May 27, 1893: 163.

"Mr. Borden was a plain living man": Alice M. Russell, *Inquest*, 151.

"What is wrong with the house": "The Borden Mansion Empty," *New York Times*, September 10, 1893.

"odd habits": Martins and Binette, *Knowlton Papers*, 35.

"So far as I know": Ibid., 75.

INVESTIGATION

"Tell him all, Lizzie": John Fleet, *Preliminary Hearing*, 355; see also Koorey, "Fleet's Notes," 41.

"Has your father or mother ever": Koorey, "Fleet's Notes," 41.

"I think sometimes": Lizzie A. Borden, quoted by Alice M. Russell, *Trial*, 379.

"mortified": Ibid.

"I feel as if I wanted to sleep with my eyes half open": Ibid., 378.

"I did not hear anything for some time": Lizzie A. Borden, *Inquest*, 49.

"Her actions were rather peculiar for a lady": John Cunningham, *Preliminary Hearing*, 215.

"[A] young lad told me that there had been a fight": Charles E. Gardner, *Trial*, 1485.

"Some one said there was a man stabbed another one": Charles V. Newhall, *Trial*, 1432.

"on the run going up Second Street": Charles E. Gardner, *Trial*, 1425.

"the [most] ghastly thing I have ever seen: Dr. William A. Dolan, *Preliminary Hearing*, 90.

"It is no use in searching this room": Lizzie A. Borden, quoted by John Fleet, *Preliminary Hearing*, 361; see also *Trial*, 471.

"Just wait a moment": Dr. Seabury W. Bowen, quoted by John Fleet, *Preliminary Hearing*, 359.

"Is it absolutely necessary that you should search this room": Ibid.

"Yes, I have got to do my duty as an officer": John Fleet, *Preliminary Hearing*, 359.

"How long will it take you?": Lizzie A. Borden, quoted by John Fleet, *Preliminary Hearing*, 359.

"It won't take me long": John Fleet, *Preliminary Hearing*, 359.

"I wish to ask you some questions": John Fleet, quoted by Marianna Holmes, *Trial*, 1501.

"You said this morning": John Fleet, *Trial*, 469.

Lizzie's sharpness: see "Bad Day for Lizzie Borden," *New York Times*, August 30, 1892.

"I don't like that girl": Philip Harrington, *Witness Statements*, 7.

"stifling hot": Patrick Doherty, *Trial*, 600.

"No, I can tell you all I know": Lizzie A. Borden, quoted by Philip Harrington, *Preliminary Hearing*, 392.

"I want you men to go give this place": Rufus B. Hilliard, quoted by Philip Harrington, *Witness Statements*, 7.

"If any girl can show you or me": Philip Harrington, *Witness Statements*, 7.

"Incredible": Ibid.

"as if she had run around the bed as far as she could": Jennings's notes, quoted in Allard; see also "Twelve Cuts," *Boston Daily Globe*, August 5, 1892.

"away from the door": Ibid.

"had no thought of a greater calamity": "She Will Be Held," *Fall River (MA) Daily Herald*, September 1[?], 1892, in Kent, *Sourcebook*, 192.

"overcome": "Thursday's Affray," in Kent, *Sourcebook*, 9.

"[T]here was so much going on": Emma L. Borden, *Inquest*, 114.

"Rather a singular coincidence": Frank Kilroy, quoted by Eli Bence, *Inquest*, 161.

"Why, I understand they are suspecting Miss Borden": Eli Bence, *Inquest*, 161.

"Well my good lady": Ibid., 160.

"That is Andrew J. Borden's daughter": Frank Kilroy, quoted by Eli Bence, *Inquest*, 161.

"What she did I don't know": Joseph Hyde, *Trial*, 835.

"I will go down with that": Alice M. Russell, *Inquest*, 155.

"Lynch him!": "Fall River's Tragedy," *New Bedford (MA) Evening Standard*, August 6, 1892.

Horrible Butchery: "Horrible Butchery," *New Bedford (MA) Evening Standard*, August 4, 1892.

Hacked To Pieces At Their Home: "Shocking Crime," *Fall River (MA) Daily Herald*, August 4, 1892, in Kent, *Sourcebook*, 1.

Mutilated Beyond Recognition: "Police Baffled," *New Bedford (MA) Evening Standard*, August 5, 1892.

"At almost any moment startling developments": "$5000 Reward," *New Bedford (MA) Evening Standard*, August 5, 1892.

Suspecting The Daughter Lizzie: "Husband and Wife Murdered in Daylight," *New York Herald*, August 5[?], 1892, in Kent, *Sourcebook*, 6.

Members of the Family Are Shadowed: "Discovery!" *Boston Daily Globe*, August 6[?], 1892, in Kent, *Sourcebook*, 11.

The Suspected Man; John V. Morse: "The Suspected Man," *New Bedford (MA) Evening Standard*, August 5, 1892.

"That's the murderer": "Fall River's Tragedy," *New Bedford (MA) Evening Standard*, August 6, 1892.

$5000 Reward: "$5000 Reward," *New Bedford (MA) Evening Standard*, August 5, 1892. (Note: Emma Borden's middle initial is incorrectly printed as J. It was L, for Lenora.)

"Her nerves were completely unstrung": "The Fall River Mystery," *New York Times*, August 7, 1892.

"was not in mourning": "Funeral Scenes in Fall River Today," *Boston Daily Globe*, August 6, 1892, in Rebello, 102.

"deep mourning": Sherwood, 128.

"is alone considered respectful to the dead": Ibid., 127.

"as thorough an examination as possible": Rufus B. Hilliard, *Preliminary Hearing*, 424–5.

"I slept here last night": Alice M. Russell, quoted by Joseph Hyde, *Witness Statements*, 39.

"I was terribly alarmed": Alice M. Russell, *Inquest*, 153.

"a body that might rightly": "Seen in Court," *Boston Daily Globe*, August 29, 1892.

"considered one of the ablest corporation lawyers": "Life and Honor at Stake,"
  Boston Daily Globe, June 5, 1893.

"handled most everything that was moveable": Dennis Desmond, *Trial*, 724.

"unless the paper was torn from the walls": Dr. William A. Dolan, quoted by
  Emma L. Borden, *Trial*, 1533.

"Is there anybody in this house suspected?": Lizzie A. Borden, quoted by Dr.
  John W. Coughlin, *Trial*, 1163.

"I have a request to make of the family": Dr. John W. Coughlin, *Trial*, 1162–3.

"Well, perhaps Mr. Morse": Ibid, 1163.

"I want to know the truth": Lizzie A. Borden, quoted by Dr. John W. Coughlin,
  Trial, 1163.

"Well, Miss Borden": Dr. John W. Coughlin, *Trial*, 1163.

"We have tried to keep it from her": Emma L. Borden, quoted by Dr. John W.
  Coughlin, *Trial*, 1163.

"Well, I am ready to go any time": Lizzie A. Borden, quoted by Rufus B. Hilliard,
  Trial, 1119 and Dr. John W. Coughlin, *Trial*, 1166.

"I shall see that you receive all the protection": Dr. John W. Coughlin, *Trial*, 1163.

"We want to do everything we can in this matter": Emma L. Borden, quoted by Dr.
  John W. Coughlin, *Trial*, 1163–4.

"I wouldn't let anybody see me do that, Lizzie": Alice M. Russell, *Trial*, 391.

"What are you going to do?": Emma L. Borden, quoted by Alice M. Russell, *Trial*,
  391.

"I am going to burn this old thing up": Lizzie A. Borden, quoted by Alice M.
  Russell, *Trial*, 391.

You might as well or *Why don't you*: Emma L. Borden, *Trial*, 1571.

"I wouldn't let anybody see me do that, Lizzie": Alice M. Russell, *Trial*, 391.

"Why didn't you tell me?": Lizzie A. Borden, quoted by Alice M. Russell, *Trial*, 393.

"sung out": William H. Medley, *Trial*, 713.

"bright": Rufus B. Hilliard, *Trial*, 1125; George Seaver, *Trial*, 744.

"told Mr. Hanscom a falsehood": Emma L. Borden, *Trial*, 1545.

"What was there to tell a falsehood about?": Ibid.

"I am afraid, Lizzie": Alice M. Russell, *Trial*, 393.

"Oh, what made you let me": Lizzie A. Borden, quoted by Alice M. Russell, *Trial*, 393.

"Let us ourselves curb our tongues": "Nothing But Theories," *New Bedford (MA)
  Evening Standard*, August 8, 1892.

"At this moment I can say": "Butchery of the Bordens," *Rochester (NY) Democrat &
  Chronicle*, August 8, 1892.

"[M]en walked slowly": "Nothing But Theories," *New Bedford (MA) Evening Standard*, August 8, 1892.

"Two interpretations are not placed side by side": "Full of Interest," *Fall River (MA) Daily Herald*, August 31[?], 1892, in Kent, *Sourcebook*, 172.

"34 Columns of reading matter": undated *Fall River (MA) Daily Herald* squib, in Kent, *Sourcebook*, 124.

"concocted the deed, and hired someone to do it": "Lizzie Borden Case," *Rochester (NY) Democrat & Chronicle*, August 9, 1892.

"that there had been ill-feeling": "Mrs. Borden Was Dead . . . ," *New York Herald*, August 7 or 8[?], 1892, in Kent, *Sourcebook*, 31–2.

"She told me she helped him": "No Clearer!" *Fall River (MA) Daily Herald*, August 6, 1892, in Williams, 42–3.

"Money, unquestionably money": Ibid., in Williams, 42.

"The Fall River police": quoted in an untitled *Fall River (MA) Daily Herald* article of approx August 9, 1892, in Kent, *Sourcebook*, 32.

INQUEST

"it was hard to be watched so closely": "The Crisis Reached," *New Bedford (MA) Evening Standard*, August 9, 1892.

a "leaky place": "Released From Custody," *New Bedford (MA) Evening Standard*, August 10, 1892.

"In the past few days": "Inquest Begun," *Fall River (MA) Daily Herald*, August 9[?], 1892, in Kent, *Sourcebook*, 38.

"I don't know how to answer it": Lizzie A. Borden, *Inquest*, 51.

"disinterested expression": "Last Day of Testimony," *New Bedford (MA) Evening Standard*, September 1, 1892.

"Give me your full name": Hosea M. Knowlton, *Inquest*, 47.

"does not differ widely": Pearson, *Smutty Nose*, 240.

"the two vary only in slight detail": Sullivan, 211.

less than 5 percent: Duniho & Koorey, 11.

"I made no effort": Sullivan, 216.

"You made no effort": Hosea M. Knowlton, *Inquest*, 78.

"Not that I know of": Lizzie A. Borden, *Inquest*, 49, 50, 57.

"I cannot locate the time exactly": Ibid., 49.

"I think, I am not sure, but I think": Ibid., 47.

"simply a difference of opinion": Ibid., 51.

"You have been on pleasant terms with your stepmother": *Inquest*, 51.

"You did not regard her as your mother": Ibid.

"I did not finish them": *Inquest*, 60.

"I am so confused I don't know one thing from another": Ibid., 61.

"Where were you when [your father] returned?": Hosea M. Knowlton, *Inquest*, 60.

"I was down in the kitchen": Lizzie A. Borden, *Inquest*, 60.

"almost identical": Martins and Binette, *Knowlton Papers*, 176.

"Are you sure you were in the kitchen": *Inquest*, 60.

"Where were you when the bell rang": Ibid., 61.

"mental distress and nervous excitement": Dr. Seabury W. Bowen, *Trial*, 327.

"You remember, Miss Borden": *Inquest*, 61–2.

"You did not answer my question, and you will, if I have to put it all day": Hosea M. Knowlton, Ibid., 76.

"Do you think she might have gone to work": *Inquest*, 70.

"I said to myself": Lizzie A. Borden, *Inquest*, 71.

"I thought I would find out": Ibid., 73.

"You were feeling better": *Inquest*, 76.

"I cannot tell you any reason": Lizzie A. Borden, *Inquest*, 76.

"No, only that I can't do anything in a minute": Ibid., 77.

"I opened the door and rushed back": *Inquest*, 79.

"being entirely decomposed": Martins and Binette, *Knowlton Papers*, 16.

"far advanced": Ibid., 10.

"evacuated in a fluid condition": Ibid, 16.

"bound down behind but normal": Ibid.

"I don't know as I could put enough of it together now": Hiram C. Harrington, *Inquest*, 135.

"[A]t 3 o'clock": "Arrested at Last" *New Bedford (MA) Evening Standard*, August 12, 1892.

"Miss Borden, of course you appreciate": Hosea M. Knowlton, *Inquest*, 90.

"Is there anything else that you can suggest": Ibid., 92.

I am only guessing: Dr. Seabury W. Bowen, *Inquest*, 125.

I don't know, because I was so shocked: Adelaide B. Churchill, *Inquest*, 129.

"I have omitted a good many questions": Hosea M. Knowlton, *Inquest*, 114.

"cut [Mr. Borden's] acquaintance": Hiram C. Harrington, *Inquest*, 134.

"I don't know as I could put anything together now": Ibid.

"sneeringly": Ibid., 135.

"mentioned in a joking way": Ibid.

"For several years, I guess": Ibid.

"Lizzie told me she thought her stepmother": Augusta Tripp, *Witness Statements*, 31.

"a mean old thing": Hannah H. Gifford, *Inquest*, 158.

"She said that": *Inquest*, 158.

"peculiar expression around the eyes": Eli Bence, *Inquest*, 162.

ARREST

"I have here a warrant for your arrest": Porter, 65.

"grim and self-composed": "Gathering Evidence of the Borden Murder," *New York Herald,* August 9[?], 1892, in Kent, *Sourcebook,* 40.

"I have here a warrant for your arrest": Porter, 65.

"I shall read it to you if you desire": Ibid.

"*Not* guilty": "The Police Move," *Fall River (MA) Daily Herald,* August 12[?], 1892, in Kent, *Sourcebook,* 104.

"a drenching rain": Porter, 70.

"more like one who did not fully understand": "Her Father's Murder Charged Against Her," *New York Herald,* August 12[?], 1892, in Kent, *Sourcebook,* 109.

"Your Honor, before the prisoner": Porter, 71.

"disqualified": Ibid.

"This is a complaint charging you with homicide": "Her Father's Murder Charged Against Her," in Kent, *Sourcebook,* 109.

"What is your plea, Lizzie A. Borden": "The Police Move," in Kent, *Sourcebook,* 104.

"Lizzie Borden, stand up": "Her Father's Murder Charged Against Her," in Kent, *Sourcebook,* 110.

"It is beyond human nature": Ibid., in Kent, *Sourcebook,* 109.

"The Commonwealth demurs to the plea": Ibid.

"apparent and glaring": Ibid., in Kent, *Sourcebook,* 110.

"The motion is overruled": Porter, 73.

"Exception!": "Her Father's Murder Charged Against Her," in Kent, *Sourcebook,* 110.

"Your Honor, we are ready for trial": Porter, 73.

"The evidence in this case could not be completed": Ibid.

"We are very anxious to proceed at once": Ibid.

"That's the murderess!": "Lodged in Jail," *New Bedford (MA) Evening Standard,* August 13, 1892.

"Oh, there she is!": Ibid.

"[H]er step as she alighted from the carriage": Ibid.

"Are you not the Lizzie Borden": "Taken to Taunton," *Fall River (MA) Daily Herald,* August 14[?], 1892, in Kent, *Sourcebook,* 115.

"an inflexible prison rule": Martins and Binette, *Parallel Lives,* 474.

"she hoped he would come home a corpse": *New York Times,* August 20, 1892.

"No matter where a person goes": "Divided Opinion," *Fall River (MA) Daily Herald,* August 16[?], 1892, in Kent, *Sourcebook,* 119.

"I do not believe that the public has a right": Ibid., in Kent, *Sourcebook,* 120; see also "First Day in Jail," *Boston Sunday Globe,* August 14, 1892.

"No, I can't": Ibid.

"I believe firmly in my sister's innocence": "I Believe Her Innocent, So Says Sister Emma, Morse, and Buck—Interviewed," *New Bedford (MA) Daily Mercury,* August 13, 1892, in Rebello, 156.

"embittered": "Still No Light on the Mystery," *Springfield (MA) Daily Republican,* August 8, 1892.

"I am sorry": "Blow Falls," *Boston Daily Globe,* August 12, 1892.

"[F]rom Lizzie's face I read": Martins and Binette, *Knowlton Papers,* 5.

"The rights of a noble woman have been trampled": Ibid., 24.

"ruined the peace of the household": "'Told to Friend," *Boston Daily Globe,* August 20, 1892.

"[W]hen he left the house Lizzie told him": *New York Times,* August 20, 1892.

"The story that she would not sit": "Awaiting Monday," *Fall River (MA) Daily Herald,* August 20, 1892, in Kent, *Sourcebook,* 136–7.

"It is hardly necessary to say": quoted in "Lizzie Borden's Arrest," *New Bedford (MA) Evening Standard,* August 15, 1892.

"You and every other citizen must remember": Ibid.

"I think if you were to publish tomorrow": "A Motive for Murder," *New Bedford (MA) Evening Standard,* August 18, 1892.

"Under no circumstances will she open her mouth": "Taken to Taunton," in Kent, *Sourcebook,* 118.

PRELIMINARY HEARING

"that is the first thing that I undertook to do that I never could": Lizzie A. Borden, quoted by Hannah H. Reagan, *Trial,* 1222.

"[a] record of unvarying success": "Seen in Court," *Boston Daily Globe,* August 29, 1892.

"If it please Your Honor": "Knowlton Not Ready," *New Bedford (MA) Evening Standard,* August 22, 1892.

"a sanctuary": undated *New York Telegram* excerpt, in Kent, *Sourcebook,* 127.

"I was surprised to find the house extremely pretty": quoted in "Element of Time," *Fall River Daily Herald,* August 24, 1892, in Kent, *Sourcebook,* 145.

"Well, I can break an egg": Lizzie A. Borden, quoted by Hannah H. Reagan, *Trial,* 1221.

"There, that is the first thing that I undertook to do that I never could": Ibid., 1222.

"That reporter has come after me again": Hannah H. Reagan, quoted by Mary Ella Brigham, *Trial,* 1590.

"Lizzie was back to her old mood": "Court-Room Scenes," *New Bedford (MA) Evening Standard,* August 26, 1892.

"Did you remove anything from those bodies": *Preliminary Hearing,* 185.

"Do you mean to say these bodies are now buried": Ibid., 185–6.

Barbarous: "Belief in Guilt," *New Bedford (MA) Evening Standard,* August 27, 1892.

"The bodies have been made sausage meat of": undated *Holyoke (MA) Democrat* squib, in Kent, *Sourcebook,* 170.

wonderful: "Have a Clew!" *New Bedford (MA) Evening Standard,* August 5, 1892; "Story of a Great Crime," *New York Times,* August 14, 1892.

dignified: "Said Not Guilty!" *New Bedford (MA) Evening Standard,* August 12, 1892.

remarkable: "Lodged in Jail," *New Bedford (MA) Evening Standard,* August 13, 1892.

strange: "Lizzie Borden's Hearing," *New York Times,* August 26, 1892.

indifferent: "Bridget's Story," *New Bedford (MA) Evening Standard,* August 27, 1892.

unfeeling: undated *Pawtucket (RI) Times* excerpt, in Kent, *Sourcebook,* 177.

abnormal: undated *Boston Herald* excerpt, in Kent, *Sourcebook,* 166.

"Even at the recital of the gory details": "Lizzie Borden's Hearing," *New York Times,* August 26, 1892.

"Miss Lizzie closed her eyes": "Court-Room Scenes," *New Bedford (MA) Evening Standard,* August 26, 1892.

"to a fringe": "Bridget's Story," *New Bedford (MA) Evening Standard,* August 27, 1892.

"Mr. Borden was in my place of business": "Morse Testifies," *New Bedford (MA) Evening Standard,* August 27, 1892.

"I live on Main Street": "The Borden Inquiry." *New Bedford (MA) Evening Standard,* August 29, 1892.

Q. Do you know what time of day that was: *Preliminary Hearing,* 290.

"Do you remember anything that took place at all": Ibid., 291.

"You gave me away, Emma": "Awaiting Her Fate!" *Fall River (MA) Daily Herald,* August 25[?], 1892, in Kent, *Sourcebook,* 150.

THE TWO SISTERS . . . : "The Two Sisters," *New Bedford (MA) Evening Standard,* August 26, 1892.

"You gave me away, Emma, didn't you": "Awaiting Her Fate!" in Kent, *Sourcebook,* 150.

"If approached I have no doubt": "You Gave Me Away, Emma," *New Bedford (MA) Evening Standard,* August 25, 1892.

"Naturally it was denied": "The Two Sisters," *New Bedford (MA) Evening Standard,* August 26, 1892.

"Mrs. Reagan refused": Porter, 85–6.

"If you sign this": "Bridget's Story" *New Bedford (MA) Evening Standard,* August 27, 1892.

"The man that wrote it": Ibid.

"My heart almost stood still with anxiety": Porter, 131.

"It was doubtful": "Unabated Interest," *New Bedford (MA) Evening Standard*, August 31, 1892.

"I found that both stomachs": Edward S. Wood, *Preliminary Hearing*, 370.

"Did you find any trace of any poison": *Preliminary Hearing*, 371.

"pulled out an innocent-looking hatchet": "The Tide Turns," *Boston Advertiser*, August 31[?], 1892, in Kent, *Sourcebook*, 183.

"The hatchet contained quite a number": Edward S. Wood, *Preliminary Hearing*, 372.

"flea bites": Lizzie A. Borden, *Inquest*, 87.

"The hair taken from the hatchet": Edward S. Wood, *Preliminary Hearing*, 373.

"God grant Your Honor wisdom to decide": Porter, 132.

"Lizzie Borden did not do this crime!": "She Will Be Held," in Kent, *Sourcebook*, 190.

"Her form was convulsed": Porter, 126.

"Every blow was distinct and parallel": Ibid.

"Evidently Mr. Jennings feels": "Moved to Tears," *New Bedford (MA) Evening Standard*, September 1, 1892.

"Why have not the police": "She Will Be Held," in Kent, *Sourcebook*, 190.

"That brings it down to Lizzie and Bridget": Ibid., in Kent, *Sourcebook*, 191.

"the pet of the family": "Moved to Tears," *New Bedford (MA) Evening Standard*, September 1, 1892; "Held for Trial," *Boston Advertiser*, September 2[?], 1892, in Kent, *Sourcebook*, 195.

"Understand me, I don't believe": "She Will Be Held," in Kent, *Sourcebook*, 191.

"Was Bridget Sullivan compelled": Ibid.

"Here is Lizzie Borden": Ibid., in Kent, *Sourcebook*, 192.

"I demand her release!": Ibid.

"Don't, Your Honor": Porter, 132.

"in a most impassive manner": "Judge Blaisdell's Decision," *New Bedford (MA) Evening Standard*, September 2, 1892.

"They are not such blows": "Probably Guilty," *New Bedford (MA) Evening Standard*, September 2, 1892.

"stubborn fact": Ibid.

"Next comes the servant girl": Ibid.

"She could have but one alibi": Porter, 136.

"While everybody is dazed": Ibid., 138.

"This somewhat removes from our minds": Ibid.

"we would all be proud of it": Ibid., 139.

"there is only one thing to do": Ibid., 140.

"The long examination is now concluded": Ibid., 139.

"The judgment of the Court": Ibid.

"Lizzie A. Borden, stand up": "Probably Guilty," *New Bedford (MA) Evening Standard*, September 2, 1892.

"Don't be afraid": "Bound Over to the Grand Jury," *Boston Daily Globe*, September 2, 1892.

THE WAITING TIME

"flap-doodle, gush, idiotic drivel": Radin, 97.

"shivering in the chilliness": "Lizzie Borden: A Vigorous Letter from Mrs. Livermore," *Maine Farmer*, October 6, 1892.

I was anxious to see if this girl: "In a New Light," *New York Recorder*, September 20, 1892, in Williams, 130.

"The hardest thing": Ibid., in Williams, 131.

"They will not allow me": Ibid.

"of moving up 'on the hill' ": Ibid., in Williams, 133

"There is one thing that hurts me very much": Ibid., in Williams, 131.

She spoke slowly: Ibid., in Williams, 130.

"Why, I had seen so many": Ibid., in Williams, 131.

"As to our not putting on mourning": Ibid., in Williams, 132.

"Petticoat propaganda": Radin, 97.

"a magnificent 'fake'": Porter, 141.

"Lizzie Borden took an axe"

LIZZIE BORDEN'S SECRET: "Lizzie Borden's Secret," *Boston Daily Globe*, October 10, 1892.

"You can make your own choice": Ibid.

"Quarreling will not fix the thing": Ibid.

"Keep your tongue still": Ibid.

A $500 FAKE: Sullivan, 188.

"They'll hang her, sure": "The Jurymen Talk," *New York Times*, December 7, 1892.

"clinched": "In That Grand Jury Room," *New Bedford (MA) Evening Standard*, December 5, 1892.

"the same stolid demeanor": "Indicted!" *New Bedford (MA) Evening Standard*, December 2, 1892; "Lizzie Borden Indicted," *Boston Daily Globe*, December 3, 1892.

"much distressed": "The Jurymen Talk," *New York Times*, December 7, 1892.

"I have scarcely expected a verdict of guilty": Martins and Binette, *Knowlton Papers*, 159.

"lay awake half of the night": "Borden Murder Trial," *New Bedford (MA) Evening Standard,* December 17, 1892.

"a prominent figure": "Life and Honor at Stake," *Boston Daily Globe,* June 5, 1893.

"It's all right, little girl": Pearson, *Trial,* 84.

"one of the most skillful": "Life and Honor at Stake," *Boston Daily Globe,* June 5, 1893.

One thing is sure: Martins and Binette, *Knowlton Papers,* 72.

We, the members of the Young People's Society of Christian Endeavor: Radin, 90.

"unshaken faith": "The Work of the Police," *New Bedford (MA) Evening Standard,* August 16, 1892.

"Personally I would like very much": Martins and Binette, *Knowlton Papers,* 158.

"[I]t does not seem to me": Ibid., 158–9.

"The situation is this": Ibid., 159.

"I try to fill up the waiting time as well as I can": Martins and Binette, *Parallel Lives,* 487.

"[I]t is singular": Martins and Binette, *Knowlton Papers,* 200.

"wonderful nerve": Ibid., 351.

"No sudden, frantic scream": Ibid., 132–5 (see also 348).

"Why did she not rush": Ibid., 158.

"Her religious pretences": Ibid., 144.

"A MAN NAMED RODMAN": Ibid., 136.

"What would they have me do": "A Talk With Lizzie Borden," *Woman's Journal,* May 27, 1893: 163.

"My head troubles me so much": Martins and Binette, *Parallel Lives,* 483.

"Do you know": Ibid.

"To me, I see nothing but the densest shadows": Ibid., 484.

"My spirits are at ebb tide": Ibid., 487.

"crushed to a jelly": "Again the Axe," *Boston Daily Globe,* May 31, 1893.

"fully as revolting": "The Manchester Murder," *New Bedford (MA) Evening Standard,* May 31, 1893.

"struggled for her honor and her life": "A Clew," *New Bedford (MA) Evening Standard,* June 1, 1893.

TRIAL OF THE CENTURY

DAY ONE

"Those who saw Miss Borden for the first time": "Borden Jury Found," *Boston Daily Globe,* June 6[?], 1893, in Kent, *Sourcebook,* 206.

"It has been said": Radin, 39.

"Some have made her out": "Borden Jury Found," in Kent, *Sourcebook,* 206.

"common sense, broad-toed, brand new shoe": Ibid.

"cut in the latest style": "The Court Room Scene," *New Bedford (MA) Evening Standard,* June 5, 1893.

"of a very old fashion": "Borden Jury Found," in Kent, *Sourcebook,* 206.

"modest": "Selected," *Boston Daily Globe,* June 6, 1893.

"rather loud": "Borden Jury Found," in Kent, *Sourcebook,* 206.

"Her dress fitted her as perfectly": Ibid.

"obstinate and stubborn": "Selected," *Boston Daily Globe,* June 6, 1893.

Day Two

"in the plainest, simplest and most direct manner": William H. Moody, *Trial,* 48.

"On the morning of Sunday": Ibid., 81.

"The Commonwealth will prove": Ibid., 86–8.

"like a graven image": "Lizzie Borden Swooned," *Boston Daily Globe,* June 7[?], 1893, in Kent, *Sourcebook,* 214.

"the fan and the arm that held it": Ibid., in Kent, *Sourcebook,* 219.

"Her hand went into her pocket": Ibid.

"Lizzie Borden, the sphinx of coolness": *Fall River (MA) Daily Globe,* June 7, 1893, in Robertson, 397–8.

Day Three

"Since her fainting yesterday": "A Flimsy Structure," *Rochester (NY) Democrat & Chronicle,* June 8, 1893.

"Valentines and daisies": Robertson, 391–2.

"To-day she held her head up": "A Flimsy Structure," *Rochester (NY) Democrat & Chronicle,* June 8, 1893.

"At the time you were making measurements": *Trial,* 106.

"A smile played about the lips": *Fall River (MA) Daily Herald,* June 8, 1893, in Rebello, 91.

"I asked her what did she want for her breakfast": Bridget Sullivan, *Trial,* 224.

"She said she wanted the windows washed": Ibid., 226.

"Yes. You needn't lock the door": Ibid., 229.

"With his queer spectacles": "A Flimsy Structure," *Rochester (NY) Democrat & Chronicle,* June 8, 1893.

"On the outside of the parlor": *Trial,* 279.

"Can't see in, can you?": Ibid., 280.

"Maggie, are you going out": Lizzie A. Borden, quoted by Bridget Sullivan, *Trial,* 237–8.

"Maggie, come down!": Ibid., 240.

Day Four

"[E]xtremely trim in her manner": "Even Fight," *Boston Daily Globe,* June 9, 1893.

"Do you remember anything that took place at all?": Hosea M. Knowlton, *Preliminary Hearing,* 291.

"I cannot tell it in order": Alice M. Russell, *Trial,* 380–1.

"I couldn't tell what dress the girl had on": Bridget Sullivan, *Trial,* 224.

"It looked like a light blue and white": Adelaide B. Churchill, *Trial,* 352.

"[I]t was loose here": Alice M. Russell, *Trial,* 400.

"It was an ordinary, unattractive": Dr. Seabury W. Bowen, *Trial,* 311.

"I couldn't tell you the colors, as I know of": Charles S. Sawyer, *Trial,* 1472.

"I thought she had a light blue dress": Patrick Doherty, *Trial,* 599.

"kind of a brown": Ibid., 608.

"[a] white dress": Phoebe B. M. Bowen, *Trial,* 1588.

"It is not a spray": Ibid., 1587.

"I did not mean a dress with any white": Ibid., 1588.

"navy blue, sort of a bengaline": Lizzie A. Borden, *Inquest,* 53.

"Would you have seen any paint": *Trial,* 497.

"Did you see a light blue dress": William H. Moody, *Trial,* 746.

"Was you actually looking": *Trial,* 762.

Day Five

"I didn't notice any ashes": John Fleet, *Trial,* 536.

"He did not look like a powder magazine": "A Dramatic Sensation," *Rochester (NY) Democrat & Chronicle,* June 10, 1893.

"What did you do": *Trial,* 617.

"looked so as though it was rubbed on": Michael Mullaly, *Trial,* 618.

"What did Mr. Fleet do": *Trial,* 618.

"Do you know anything": Ibid., 631.

thunderbolt: "A Dramatic Sensation," *Rochester (NY) Democrat & Chronicle,* June 10, 1893.

"Handle": Michael Mullaly, *Trial,* 631.

"Well, did you take it out": *Trial,* 631.

"Did you see it taken out": Ibid., 632.

"Have you that handle here": Ibid.

"I don't know where it is": Hosea M. Knowlton, *Trial,* 632.

"I found a hatchet head": John Fleet, *Trial,* 634.

"Was this what you found": *Trial,* 635.

"Now, if I understand you": Ibid.

"You would have seen it": Ibid., 636.

Day Six

"I didn't see any": William H. Medley, *Trial*, 691.

"How distinctly could you see": *Trial*, 691–2.

"I could see them quite distinctly": Ibid., 692.

"Then I stepped up": Ibid.

"And you didn't look to see": Ibid., 712.

"You wrapped it up": George D. Robinson, *Trial*, 715.

"I am not very tidy": William H. Medley, *Trial*, 715.

"Now that, as near as I can think": *Trial*, 715–16.

it sounded as if the officers had all memorized the same basic script: "A Handleless Hatchet," *Rochester (NY) Democrat & Chronicle*, June 12, 1893; see also "Not Guilty—Lizzie Borden Is Free," *Rochester (NY) Democrat & Chronicle*, June 21, 1893.

"It was all dirty": Dennis Desmond, *Trial*, 720.

"I gave it to him": Ibid., 723.

"Positive": *Trial*, 740–1.

"a great newspaper bundle": "Broken Hatchet," *Boston Herald*, June 11, 1893, in Kent, *Sourcebook*, 248.

"The handleless hatchet": Ibid., in Kent, *Sourcebook*, 248.

Day Seven

"the City Marshal stood": George D. Robinson, *Trial*, 797.

"If that is freedom": Ibid., 798.

"[w]orse than burning a dress": Ibid., 799.

"May it please Your Honors": William H. Moody, *Trial*, 819.

"because the law expressly gives [the courts]": William H. Moody, *Trial*, 823.

"And Your Honors can have no doubt": Ibid., 824.

"There was nothing in that warrant": Ibid., 827.

"From the agreed facts": Albert Mason, *Trial*, 830–1.

Day Eight

"Would the skull itself be of assistance": *Trial*, 1046.

"sat with red eyes and trembling lips": *New York Tribune* quoted in "Miss Borden Breaking Down," *New Bedford (MA) Evening Standard*, June 15, 1893.

"done up in a white handkerchief": undated, unidentified article, in Kent, *Sourcebook*, 270 (possibly *Boston Herald*, June 14, 1893).

"Will you tell us what it is": Hosea M. Knowlton, *Trial*, 1047.

"Are you able to say whether that hatchet head": *Trial*, 1048–9.

"The handleless hatchet is not": Ibid., 1067.

"He may answer": *Trial*, 1017.

Day Nine

I am ready to go at any time: Rufus B. Hilliard, *Trial,* 1119; John W. Coughlin, *Trial,* 1166.

"a mean, good for nothing thing": Hannah H. Gifford, *Trial,* 1169.

"Now will you go on and describe": William H. Moody, *Trial,* 1214.

noticeable zeal and encyclopedic detail: "Even So!" *Boston Daily Globe,* June 15, 1893.

"Did Miss Emma come again that day": *Trial,* 1217.

"Are you sure he came that same afternoon": *Trial,* 1218.

"Now let me go a little further": Andrew J. Jennings, *Trial,* 1221.

"Had quite a pleasant time": *Trial,* 1222.

"Had quite a pleasant afternoon": Ibid.

"Wasn't that afternoon": Ibid.

"You propose to bring evidence upon attempts": George D. Robinson, *Trial,* 1242.

"Yes, sir": Hosea M. Knowlton, *Trial,* 1242.

"She is charged in this indictment": George D. Robinson, *Trial,* 1242.

lean evidence: Ibid., 1244.

"I can conceive of no more significant act": William H. Moody, *Trial,* 1262–3.

"But here there is nothing of that": George D. Robinson, *Trial,* 1265.

"Well, people buy prussic acid to kill animals": Ibid., 1267.

Day Ten

"dull thud": undated *Springfield (MA) Union* article, in Kent, *Sourcebook,* 286.

"I want to say right here and now": Andrew J. Jennings, *Trial,* 1305.

"We shall show you": Ibid., 1306.

"I say this is a mysterious case": Ibid., 1309.

"There is not a spot of blood": Ibid., 1310.

"there has not been a living soul": Ibid., 1321.

"people who have not been located or identified": Ibid.

"[W]e shall ask you to say": Ibid., 1322–23.

"She had learned to brace herself": "Lizzie Borden's Turn Now," *Boston Herald,* June 15, 1893, in Kent, *Sourcebook,* 288.

"punctured with smiles": "It is a Dire Failure," *Rochester (NY) Democrat & Chronicle,* June 16, 1893.

"just nerving himself up": "On the Motive," *Boston Daily Globe,* August 16, 1892.

"He was moving very slowly": *Trial,* 1376.

"the most uniquely locked house in Fall River": Martins and Binette, *Knowlton Papers,* 129; see also "Held for Trial," in Kent, *Sourcebook,* 196.

"Did you ring before": *Trial,* 1383.

"I found that unless the bolt was used": Mary E. Brigham, *Trial,* 1592.

"What is your name": *Trial*, 1408.

"Well, when you got to the Borden house": Ibid., 1409.

"Had you ever seen the servant": Ibid., 1410.

"You ask too fast": Hymon Lubinsky, *Trial*, 1422.

"What has a person got eyes for": Ibid.

"When you arrived": *Trial*, 1442–3.

"How was the heat": Ibid., 1443.

Extremely hot: Philip Harrington, *Trial*, 535.

Close: John Fleet, *Trial*, 482.

Stifling: Patrick Doherty, *Trial*, 600.

83 degrees: *Lizzie Borden Quarterly* IV, no. 1 (1997): 9.

79 degrees: Masterton, 7.

"Do you know Officer Medley": *Trial*, 1443.

"I seen Officer Fleet": Everett Brown, *Trial*, 1438; see also Thomas Barlow, *Trial*, 1444.

"a minute or two": William H. Medley, *Trial*, 688.

"I've found Lizzie Borden's hatchet!": "The New Sensation," *New Bedford (MA) Evening Standard*, June 16, 1893.

"[O]n one of the cuts": Martins and Binette, *Knowlton Papers*, 212.

DAY ELEVEN

Medley's cake walk: Andrew J. Jennings, *Trial*, 1321.

"Now where was that dress": Ibid., 1540.

"[U]pon Mr. Knowlton": "The Evidence Complete," *Rochester (NY) Democrat & Chronicle*, June 17, 1893.

"And do you say that the relations": *Trial*, 1557–8.

"Wasn't the first thing said by anybody": Ibid., 1571.

"Why doesn't it seem so to you": Ibid., 1572.

DAY TWELVE

"You will need at the outset, gentlemen": George D. Robinson, *Trial*, 1623.

"I have no right to tell you": Ibid., 1638.

"never reached into the heart": "The Arguments," *New Bedford Evening Standard*, June 21, 1893.

"Gentlemen, with great weariness on your part": George D. Robinson, *Trial*, 1750.

"You couldn't see the gestures": "Not Guilty," *Boston Daily Globe*, June 21, 1893.

"Murder is the work of stealth and craft": Hosea M. Knowlton, *Trial*, 1766.

"Nobody that has told of it": Ibid., 1766–7.

"But Lizzie Andrew Borden, the daughter of Andrew Jackson Borden": Ibid., 1806–7.

"a wicked and dreadful necessity": Ibid., 1808.

DAY THIRTEEN

"Lizzie Andrew Borden": *Trial*, 1885.

"the general tenor of their lives": Justin Dewey, *Trial*, 1894.

"There is so little absolute evidence": "Will It Remain a Mystery?" *New York Times*, June 17, 1893, in Kent, *Sourcebook*, 296.

"Lizzie Andrew Borden, stand up": *Trial*, 1929.

"Thank God!": "Not Guilty," *Rochester (NY) Democrat & Chronicle*, June 21, 1893.

"Mr. Robinson dodged under the rail": "Not Guilty; Lizzie Borden Is Free," *Rochester (NY) Democrat & Chronicle*, June 21, 1893.

"She gave them a wealth of glad smiles": Ibid.

"I want to go home": "Not Guilty," *Boston Daily Globe*, June 21, 1893.

Three of every four people believed Lizzie Borden was guilty: "Not Guilty; Lizzie Borden Is Free," *Rochester (NY) Democrat & Chronicle*, June 21, 1893.

"the happiest woman in the world": "The News At Fall River," *New Bedford (MA) Evening Standard*, June 21, 1893.

IT WASN'T MISS BORDEN: Rebello, 270.

IN JAIL!: Kent, *Forty Whacks*, 208; see also Radin, 234.

NOT AT CHURCH: "Not at Church," *Boston Daily Globe*, June 26, 1893.

AFTERMATH

"THE 'THING' That Butchered the Bordens Still at Large": Martins and Binette, *Parallel Lives*, 515.

"Never, never had girls such faithful friends": "Her Old Home," *Boston Daily Globe*, June 22, 1893.

"[I]f any of my old friends sees fit to ignore me": Ibid.

"jolly crowd": Martins and Binette, *Parallel Lives*, 513.

"[A]lways shall I think of you . . .": Ibid., 514.

"That cat won't ever bother you again": Martins and Binette, *Knowlton Papers*, 242.

"voluntarily": "Personal Gossip," *New York Times*, July 16, 1893.

Dear Sir: Martins and Binette, *Parallel Lives*, 520.

"You are therefore hereby notified": Rebello, 359.

"[L]ike most of Fall River": Lincoln, 27.

"Can't anybody frighten her out of doing what she wants to": "They Are Like Prisoners," *Rochester (NY) Democrat & Chronicle*, June 19, 1893.

"A good many persons": Radin, 233.

"the house of horrors": "The Work of the Police," *New Bedford (MA) Evening Standard*, August 16, 1892.

"When the truth comes out about this murder": undated *Boston Globe* article, in Kent, *Sourcebook*, 332.

"LIZZIE BORDEN AGAIN": "Lizzie Borden Again," *Providence (RI) Daily Journal,* February 16, 1897, in Williams, 235.

"Investigation followed": Ibid., in Williams, 236.

"He will not deny, however": Ibid., in Williams, 236–7.

"adjusted": Pearson, *Trial,* 79.

"I did not go until conditions became absolutely unbearable": "Guilty—No! No!" in Williams, 252.

"After repeated disagreements": "Lizzie Borden Left by Sister," *Boston Sunday Herald,* June 3, 1905, in Kent, *Sourcebook,* 329.

"jolly crowd": Martins and Binette, *Parallel Lives,* 513.

"[A]lways shall I think of you . . .": Ibid., 514.

"imperative that I should make my home elsewhere": "Guilty—No! No!" in Williams, 252.

"a fine looking young man": "Lizzie Borden Left by Sister," in Kent, *Sourcebook,* 329.

"Miss Emma's dislike": Ibid.

"Guilty?—No! No!": In Williams, 248.

"Nothing to say": Ibid., 250.

"[p]robably the most remarkable": "Lizzie Borden Twenty Years After the Tragedy," *Boston Sunday Herald,* April 6, 1913, in *Hatchet* 2 no. 4 (2005): 9.

"The tragedy seems but yesterday": this and all following quotes by Emma Borden from "Guilty—No! No!" in Williams, 248–54.

"She constantly hoped": "Took 35-Year Hope to Grave," *New Bedford (MA) Sunday Standard,* June 5, 1927, in Kent, *Sourcebook,* 354.

"were very glad that it had come to an end": Ibid.

"strictly private": Martins and Binette, *Parallel Lives,* 980.

"The undertaker unlocked the door": Williams, 263.

EPILOGUE

"Auntie Borden": Martins and Binette, *Parallel Lives,* 904.

"Now you remember": Ibid., 874–5.

"I would give every cent I have": "Took 35-Year Hope to Grave," in Kent, *Sourcebook,* 354.

"When I know how easy it is to be accused": Ibid., in Kent, *Sourcebook,* 355.

RESEARCHING THE BORDENS

"garbled and wickedly sensational": Martins and Binette, *Knowlton Papers,* 179.

BIBLIOGRAPHY

PRIMARY SOURCES

The Witness Statements for the Lizzie Borden Murder Case, August 4–October 6, 1892.
(Digitized by Stefani Koorey)

Inquest Upon the Deaths of Andrew J. Borden and Abby D. Borden. Annie M. White, Stenographer. (Digitized by Stefani and Kat Koorey)

Preliminary Hearing (Stenographer's Minutes): Commonwealth of Massachusetts vs. Lizzie A. Borden, August 25, 1892–September 1, 1892, Judge Josiah Coleman Blaisdell, presiding, Second District Court, Fall River, MA. Annie M. White, Stenographer.
(Digitized by Faye Musselman)

Trial of Lizzie Andrew Borden Upon an indictment charging her with the Murder of Abby Durfee Borden and Andrew Jackson Borden Before the Superior Court for the County of Bristol; Mason, C. J. and Blodgett and Dewey, J. J. Presiding. Official Stenographic Report by Frank H. Burt, 1893. (Digitized by Harry Widdows)

BOOKS

Chapman, Sherry. *Lizzie Borden: Resurrections.* Fall River, MA: PearTree Press, 2014.

Cole, George S. *A Complete Dictionary of Dry Goods.* Chicago: W. B. Conkey Company, 1892.

Earl, Henry H. *Fall River and Its Manufactories 1803–1890.* Fall River, MA: George E. Bamford, 1890.

Historical Briefs. *Lizzie Borden. Did She? Or Didn't She?* Verplanck, NY: Historical Briefs Inc., 1992.

Hoffman, Paul Dennis. *Yesterday in Old Fall River: A Lizzie Borden Companion.* Durham, NC: Carolina Academic Press, 2000.

Kent, David. *Forty Whacks: New Evidence in the Life and Legend of Lizzie Borden.* Emmaus, PA: Yankee Books, 1992.

———. *The Lizzie Borden Sourcebook.* Boston: Branden Publishing Company, 1992.

Lincoln, Victoria. *A Private Disgrace: Lizzie Borden by Daylight.* New York: Putnam, 1967.

Martins, Michael and Dennis Binette, eds. *Commonwealth of Massachusetts vs. Lizzie A. Borden: The Knowlton Papers.* Fall River, MA: Fall River Historical Society, 1994.

———. *Parallel Lives: A Social History of Lizzie Borden and Her Fall River.* Fall River, MA: Fall River Historical Society, 2011.

Pearson, Edmund. *Murder at Smutty Nose and Other Murders*. Garden City, NY: Dolphin Books, 1926.

———, ed. *The Trial of Lizzie Borden*. Garden City, NY: Doubleday, Doran & Company, 1937.

Phillips, Arthur S. "The Borden Murder Mystery: In Defence of Lizzie Borden." *The Phillips History of Fall River, Fascicle III*. Fall River, MA: Dover Press, 1946.

———. *The Phillips History of Fall River, Fascicle I*. Fall River, MA: Dover Press, 1941.

Porter, Edwin H. *The Fall River Tragedy*. Fall River, MA: Geo. R. H. Buffinton, 1893.

Radin, Edward D. *Lizzie Borden: The Untold Story*. New York: Simon & Schuster, 1961.

Rebello, Leonard. *Lizzie Borden: Past and Present*. Fall River, MA: Al-Zach Press, 1999.

Sargent, Porter E. *A Handbook of New England*. Boston: George H. Ellis, 1921.

Sherwood, M. E. W. *Manners and Social Usages*. New York: Harper & Brothers, 1884.

Sullivan, Robert. *Goodbye Lizzie Borden*. Brattleboro, VT: S. Greene Press, 1974.

Williams, Joyce G., et al. *Lizzie Borden: A Case Book of Family and Crime in the 1890s*. Bloomington, IN: T.I.S. Publications, 1980.

ARTICLES

Both *The Hatchet: A Journal of Lizzie Borden & Victorian Studies* and *The Lizzie Borden Quarterly* are troves of Borden minutiae. I harvested dozens of details from many more of their articles than are cited here. Those listed below are the handful I found most valuable in their entirety.

Bertolet, Maynard F. "The Lizzie Borden and Bridget Sullivan Missing Inquest Transcripts." *The Lizzie Borden Quarterly* VIII, no. 4 (October 2001): 7, 15–19.

Demakis, Denise. "The Rocky Point Picnic." *The Lizzie Borden Quarterly* VII, no. 4 (October 2000): 6, 21.

Duniho, Terence, and Stefani Koorey. "Will the Real Inquest Testimony of Lizzie Borden Please Stand Up." *The Lizzie Borden Quarterly* VIII, no. 4 (October 2001): 1, 10–14.

Dziedzic, Shelley. "The Victorian Celebration of Death." *The Hatchet* 6, no. 1 (Spring 2009): 22–32.

Dziedzic, Shelley, and Stefani Koorey, PhD. "Emma Lost and Found." *The Hatchet* 4, no. 3 (August 2007): 6–25.

Holba, Annette. "Shattering the Myth." *The Lizzie Borden Quarterly* X, no. 3 (July 2003): 1, 10–17.

Koorey, Kat. "'The Borden House: Frame by Frame, Part 4: The Cellar." *The Hatchet* 1, no. 6 (December 2004): 24–31.

———. "One's Idea of Cordiality: Miss Lizzie on the Stand." *The Hatchet* 2, no. 4 (August 2005): 32–36.

Koorey, Stefani, PhD. "Fleet's Notes." *The Hatchet* 7, no. 2 (Spring 2012): 38–48.

Masterton, William L. "Weather We Do: Some Like It Hot!" *The Lizzie Borden Quarterly* IV, no. 1 (January 1997): 7–8.

Naugle, Mary Elizabeth. "Let's Call It a Wrap or What Did the Bordens Wear?" *The Hatchet* 2, no. 3 (June 2005): 52–57.

Pavao, William L. "Abby Durfee Borden: Portrait of a Stepmother." *The Lizzie Borden Quarterly* IX, no. 1 (January 2002): 10–20.

Pearson, Edmund. "Legends of Lizzie." *The New Yorker,* April 22, 1933: 20–23.

ONLINE SOURCES

Allard, Deborah. "Excerpts from lawyer's journal reveal new insight into Borden case." *The Herald News* (Fall River, MA), August 2, 2013. heraldnews.com/article/20130802/News/308029408. Accessed August 22, 2013.

Dziedzic, Shelley. "Abby's Sisters." *Lizzie Borden Warps and Wefts.* 2010. lizziebordenwarpsandwefts.com/september-muttoneaters-online-the-sisters-of-abby-borden/. Accessed July 19, 2013.

Robertson, Cara W. "Representing 'Miss Lizzie': Cultural Convictions in the Trial of Lizzie Borden." *Yale Journal of Law & the Humanities* 8, no. 2: 351–416. (digitalcommons.law.yale.edu/yjlh/vol8/iss2/2)

INDEX

Turn the page to read an excerpt of

THE MIRACLE & TRAGEDY
OF THE DIONNE QUINTUPLETS,

the next book from Sarah Miller,
coming in August 2019!

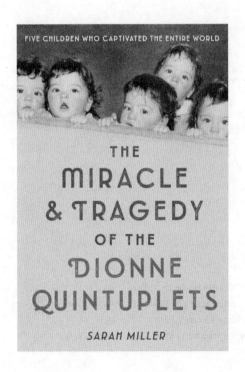

PROLOGUE

In an empty nursery, behind two woven wire fences topped with barbed wire, five nine-year-old girls waited for their father. Five suitcases sat alongside them. Five smiling Shirley Temple dolls were clutched in their arms. Yvonne stared out the window at the yellow brick mansion up the hill. Annette quietly seethed, pretending not to be afraid. Cécile sat in a corner, rocking her doll. Émilie prayed that it was all just a bad dream. Marie tried to tell a silly story, but no one laughed.

At the sound of their father's footsteps in the hall, all five sisters hugged their Shirley Temples closer to their chests. The moment they dreaded had come.

For the first time in their lives, the Dionne Quintuplets were going home.

Oliva Dionne did not speak as he and his five identical daughters walked through the hospital's guarded gate, down the road, and through another gate that led to the colossal Georgian house that was to be their new home. He did not lead them up the steps to the grand front door. Instead, he entered through a service door into the kitchen. Yvonne followed first, trying to be brave for her sisters' sake. Though Yvonne was no more than a few minutes older than Annette, Cécile, Émilie, and Marie, she had acted the part of the little mother since she was a toddler.

For nine years Mr. Dionne had battled with the government to unite his family under a single roof. Now that his triumphant moment had arrived, the man who had once crawled through a drainpipe to elude hospital guards just so he could glimpse his five famous babies through a window spoke a single sentence.

"The little girls are here," he told his wife, and continued into the house, leaving his daughters standing in the unfamiliar kitchen with their dolls and suitcases.

"Bonsoir, Mom," Yvonne, Annette, Cécile, Émilie, and Marie said, greeting their mother in a mixture of French and English.

"Supper will be ready soon," Mrs. Dionne replied in French, then called for two of her elder daughters. "Show the little girls around the house," she instructed.

Without a word, "the little girls" followed as their big sisters pointed into one doorway after another. The living room, the den, the sewing room, their father's office. Redolent of fresh paint and filled with pristine furniture, the house felt new and sterile, more sterile by far than the hospital that had been their home since they were four months old.

Then they reached the dining room. Like everything else in the house, it was big, in this case big enough to seat fourteen—Mr. and Mrs. Dionne, Yvonne, Annette, Cécile, Émilie, Marie, and their seven brothers and sisters, Ernest, Rose-Marie, Thérèse, Pauline, Daniel, Oliva Jr., and Victor. An archway divided the room in half, with a table on each side. "This side is for our family," the little girls remembered one of their elder sisters saying. "The other side is for your family."

Not one of the bewildered nine-year-olds knew what to say.

PART ONE

1 IN 57,000,000 BIRTHS

May 28, 1934–March 15, 1935

CHAPTER 1

Quintuplets Born to Farm Wife

North Bay Nugget, Monday, May 28, 1934

The knock at the back door roused Douilda Legros from her bed. "Auntie, please hurry and dress and come over," Oliva Dionne called. "Elzire, she is very sick. Please hurry," he said again.

Auntie Legros was on her way in minutes.

It was only a short drive across the road to the Dionne farm, but it was long enough for Douilda Legros's worries to unreel through her mind. Poor Elzire had never had such a difficult pregnancy. Headaches, dizzy spells, vomiting. Painful legs and feet swollen to twice their normal size. A finger pressed into her skin left a deep dent. Now and then the edges of her vision went black.

Two, perhaps three weeks ago it had become so bad Elzire had finally consented to let her husband, Oliva, consult the doctor in spite of the cost. The doctor had ordered Elzire off her feet entirely, but that was next to impossible on a three-hundred-acre farm with five young children to care for.

And now? The urgency in Oliva's voice could only mean something worse yet. Perhaps the worst thing of all—the baby, coming too soon.

Auntie Legros let herself in the front door without waking Ernest, Rose-Marie, Thérèse, and Daniel, asleep upstairs, and made her way to the bedroom at the back of the house. Eleven-month-old Pauline slept in a crib at the foot of the big wooden bed where Elzire lay. Her niece's black eyes peered up out of a pale and puffy face. "Auntie," she said weakly in French, "I don't think that I will be able to pull through this time."

Auntie Legros could hardly contradict her. Even by the light of the kerosene lamp, it was clear that Elzire was ailing badly. The young mother's legs and feet were so distended, her toes had nearly disappeared. She could neither stand nor walk. There was a bluish cast to her fingernails. Her labor pains had woken her sometime near midnight—mild at first, steadily advancing until there could be no doubt that the baby was insisting on being born.

Nevertheless, Auntie Legros did her best to comfort her niece. "Don't you worry, my dear. I will stand by you now as I always did before," she promised. This child would be the fifth Dionne she had helped bring into the world.

Elzire asked for her rosary, and the two women paused to say a prayer to the Blessed Virgin. Elzire kissed the feet of the crucifix and recited aloud the Ave Maria. Both women cried a little. Then Auntie Legros set to work.

Herself a mother of nine, Douilda Legros had been helping deliver her neighbors' children for eighteen years, sometimes assisting the midwife or doctor, sometimes working alone. In all that time, she'd lost only one baby—a premature infant, born with the umbilical cord around its neck. And now Elzire's baby was coming two months too early.

O God, inspire me in my work, Auntie Legros prayed.

Nothing was prepared. No clothing, no diapers. Elzire should have had most of the summer to sew new baby things and accustom little Pauline to sleeping upstairs with her brothers and sisters. But that could not be helped now. Auntie Legros did what she could. She lit the wood stove and put a pan and a teakettle on to boil. She found a stack of newspapers to spread over the mattress, easing Elzire back and forth as she rearranged the bedding for the birth. Elzire was too weak to move without assistance, but the prayer, to Auntie Legros's relief, had bolstered her niece's spirits. Douilda Legros had never before seen Elzire discouraged or fearful, even during the most difficult of her deliveries, when Thérèse had been turned the wrong way.

Just the same, Auntie Legros herself was growing more ill at ease as Elzire's suffering increased. The prospect of losing another newborn was difficult enough; the memory of that failed premature delivery still haunted her. But to lose Elzire? Though they were not related by blood (Elzire was Douilda's husband's niece), Elzire had been like a daughter to her since she was a little girl. Auntie Legros had taken Elzire in after her mother's long illness and death—until the eleven-year-old was compelled to leave school and return home to help her father care for a houseful of brothers. She had seen Elzire married to Oliva Dionne at sixteen, and watched her become the mother of six children before turning twenty-five. Hardest of all, she had supported Elzire when her fourth baby, two-month-old Leo, died of pneumonia.

After all that, Auntie Legros would take no chances with Elzire's health. Within an hour of her arrival at the Dionne house, she sent Oliva a mile down the road for Madame Lebel.

To the French Canadians of Corbeil, Ontario, *midwife* and *Madame Lebel* were interchangeable terms. A large "weather-beaten" woman with "a heart as big as a washtub," Madame Lebel had borne eighteen children of her own and delivered her neighbors of at least three hundred more, most of them without a doctor's assistance. She never expected so much as a penny for her services—something that endeared her more and more each year to the small rural community, now that times were harder than anyone could remember.

Madame Lebel recognized the gravity of the situation at once. Warmth and color were draining from Elzire's body as the frequency of the pains increased. She ignored Elzire's requests not to send for the doctor. "Elzire's pulse is bad," Madame Lebel told Oliva. "So is her general condition. Get Dr. Dafoe here quick as you can."

Oliva obeyed instantly.

With her rosary pressed tightly to her heart, Elzire begged Madame Lebel to hurry the baby's arrival. Though the Dionnes were one of the few families in Corbeil who were not receiving relief payments from the government, Elzire knew there wasn't a cent to spare for the doctor. Since the Depression had hit, their savings had "melted away." Not a day went by that she wasn't thankful for Oliva's $4-a-day job as a gravel hauler, but with a $3,000 mortgage on the farm and seven—soon to be eight—mouths to feed, $20 a week stretched barely far enough. Dr. Dafoe's last visit had spread them tissue-thin; another might cost as much as a week's wages. Elzire's lips were white as she formed the request.

Fewer than three miles separated Oliva Dionne from the doctor's neat brick house in Callander, but it was dark, rocky going, more a rutted lumber trail than a road. Aside from the priest, not another man in the Corbeil parish had the good fortune to own an automobile, but it still might not get him there in time.

When he reached the house with its plaque reading *Dr. A. R. Dafoe,* Oliva pounded on the door and rang the bell.

Dr. Allan Roy Dafoe himself answered, wearing a pair of pants under his rumpled nightshirt. The doctor was an odd-looking man at any hour of the day—short enough that folks called him "the Little Doc," with hands so small he had to buy gloves in the children's department. Yet his head was so large he was rarely able to find a hat that fit properly. And he stuttered. The next day would be his fifty-first birthday.

At first, the doctor could make little sense of Oliva Dionne's presence on his doorstep. Elzire Dionne was not expected to deliver until late July. Besides, it was something like four o'clock in the morning, and Dafoe had had less than three hours' sleep. Returning home from a delivery well after midnight, he'd sat up past one to read a detective story.

"My wife is very sick," Oliva said in English. (The doctor, like most who lived outside the tiny Catholic community of Corbeil, did not speak French.) "I think she soon have a baby. Can you come right away, Doctor?"

"You go on back," Dafoe told the worried father. "I'll dress and come along in my own car."

Oliva had to know how long he would be.

"A few minutes," Dafoe answered, and shut the door.

If the doctor was short with Oliva, it was not only because of the stutter that obliged him to get straight to the point. Dr. Dafoe had warned the Dionnes about Elzire's condition, and they had not complied. She ought to have been in bed these last two weeks. No housework, no farm chores. Get a hired girl to take over Elzire's work, Dafoe instructed Oliva, or else start looking for a new wife. Yet when the doctor visited the Dionne farm the next day, there was Elzire, waddling around the kitchen on feet puffed up like bread dough, aggravating the swelling as well as her blood pressure. The results of the test he'd conducted indicated the beginnings of toxemia—a condition better known today as preeclampsia, guaranteed back then to be fatal to mother and baby if it progressed—but Dr. Dafoe seems not to have bothered to explain all that to the Dionnes. He took it for granted that a doctor's orders would be obeyed, regardless of whether his patient understood why.

Now that their ignorance had made things worse, they wanted him to hurry. And, of course, he would.

The doctor was already too late. Around ten past four, Elzire's baby was born.

Between them, Auntie Legros and Madame Lebel had delivered hundreds of babies, but the size of this infant left the two midwives terror-stricken. Arms barely bigger around than sticks of chalk, and every bit as breakable. Fingers that seemed too tiny to contain bones at all. Bruise-colored skin so thin and tender, it might as well have been cellophane. Lamplight glanced off the shining outline of her delicate ribs. The whole of the baby's torso fit within Madame Lebel's palm; a bulbous head the size of a small orange wobbled on a frail neck. Like an insect's, her head and belly were entirely out of proportion with her long, spindly limbs.

Everything about the tiny little girl looked raw and unfinished, with one startling exception: a beautiful set of long black eyelashes.

She was not breathing.

The midwives rubbed her back and chest and blew into her mouth, desperate to inflate her lungs. Precious seconds ticked by as the two women struggled to make her live without injuring her impossibly fragile body. Suddenly a mewling sound rose from the thin blue lips.

A moment's exultation, then the realization: a child so small could not live more than a few minutes. Auntie Legros dashed to the kitchen pump for a dipper of water. "Ego te baptizo in nomine Patris et Filii et Spiritus Sancti," she murmured as she sprinkled the water over the child's silky dark hair. *I baptize you in the name of the Father and of the Son and of the Holy Spirit.* They could do no more than that. The midwives tied off the cord with a length of cotton thread from Elzire's sewing basket, wrapped the baby in a torn bit of wool blanket warmed before the oven door, and laid her near her mother, certain that death was imminent for one or both of them.

Within minutes, Elzire's pains returned. But instead of the afterbirth, out came another baby girl, smaller yet than the first. Again Auntie Legros and Madame Lebel persuaded the baby to breathe. Immediately they baptized her, too, and laid her next to her sister, who, miraculously, was also still breathing.

Madame Legros and Auntie Lebel had no time to congratulate themselves before yet another infant's head began to emerge. Not twins, but triplets! At almost the same moment, Dr. Dafoe arrived. "Good God, woman, put on some more hot water!" he exclaimed as he headed to scrub up in the kitchen basin.

The third baby, delivered by the midwives before the doctor had taken his coat off, was even smaller, even more reluctant to breathe than her sisters. Undaunted, Dr. Dafoe and the two women worked her over until they coaxed her into making that strange but encouraging mewling. Auntie Legros baptized her, and she joined the widening row of dark-haired baby girls at the foot of the bed.

By now Elzire was so exhausted, she appeared to be unconscious. What little of her strength remained, she devoted to pressing her rosary beads to her heart and praying silently to herself. She desperately needed rest. But her body had not finished its work.

"My God, there are still more there," Madame Lebel said to the doctor.

"Gosh!" he exclaimed. Realizing that Elzire had become too weak to bring yet another child into the world without assistance, Dafoe put "a little pressure" on her abdomen, and a fourth baby made its way into the lamplight. "Gosh!" he said again as a fifth followed two minutes later.

Through the transparent walls of the unbroken amniotic sacs, Dafoe could see arms and legs moving: two more miniature baby girls, these the smallest of all. In his sleepy state, the scene was "unreal and dream-like," he remembered, "but I mechanically went about the business of looking after the babies."

Madame Lebel and Auntie Legros were every bit as stunned. Five babies in a single hour! "We just looked at each other with amazement," Auntie Legros recalled of the fifth birth. And the last two were born in "angel veils"—an uncommon sign of good luck. It was clear from their size that this pair would need every ounce of luck imaginable.

Quickly, Dr. Dafoe ruptured the sacs and got the last two babies breathing. Auntie Legros baptized them. (Or perhaps it was the doctor. Maybe both—certainly both remembered doing so.) Madame Lebel swaddled the infants in napkins and sheets and laid them alongside the first three. Then a warmed blanket was spread over all five babies.

"Auntie, have I twins, this time?" Elzire asked.

"Yes, my dear," Madame Lebel answered, "twins and three more." She held up her fingers and counted off five daughters—"Cinq fillettes."

Elzire burst into tears. "What will I do with all them babies?" she wailed.

Satisfied that the birth was finally over, Auntie Legros ran home for supplies. Into a butcher's basket went an old woolen blanket, a bottle of olive oil, and some flatirons. When she returned, everything had changed. Elzire had gone into shock. She was cold to the touch. Her fingertips were black, her pulse nearly imperceptible. Frightened, Auntie Legros called the doctor in from the yard.

Dr. Dafoe injected Elzire with pituitary hormone to raise her blood pressure, and ergot solution to slow any internal bleeding. A little color appeared in her face. Her pulse quickened, but not enough to bring her out of danger. For forty-five minutes, Auntie Legros and the doctor worked to keep her from slipping away. When Elzire looked no better, Auntie Legros told Dafoe it was time to send for the priest. Dafoe agreed—he had been thinking the same thing.

Auntie Legros went out to the living room, where Oliva was pacing the floor. "My God, what am I going to do with five babies!" he exclaimed, just as Elzire had done. In the space of an hour his family had doubled, leaving his wife on the verge of death. He felt as though he had been "punched." The news put Oliva in such a frantic state of nerves, Auntie Legros did not trust him behind the wheel. Instead, it was Dr. Dafoe who left Elzire's bedside and sped off to Corbeil to alert Father Routhier. There was not much else Dafoe could do for her.

Elzire had watched the doctor's face and heard his grave tone as he spoke with the midwives in English. She did not need to understand the words to guess what he was telling them. Elzire had never felt so feeble and helpless in all her life. She tried to say Oliva's name. She wanted to touch her babies once while they were still living. But she was too weak to speak, too weak to lift her hand.

In the time it took Dafoe to return, Elzire had rallied somewhat. He left a prescription for her and instructed the midwives to administer it if she had any more pains. He had done everything he knew how to do. If that was not enough, the priest would be along soon.

"As we did not anticipate his return, I asked Dr. Dafoe what to do with the babies," Madame Lebel recalled. In all the commotion over Elzire, hardly anyone had given a thought to the five infants at the foot of the bed. Every last one of the "little mites" was still living.

"All we can do is to keep them warm and quiet," Dafoe answered. "Leave 'em alone, except to give them a few drops of warm water every couple of hours—if they live."

What about bathing them in warm olive oil? Madame Lebel wondered.

"He told her to please herself," Auntie Legros remembered, "as he did not think there was much use in her troubling herself a great deal as the babies would all die." Perhaps the biggest one might have a chance, he conceded, but certainly not the others. No set of quintuplets had ever lived before, and he had no reason to hold out hope for these five. Twenty-six years earlier, Dafoe had assisted at the birth of a set of quadruplets; all four were dead within a week. "However, you can please yourself," he repeated.

Madame Lebel warmed flatirons on the stove. The midwives positioned two chairs before the open oven door and balanced the basket across the two seats while one at a time they sponged each of the infants with warm olive oil. Careful to preserve the order in which they had been born, Madame Lebel and Auntie Legros arranged the babies in the butcher's basket from biggest to smallest.

By the time Oliva came in to see his five daughters for the first time, they were back in the basket on the foot of their mother's bed, with hot flatirons propped near their toes and a big wool blanket draped over the top.

Elzire lay watching as her husband approached on tiptoe, hesitating in the bedroom doorway. His brown-black eyes were red from crying. She knew what kind of tragedy or sorrow it took to bring Oliva Dionne to tears. "Realizing this, near death as I was," Elzire remembered, "I made up my mind to be as brave as possible. So when Oliva grasped my hand and asked me how I felt I replied: 'Not too bad.'"

Oliva glanced at the butcher's basket. Then he took a few steps to the end of the bed. Elzire watched him stare into the basket. She could not guess his feelings. He looked sheepish, embarrassed, bewildered.

"What do you think of . . . of . . ." Elzire stammered. She could not bring herself to say *our five babies*. It still seemed too much. ". . . of them?" she finished.

Oliva did not take his eyes from the basket. "I don't know what to think, Elzire," he answered slowly, "for the unheard of has just happened to us, hasn't it? But I do know that I never could have imagined any babies so small. Aren't they the tiniest things to be alive and breathing?"

"They're still alive and breathing, all five of them?"

"Yes," Oliva answered, "I'm watching them breathe."

It was a miracle, she decided. A miracle from on high. That was the only way Elzire could explain it to herself. But already Elzire knew better than to expect anyone else to see it the same way.

"What will people say when they find out about this?" she wondered aloud. Only animals gave birth in such numbers. "They will say we are pigs."